MARKETING
SIDEKICK

IMPORTANT LEGAL STUFF

The author may be contacted at the following addresses:

Matt Bacak

www.contactmattbacak.com

mattbacak@gmail.com

Credits

Managing Editor, Cover/Interior Design/Illustration, Layout:
Christopher L. May

AUTHORS PREFACE

First, I wanted to say thanks for grabbing this book.

As stated, this is "a collection high converting, attention grabbing words, phrases and headlines to help you promote your products, service and ideas."

Basically, this book contains a massive swipe file of material you can swipe, adapt, tweak & alter as you please.

Marketers usually always have swipe files next to them, within arm's reach, as their sidekick.

Hence the title "*Marketing Sidekick*".

Check out what *Wikipedia* said about the word Swipe file:

Oh, yea I swiped it...

"A swipe file is a collection of tested and proven advertising and sales letters. Keeping a swipe file (templates) is a common practice used by advertising copywriters and creative directors as a ready reference of ideas for projects.

Copywriters are not the only ones who can benefit from having a swipe file. As book publishing coach Diane Eble points out, authors and publishers can benefit from creating a swipe file of best-selling titles to give them ideas for their own titles. Publicists can create a swipe file of great press release headlines. Swipe files are a great jumping-off point for anybody who needs to come up with lots of ideas.

Swipe files are also commonly used by Internet Marketers who need to gather a lot of resources not only about products but also about marketing methods and strategies."

Now, why do you need to keep this next to your desk?

A swipe file, especially one compiled like this, is arguably your "Marketing Sidekick", just as Robin is to Batman, like Chewy is to Han, and Tonto is to the Lone Ranger.

However, you can take this a bit further, because it can also can be used a lot like trusty Alfred, Bruce Wayne's butler as 'guided inspiration'...

and a powerful reference getting unstuck fast.

Swipe away!

Matt Bacak

TABLE OF CONTENTS

PART ONE

MAGNETIZERS

PART TWO

INFLUENCERS

PART THREE

DEAL SEALERS

INTRODUCTION

Words. For 100,000 years, language has been used by humans to communicate complex thoughts and ideas. They have helped man express himself through spiritual ideas, myths, hymns, songs and philosophies. Words were compiled to form monumental works such as The Holy Bible, The Torah, and The Quran; the cornerstones of the world's great monotheistic religions. Skillfully used by the greatest thinkers, explorers and scientists, men such as Galileo, Columbus, Copernicus, Shakespeare, Locke, Jefferson, Lincoln, Churchill, and Kennedy used words to vividly express radical new ideas that would explain revolutionary complex scientific ideas regarding our world, influence others. Influence being the key word. Words have been used by great men to sell a myriad of ideas, often religious, political, or commercial.

With the invention of the printing press, the advertisement could be distributed far and wide which changed marketing forever. The first American print advertisement was printed in 1704 and by the mid 1800's, billboards began to be used and ad agencies came into existence. By the 1890's, brands began to attract mass followings and consumer loyalty. By the 1920's words could be spoken to anyone who would listen by radio, and by 1941, the first television commercial was aired. Eventually by the 1960's focus groups turned the word with intention to sell and influence into a science. And finally, today words can be transferred from one corner of the globe to the other with a single click.

Words today still serve the same function and purpose that they did when they were first uttered by cave men. They are used to express, convey, explain, and influence. Effective marketing is similar to creating music or creating a work of art. The artist empathizes with his audience, expresses his thoughts through complex means, and ultimately influences his audience with his creation. The same is done when crafting an email or writing a sales letter. We empathize with our audience, we visualize the best possible way to convey our message, to gain someone's trust, to request someone's time, and ultimately ask for one's business.

In this collection, you will find some of the most effective words in the English language. You will find words and word combinations that have been proven to capture attention, gain trust, convey excitement, and ultimately generate sales. This collection has been thoughtfully compiled and utilized by myself and my employees for over a decade now, and I use this compendium daily when I create copy, generate sales letters, and formulate emails. To use this sidekick effectively, replace the placeholders accordingly. For instance, I might want to craft an email to capture attention on how to boost sales, so I will pick a title from **Chapter 4, #1** – It reads - *"<number> powerful methods for <person> who want to <benefit>"* and I will simply replace the place holders with words of my choosing. *"47 Powerful methods for copywriters who want to influence."* It's as simple as that! I hope that you get as much out of this book as I have!

Matt Bacak

PART I
MAGNETIZERS

CHAPTER ONE

DO YOU FIND IT DIFFICULT TO WRITE GREAT EMAIL SUBJECT LINES?

THERE ARE A NUMBER OF THINGS TO DO AND TRY, BUT IT CAN STILL BE HARD TO KNOW IF WHAT YOU'RE WRITING IS REALLY RESONATING WITH YOUR AUDIENCE AND COMPELLING THEM TO ACTUALLY OPEN YOUR EMAILS.

BETTER SUBJECT LINES MEAN MORE "OPENS" OF YOUR EMAIL CAMPAIGNS, AND MORE OPENS LEADS TO MORE CLICK-THROUGHS, MORE CONVERSIONS, AND ULTIMATELY MORE REVENUE FOR YOUR BUSINESS.

YOU CAN ALWAYS GO TO PLACES LIKE GOOGLE AND LOOK AT THE TITLE OF THE ADS AND USE THOSE, OR EVEN LOOK IN YOUR EMAIL BOX TO GET IDEAS.

OR SIMPLY LOOK AT THE ONES I HAVE IN THIS BOOK FOR YOU TO USE, SWIPE OR ADAPT TO GET EVEN FASTER SUBJECT LINES.

CHAPTER 1: EMAIL MARKETING SUBJECT LINES

1. This is going to be insane…

2. This is going to be so real…

3. This is going to be interesting…

4. This is unbelievable…

5. This is scary…

6. This is incredible…

7. This is magnificent…

8. This is life-changing…

9. This is so surprising...

10. He can make <number> in 4 weeks…

11. How did he make <number> in 4 weeks…

12. What a record!

13. What an amazing way to…

14. This is real magical…

15. Start with just $10?

16. You will be shocked!

17. Even the dead are alive now…

18. The next Warren Buffett?

19. First in the world to….

20. You will fall in love with this…

21. This is so irresistible…

22. What a creative idea to…

23. Earning $10k in just 1 hour…

24. Earning six-figures income with just…

25. You are just gonna scream…

26. You are gonna hit the wall…

27. You are just gonna love…

28. You are just not going to resist…

29. You are going to believe this…

30. You are gonna be singing in joy…

31. This is what your teachers did not teach you…

32. Even the rich are not aware…

33. You are not dreaming…

34. Even the experts are saying this…

35. Working has never been so easy before…

36. A 14 years old with 5 figures income?

37. You may not believe it at first…

38. Seriously? 5 figures sales in a day…

39. Even a person with low IQ can do…

40. You will want to know…

41. You never know this happens…

42. He did it in just 5 days…

43. This guy just makes a five figures income in 12 hours….

44. This fellow is earning more than his parents with only…

45. This is what you do not know…

46. The secrets behind $100k…

47. You thought it is a joke…

48. You will be dreaming for this…

49. From bankrupt to millionaire in 3 months…

50. This is why so many people suffering…

51. He has multiple streams of income from…

52. He did it with only 3 hours of work…

53. A father makes 6 figures income after learning…

54. A road sweeper relished his dream of owning a bungalow at the age of 25…

55. The real <benefit> that only <number of %> people in the world know…

56. He is the first person to show you this…

57. No one has ever shown this before…

58. He struggled with life without money and now he is…

59. You never know you can do this as well…

60. This is going to change your life permanently…

61. This is going to turn your life around…

62. See who has the last laugh…

63. Experience the wonder of this man…

64. This will be the perfect tool you are going to have…

65. This will be the missing jigsaw to you…

66. You will regret if you miss this…

67. You will never regret watching this…

68. Breaking news! <nationality> success story unveil the secret to…

69. Breaking news! Former unemployed sweeper turns himself into millionaire…

70. He just became financially free with…

71. Amazing breakthrough to his life with 6-figures income now…

72. Don't choke when you find out the reason to…

73. This is what you never learn in your school…

74. This is so overwhelming…

75. Wow! How can a normal person achieve this in just 1 month…?

76. This dream has just become real…

77. Many people have no idea how he manages to…

78. This will be vital to you…

79. This could be crucial information that you lacked…

80. Be careful! This is going to be mind-opening…

81. This will provide you information to make important decisions…

82. What a breakthrough for a person who is just a drop-out

83. This is not a laughing matter…

84. Ultimate energy now…

85. You will definitely appreciate this…

86. This is going to make you feel alive again…

87. You will be captivated…

88. You will be amazed when you see what this fellow can do…

89. This is just pure inspiring…

90. You will be impressed by the way he earns his first million in just...

91. This is so cool…

92. What the… This person just proves everybody wrong with…

93. Special case! Learn how you can do the same…

94. Let this guy show you how you can do the same…

95. How a 25 years old makes a six-figure income at home…

96. Thinking of how you can do the same too…

97. Easy money for 25 years old…

98. How he did it with nothing at all…

99. Envy about the way he is now…

CHAPTER TWO

BILLIONS OF PEOPLE ARE ON SOCIAL MEDIA.

YES, BILLIONS!

AND EVERY ONE OF THEM ARE COMPETING FOR ATTENTION!

THAT WHY YOU NEED TO MAKE SURE THAT WHAT YOU POST INSTANTLY GRABS EVERYONE'S ATTENTION BECAUSE, THEN AND ONLY THEN, YOU WILL INCREASE YOUR CLICK THROUGH RATES OR GET MORE 'LIKES' ON FACEBOOK.

SO DON'T WASTE YOUR TIME CHECKING OUT WHAT EVERYONE ELSE IS DOING JUST TO END UP IN SOME SOCIAL MEDIA RABBIT HOLE A FEW HOURS LATER...

SIMPLY, ADAPT, TWEAK & ALTER...

AND POST

CHAPTER 2: SOCIAL MEDIA ATTENTION GRABBERS

1. Who else wants _____ ?

2. How _____ game _____(how marketers game SEO)

3. Top ten _____(top ten SEO strategies)

4. _____ tips _____ should really teach

5. The evolution of the _____

6. Who makes money from _____

7. How you can _____ from _____

8. x reasons _____ will lose you _____

9. x ways to _____ by using _____

10. The Secret of_____

11. Here's the method that is helping _____ to _____

12. Little known ways to _____

13. Get rid of _____ once and for all

14. Here's a quick way to_____

15. Now you can have _____

16. _____ like_____(dance like Michael Jackson)

17. Have a _____ you can be proud of

18. Build a _____you can be proud of

19. What everyone ought to know about _____

20. What everybody ought to know about _____

21. Is _____ better than _____?

22. What if you can _____?

23. What are the secrets to _____?

24. Ways _____ can get you _____

25. _____ who _____ (marketers who tweet)

26. Ultimate list of _____ who _____

27. Can you call yourself a ____ if you have _____?

28. A list of people who _____ but are now addicted

29. x best put downs about ____

30. x _____ who _____ (10 businesses who market on facebook)

31. Why _____ will never make _____

32. How to spot a _____ on _____

33. Is _____ the new _____ hotspot?

34. Most famous fake _____

35. Top ten things people most hate about _____

36. Top ten things people love about _____

37. X _____ gurus and their advice

38. How to make _____ work for you

39. Get _____ in _____

40. Is your _____ bothering you again?

41. Will _____change the rules of _____?

42. Give me x days/week/months and I'll make you a _____.
Let me prove it!

43. Only one of these tips can help you avoid _____

44. Do you have any idea how much _____ I've made with
_____?

45. How _____ can lead to a _____

46. Is _____the fuel of _____?

47. Is the ____ higher on _____?

48. Why your _____should _____ now

49. People who should _____ more

50. People who should _____ less

51. People who really should start _____

52. People who should really stop _____

53. Is the best thing about _____that it _____?

54. X of the most stupid _____ ever

55. What defines a _____ Guru?

56. _____ you absolutely must_____ on _____

57. What is the _____of _____?

58. How _____can help _____

59. Ways _____ can help get _____

60. Why success on _____ is not about the_____

61. On _____, the _____ is crucial

62. The greatest _____ since history began

63. Will _____ really _____? (Will product x really makes me money/cure my acne)

64. X reason why you should _____

65. X reason why you should never _____

66. Get _____ with _____ (get in shape with product x)

67. New discovery on _____

68. Do you make these mistakes in _____?

69. How I improved my _____ in x weeks/months/days

70. There are 3 types of _____. Which group you belongs to?

71. To _____ who want to _____, but can't get started.

72. The right and wrong _____ techniques. This little tips can make a huge different

73. X reason why it would have paid to use _____ a few months ago

74. How a simple technique made me a _____

75. How these simple strategies made me a _____

76. I'm going to dispel a myth about <niche>

77. You will be surprised to know how easy to <benefit>

78. I'm giving away <product>

79. Let's boost your < benefit> with <product>

80. I Tripled my profit with <product> in just <time>

81. Wow my profit soar through the roof after <product>

82. Simple <skill> multiplied my <profit> manifold

83. Add a new income stream instantly with <product>

84. I laughed my way to bank upon discovering <niche>

85. Save more when you shop with < marketer>

86. How to reduce your stress by half with <product>

87. I have sneaky suspicion that this gonna be awesome.

88. I just wrote my own check <time> upon discovering <niche>

89. Ever wanted to spend more quality time with your spouse?

90. Find out how I learned <skill> in <time>

91. <Making money/ learning> <skill> is whole lot easier than you think.

92. The experience is always different when you play

93. How I put a smile on <her/his> lips

94. You can also be an expert in <market> in just <time>

95. You cannot make it a Success without a Successful team behind you.

96. <Niche> "Gurus" helped me achieved <benefit> in just <time>

97. Let me show you how you can <benefit> in <times>

98. Just imagine if you can make <benefit> in <time>

99. How much do you need to retire? It's worth discussing

100. Think about all the <benefit> you can get with our <product>

101. Making <benefit> in < niche> is simple if you know the right way

102. Let me show you why you worth it.

103. This investment will continue to pay for many years to come

104. Their objection melts away upon knowing that <benefit>

105. $50,000 banked in 2 weeks.

106. Expert strategies shows how to <benefit>

107. Time-tested <niche> allows one to <benefit>

108. Would you want to learn <skill> in <time>?

109. The key to start a successful <niche> is finding a proven and easy to follow model and duplicate it all over again

110. <Niche> is known by many names, but why should I concern?

111. In less than a year I bought over a house and a car of my dream

112. If you have the sole opportunity to seize everything you want would you interested in knowing?

113. Killing two birds with one bird is indeed practical.

114. Even the best commission is worthless if your customer don't buy

115. Nobody is born a skill <niche>. All you need is the right tools and proven blueprint

116. The reason many failed in <niche> is because of <problem>

117. Are you girded of <problem>? I was, then I found this.

118. Let's make friends to < niche>

119. There is a very simple way to use the power of <niche> and reach <benefit> easily.

120. Everybody here wants success for all, that why this system works

121. Skilled <marketer> are not born, but with the right tools and proven guidance

122. If you follow the simple steps, you will <benefit> in <market>

123. Stop daydream and start working.

124. Work less, play more and travel anywhere you want?

125. Putting the attraction back into <niche>

126. You are frustrated because you are not making <progress>?

127. You are sick and tired of wasting time and money on <niche>

128. I'm making <amount> per month and I can share with you

129. Even people with no experience in <niche> will succeed.

130. How to earn your pocket money with others idea

131. Have you ever imagined yourself as a millionaire?

132. Take the first step in faith; you don't have to see the staircase.

133. To stay on track, keep asking yourself this question, ' what must I do today to profit tomorrow'

134. Be different and never give up your passion in <niche>

135. Be FOCUS and get a good mentor

136. Success is about getting things done. So let's start the <niche>

137. If you wanna succeed and minimize failure, try out < product>

138. To success in something very well, be prepared to get messy.

139. How to invest with your only asset : YOU

140. How to retire at the age of 30 with <product>

141. Can you taste the freedom you are about to experience?

142. Focus and act fast with <product>

143. My total profit plan has been helping many to reach their goal

144. The Lazy man's way to <benefit>

CHAPTER THREE

BLOG'S CAN DRIVE SWARMS OF TRAFFIC TO YOUR MAIN WEBSITE THEY CAN GENERATE MORE PRODUCT SALES, CREATE AN ADDITIONAL STREAM OF ADVERTISING INCOME, BE A GREAT CUSTOMER SERVICE TOOL, AND MUCH MORE!

SO THE NEXT TIME YOU ARE LOST AND CAN'T FIGURE OUT WHAT ATTENTION GRABBING TITLE TO USE FOR YOUR POST – ADAPT, TWEAK & ALTER THESE.

PEOPLE AND THE SEARCH ENGINES WILL PICK IT UP.

CHAPTER 3: BLOG POST SUBJECT LINES

1. <number> steps to be <benefit>

2. <number> important tools to <goal>

3. Top <number> facts about <benefit>

4. Myths about <goal>

5. The #1 myth about <benefit>

6. The #1 myth about <problem>

7. <number> rules to control <goal>

8. <number> tips to be <goal/benefit>

9. <number> sure win methods to <goal>

10. <number> strategies I learned from <benefit>

11. The <number> different ways to <goal>

12. Simple <number> methods to <goals>

13. For those with burning desire: A <benefit>

14. <number> essential skills <person> should learn

15. Create the habit of <benefit> and <goal>

16. The <problem> that crush us

17. Your top <number> questions on <problem>, answered

18. Your top <number> queries on <benefit>, answered

19. Your top <number> confusions on <goal>, answered

20. Clearing your <problem> for <event>

21. How to tackle <problem>

22. How to have the <benefit>

23. How to have the best <goal> and <benefit> in <timeframe>

24. The <goal> challenge: transform your <problem> in <timeframe>

25. A compact guide to <benefit>

26. A compact guide to your <problem> and turn it into your <goal>

27. The essential <goal> habits

28. <number> tips for beating the <problem> habits

29. 100 days to <goal>

30. The secret rule of changing <benefit>

31. <number> simple steps to <goal> from any passion

32. <number> simple principles for becoming <goal>

33. <number> simple principles for <benefit> and <goal>

34. The <number> habits of <benefit>

35. The silliness of <problem>

36. The rules of <goal>

37. How I changed my life, with <number of steps>

38. <number> little things that make <goal> effortless

39. Becoming a god of <goal>

40. Becoming a god of learning <benefit>

41. How to \<benefit\> more: A \<goal\> guide

42. The \<benefit\> that will change your life

43. \<number\> ways to turn \<problem\> into \<goal\>

44. \<number\> shortcuts to finding your \<goal\>

45. Best \<problem\> tips ever

46. \<number\> clear reasons to \<benefit\>

47. \<number\> clear reasons to \<goal\> and \<benefit\> in \<timeframe\>

48. The \<number\> principles of a \<benefit\>

49. The amazing power of being \<goal\>

50. The Tao of \<benefit\>

51. The \<number\> productivity tips from a \<benefit\> master

52. \<number\> simple \<benefit\> fundamentals

53. When willpower is trumped by \<problem\>

54. Simple daily habits to ignite your passion to \<goal\>

55. Effortless \<benefit\>

56. Effortless \<goal\>

57. How to be \<goal\> anytime

58. \<number\> life lessons from a reluctant \<person\>

59. \<number\> \<benefit\> lessons for \<person\>

60. \<goal\>: \<number\> ideas for more \<benefit\>

61. Finally, the truth about \<benefit\>

62. Finally, the truth about \<problem\>

63. Simple <goal> and <benefit> for lazy people

64. How to be <goal> at any age

65. The myth of <goal>

66. <number> simple tips to deal with <problem> people

67. The really simple way to get <benefit>

68. The really simple way to get <goal> and <benefit> in <timeframe>

69. Get started: From <problem> to <goal>

70. The small-scale approach to <goal>

71. <number> of lessons I've learnt in <number> years

72. Breaking free from <problem>

73. The little guide to un-<problem>

74. Surround yourself with <goal> people

75. <number> mindfulness rituals to <goal>

76. <number> mindfulness rituals to <benefit>

77. The simplest cure for <problem>

78. <benefit>: How to <goal>

79. Can't find a perfect <goal>? Create your own

80. <behavior> like <person>: The first step to <goal>

81. <goal> are easy

82. The spiral of <goal>

83. <number> quick tips to identify <problem>

84. The little book of <problem> remedies

85. A Minimalist's Guide to <goal>: The least you need to know to get started

86. The importance of enjoying <benefit>

87. How to be <goal> and still <benefit>

88. <number> creative ways to avoid becoming <problem>

89. The absolute beginners guide to <benefit>

90. The absolute beginners guide to <goal> and <benefit> in <timeframe>

91. The complete beginners guide to <goal>

92. The elements of <goal>

93. <number> ways for <person> to avoid <problem> and <benefit>

94. <number> ways to combat <problem>

95. The ultimate minimalist: <number> powerful lessons you can learn from <famous person>

96. How to master the art of <goal>

97. How I became <goal> in about a day

98. How to be <goal>, in under <number of words>

99. Awesome new eBook on <benefit>

100. The ultimate <goal> guide

CHAPTER FOUR

A GREAT WAY TO DRIVE TARGETED TRAFFIC TO YOUR WEBSITE IS BY WRITING ARTICLES.

YOU'LL FIND ARTICLES QUICKLY HELP YOU WITH BRANDING YOUR NAME, TARGETING TRAFFIC, BUILDING YOUR OR YOUR COMPANIES OWN ONLINE PRESENCE, PLUS IT GIVES YOU A FREE ADVERTISING CHANNEL.

JUST A HANDFUL OF WELL WRITTEN ARTICLES CAN BE TRANSFORMED INTO THOUSANDS OF TARGETED VISITORS ONLINE.

SO BE SURE TO ALWAYS COME BACK TO GET YOUR NEXT POST TITLE BY ADAPTING, TWEAKING OR ALTERING ONE OF THESE.

CHAPTER 4: MAGNETIZING ARTICLE TITLES

1. \<number\> powerful methods for \<person\> who want to \<benefit\>

2. \<number\> instant working methods

3. \<number\> ways to \<benefit\> and \<goal\>

4. \<number\> ways to \<goal\> in \<timeframe\>

5. Building the best \<goal\>

6. End your worst nightmare now with \<number\> sure-fire methods to \<benefit\>

7. End your worst nightmare with \<number\> sure-fire methods to \<goal\> and \<benefit\> in the next \<timeframe\>

8. \<number\> secrets that only the smart knows

9. \<number\> misconceptions about \<problem\>

10. \<number\>misconceptions about \<goal\>

11. \<number\> misconceptions about \<benefit\>

12. Boost your \<goal\> by 5 times

13. \<number\> of secrets to \<goal\>

14. Truths of \<problem\> you never realized

15. Truths of \<benefit\>

16. Art of \<benefit\>

17. Instant boost to your \<goal\>

18. Developing the potential to <goal> in you in 2 weeks

19. <number> important tips to allow you to be <goal>

20. Discover the path to <goal>

21. Discover the truths of <benefit>

22. Discover the secrets of <problem> and overcome them

23. Discover the <number> simple tips that pushed me to make a six-figures income by <age>

24. Find out the <number> easy steps that allowed me to make a six-figures income with <timeframe>

25. Find out the <number> simple steps that allowed me to make a six-figures income by <age>

26. The truth about <benefit>

27. The truth about <problem> you are kept away from till now

28. Imagine you can achieve <goal> in 2 weeks

29. Imagine you can <benefit> in just <timeframe>

30. Imagine you can <benefit> and <goal>

31. At last, you will find out how to <benefit>

32. At last, you will find out how to <benefit> and <goal> in <timeframe>

33. <number> new tips to <benefit>

34. <number> new tips to overcome <problem>

35. <number> new tips to get <goal> within <timeframe>

36. Build your <goal> during recession

37. Harness the secret to <benefit>

38. Harness the secret to <benefit> and <goal> within the next minute

39. How you can transform your life with <benefit>

40. How you can turn your life 180 degrees with <benefit>

41. How you can turn your life 180 degrees with <benefit> and <goal> right away?

42. <number> free <benefit> that allow you to <goal>

43. How to <goal> effortlessly

44. How to <goal> and <benefit> in <timeframe> effortlessly

45. Master the <number> ways to <goal>

46. Master the <number> ways to <goal> and <benefit> in just <timeframe>

47. The best way to <goal>

48. The best way to <goal> and <benefit>

49. How to stop <problem> with <number of steps>

50. How to stop <problem> with <number of steps> in <timeframe>

51. Your shortcut to gain <benefit>

52. Your shortcut to <goal> and <benefit> in <timeframe>

53. Your shortcut to turn your <problem> into <goal>

54. Encounter <number of steps> to <goal>

55. Encounter the easiest and simplest way to <benefit> and <goal>

56. Encounter the <number> methods you can use immediately to <benefit>

57. Announcing <number of ways> you can <benefit>

58. Announcing <number of ways> you can <benefit> and <goal> easily

59. Announcing <number of ways> you can <benefit> and <goal> within <timeframe>

60. <number> types of different methods you can <benefit>

61. <number> types of different methods you can <goal> and <benefit> in <timeframe>

62. Unlock the <number> secret to <benefit>

63. Unlock the <number> secret to <goal> and <benefit> in just <timeframe>

64. The top <number> reasons to <problem>

65. The top <number of steps> to <benefit> and <goal>

66. The top <number of steps> to <benefit> and <goal> with <timeframe>

67. Should you still continue to <goal>?

68. Best <number> tips for <person> to <goal> instantly

69. How to <goal>

70. Are you protecting yourself from <problem>?

71. Looking for <benefit>? Simply read on

72. Improving the <benefit> for <person>

73. The rise of <benefit> and <goal>

74. <benefit> basics

75. <goal> basics

76. Top opportunities to <goal> and <benefit> by <timeframe>

77. The do's and don'ts of <goal>

78. <goal> and the importance of it

79. <benefit> and the importance of it

80. Cheapest way to <benefit>

81. Cheapest way to <goal> and <benefit>

82. The fundamentals when it comes to <goal>

83. The <number> fundamental tips when it comes to <goal> and <benefit>

84. <number> extra <goal> ideas

85. <number> steps guide to <benefit>

86. <number> steps guide to <goal>

87. <number> reasons why you need <benefit>

88. <number> reasons why you need to <goal> and <benefit>

89. <number> breakthrough in <benefit>

90. <number> breakthrough in <goal> and <benefit>

91. An introduction to <benefit>

92. An introduction to <goal> and <benefit>

93. <number> creative ideas to <goal>

94. Why you are not <benefit>?

95. <number> guides to successful <goal>

96. <number> razor-sharp guides for <goal> and <benefit>

97. <number> truths about <goal> you should know

98. One secret of that they will never let you know

99. Starting <goal> with only a small budget

100. The biggest secret that will cement your <goal> success

CHAPTER
FIVE

BELIEVE IT OR NOT, PEOPLE STILL READ THE NEWSPAPER.

DESPITE THE FACT THAT IT HAS TAKEN A HIT IN POPULARITY THAT DOES NOT MEAN THAT IT SHOULD BE IGNORED WHEN IT COMES TO RUNNING ADS.

IT IS STILL AN EFFICIENT AND TRUSTED SOURCE FOR INFORMATION AND ADVERTISING.

IF YOU EVER GET A WILD HAIR TO PUT DOWN YOUR ONLINE DEVICE AND GO OFFLINE, MAKE SURE YOU COME BACK AND ADAPT, TWEAK & ALTER THESE.

CHAPTER 5: NEWSPAPER, PRINT AND TEXT ADS

1. Get _____ fast & easy!

2. We offer _____ and faster _____

3. Do you want faster results in _____?

4. Now you can _____ unbelievably fast

5. No one would expect to see _____ so fast

6. If you want fast results, it has to be _____

7. _____ is going to work so fast and effective

8. Who else wants to _____faster than others?

9. No risk _____solution. Guaranteed!

10. You're fully protected when you purchase_____.

11. Peace of mind with _____. 100% guaranteed results.

12. No Hassle, Get your money back if _____ don't work for you!

13. 100% Risk Free when you get _____

14. The first 50_____ will get a FREE_____.

15. Only x units will be sold at this price

16. We are offering 50% discounts for first 30 customers

17. You better get _____ fast. Only limited units available!

18. We are extending the_____ offer for 2 more days.

19. Our customer have witness remarkable results with _____

20. _____ is never this easy. Get _____ now!

21. Simply _____ and see the results in no time!

22. Try _____ and see how you can _____ easily!

23. You're not going to believe how easy _____ could be with _____

24. Easy ways to _____ in _____days/weeks

25. Even a 5 year old can _____ with _____

26. _____ is as easy as A B C.

27. Our customers never thought _____could be this easy

28. Mr. X made _____ by using _____

29. More than 3000 satisfied customer. Join them now!

30. Be amazed just like our 3000 happy customers!

31. Mr. X has tried many other _____ products but only _____ works!

32. Find out what our 1000 customers think about our products!

33. Get 30% discount on our _____ sales (X-mas, Black Friday, etc.)

34. Get _____ this _____for up to 50% discount!

35. Celebrate _____ with us & received a complimentary _____

36. Its _____ and we would like to offer you a _____discounts/gifts for being a loyal customer.

37. Get yourself a FREE _____ when you purchase_____

38. This _____ worth $300 is now yours for FREE!

39. FREE____ when you purchase up to $200!

40. Receive a _____ at no cost when you visit our stores.

41. We are giving away ____ for our loyal customers

42. Thank you for being with us for ___years. We are giving ____ for FREE this anniversary!

43. Discounts up to 80% on our anniversary sale this _____ (months)

44. We're here to serve your _____ needs

45. We are assure your _____ will be taken care of when you ____ with us.

46. We are confident that you will be 100% satisfied!

47. You will be blown away when you try _____

48. Your _____need is our commitment

49. This is an important message for _____

50. Why ___ is important for you?

51. This is important if you're suffering from _____

52. New _____ that solve your ____ problem

53. We are the pioneer in ____

54. Try the New _____ and _____

55. We are the first in the world to introduce ____

56. Warning!!

57. Attention to those craving for ____

58. If you are serious about ____, then ____

59. Announcing the fastest growing <market>

60. Introducing the Blueprint of <niche>

61. Attention: Have you ever wanted to <benefit>

62. The world was shocked when <niche> revealed

63. Never revealed before the Secret of <niche>

64. Smoking hot <product> shows proven result!

65. The first of its kind has revealed <benefit>

66. Skyrocket your sale account with <product>

67. Money printing license up for grab.

68. Step by step guidance to making your first Million

69. Secret blueprint to your first Million

70. Autopilot your business in <time> with <product>

71. Maximum value of <benefit> at Minimum cost of <price>

72. Kiss <problem> goodbye with <product>

73. Buy anything you want without looking at the price tag with <product>

74. Enjoy tax free income with <niche>

75. How to write your own check with <niche>

76. Traditional <skill> won't work for everyone

77. Beware selling the Dream in your <market>

78. Learning <skill> has never been as easy as pie

79. Are you ready to use this <product> to generate absurd amount of income?

80. Step by step secret to <benefit> as early as tonight

81. 5 keys to <niche > success

82. Paving your millionaire path the easy way with <product>

83. Turn your passion profitable business the Easy way with <product>

84. The Lazy man's way to dominate in <market>

85. How to make money out of your passion that pays and pays

86. The secret killer idea that the expert refuse to reveal

87. You want to learn the most effective and high potent <niche> strategist?

88. <Niche> for this Tough Time

89. Your life will never be the same upon discovering <niche>

90. Introducing the Forbidden Fruit of <niche>

91. 24 year-old six figure earner reveals <benefit>

92. Learning <niche> is really easy if you have an Expert by your side

93. Legendary <niche> LEAKED!!

94. $50,000 banked in 2 weeks

95. The secret behind <niche> that wins

96. Here is how to profit intently and easily -- As we have done the hard work for you.

97. Time-tested <skill> shows <benefit>

98. Why we want you to be the next <market> extraordinaire.

99. The reason why I'm successful in <niche> and you are not.

100. Powerful tip and expert strategies in <niche> shows <benefit>

101. Follow our success wizard and develop your <niche>

102. Ultimate one stop guide to <benefit>

103. Brand New, Cutting edge <niche>

104. Discover the easiest way to <benefit> as soon as possible

105. How you can have <everything> on your hand in less than 72 hours

106. How I purchased my dream house in less than 6 months

107. Start <niche> even if you have completely no idea how to start

108. This is the right place with right tools to bring you <benefit> in <market>

109. First class expert shows <benefit>

110. How to turn your <passion> into your personal money maker.

111. How to <niche> - ideas for those looking for <benefit>

112. Number 1 <niche> Secret!

113. TRUTH about <niche> Unclothed

114. The Fastest, Easiest, Simplest way to <benefit>

115. Outrageous simple with proven blueprint you cannot afford to miss.

116. Be a Millionaire, all you need to do is unlock the code with <product>

117. How to stay ahead of <niche>

118. We invite you to join our <market> and ditch your corporate cubicle

119. Kill all your birds with one stone in <niche>

120. Proven record to win like a Champion in <niche>

121. Would you like to <benefit> in our FREE club?

122. A MUST for those seriously in <niche>

123. How to transform your uniqueness into profitable <niche>

124. <Niche> blueprint revealed, which will fulfill all your dream

125. Ultimate Guide to have your <problem solved>

126. The ugly Truth about your <niche>

127. Building your own brand <product> the easy way

128. World class <marketer> reveals the truth on <niche>

129. The proven system that allows you to <benefit> with expert's help

130. This WORKS even if you are newbie

131. Spending like a boss is within your reach

132. Work less, play more and free to travel

133. Your dream business/ life start with <product>

134. The <product> that gives you wealth even before you could realize

135. Just do it, but how? And our <product> knew it

136. Ultimate tip to infinite money generator

CHAPTER SIX

TALKING ABOUT YOURSELF CAN BE HARD.

HOWEVER, THINK ABOUT THIS...

PEOPLE WRITE RESUMES ALL THE TIME!

PAGES AND BIO'S, YOU NAME IT! IT'S ALL ABOUT YOU!

THESE BIO BOOSTERS, WILL HELP YOU OVERCOME THAT FEAR IF YOU HAVE IT, IF NOT, IT WILL HELP YOU GENERATE GREAT IDEAS TO USE FOR YOURSELF.

OPEN YOU MIND AND THINK ABOUT HOW YOU CAN ADAPT, TWEAK & ALTER SOME OF THESE FOR YOURSELF AND TAILOR THEM TO DESCRIBE YOU.

CHAPTER 6: BIO BOOSTERS

1. It has become an Internet sensation...

2. To this day people continue to talk about <product>

3. Here we share the <Top marketer> message and put his life lesson into action.

4. You will see this no other than here

5. Apart from here you will get this information nowhere else.

6. Let the 'gurus' show you how to <skill>

7. This <skill> is one of the greatest for <benefit>

8. This is the real money making idea that only Top Money Maker aware of

9. The Hottest <niche> in the market has yet to reveal until you finish reading what the expert have to say.

10. Though there are many "expert" out there, but let me guide you with my proven track record

11. If you are smart enough you will go to only those with proven track record

12. Never before this secret <niche

13. Let the top in the industry guide you step by step into <benefit>

14. Let us show you how to turn your <problem> into <benefit>

15. Let's make your big buck by learning from the best.

16. Discover how Top Income earner make profit in <niche>

17. This is a very specialized skill

18. Successful "Gurus" reveals his secret <skill/ product>

19. Let's team up with the <market> Extraordinaire.

20. Work only with those has proven record of <niche>

21. We know and have experience in what we are offering

22. The biggest producer in <market>

23. The fastest growing < niche> in the market

24. Expert strategies in <niche>

25. The <marketer> who provides a life time guarantee strategies

26. Let veteran show you your passport to <benefit>

27. Our record is been known far and wide enough to show <benefit>

28. The most powerful <niche> in the market today

29. Top <niche> secret revealed

30. 2 hours from now you will <prospect benefit>

31. You are to join the proven system that in just 5 minute you will start <prospect benefit>

32. Follow my secret < niche> blueprint that will make you < benefit>

33. Discover what the best has created < benefit>

34. Why my strategy are the genuine way to <benefits>

35. This Highly Specialize <skill> will help you <benefits>

36. This highly- recognize <product> will turn your <problem > into <solution>

37. Let me show you how this highly profitable <niche> help you achieve <benefit> you could ever dream for.

38. Top Rated <niche> launching < product>

39. Discover the Most Powerful <niche> ever created in the history of <market>

40. This unique <niche> has entirely transformed the....

41. The Revolutionary <skill> makes you <benefits> in 15 minutes GUARANTEED!

42. Discover the Most Profitable <niche> in the <market> as the soonest as possible.

43. The key to start a successful <career> is to find a successful and proven model and duplicating it over and over again.

44. Here is the Bullet-proof system to <solve problem>

45. Let the Fastest emerging <marketer> leads you to your <success/benefits>

46. Outrageously simple with my proven blueprint you will never <old problem>

47. Nobody is horned a skilled <talent>. All you need is the Proven Blueprint and Right Guidance

48. This <product> is a MUST for anyone who wants to <benefits/ success>

49. This is the RIGHT place with RIGHT tools to bring you <benefit>

50. Join the BEST and <benefits>

51. It is really easy when an Expert assist you in <niche>

52. The reason why I'm successful in <niche> and you are not.

53. Apart from the proven record, our expert possess the easy to follow step by step guidance to <benefit>

54. If you are in the <niche market> long enough you will know that this Block- buster <product> going to make you <benefit>

55. I'm making 5 figures/ per month and I would like to share with you.

56. Let the Top-Ranking show you how to <skill>

57. The Number One Killer <product> for <niche>

58. With Expert help,

59. This proven system allows you to <benefits>

60. Do you want to learn the High potent and Most Powerful strategies that guarantee <benefit>?

61. This is REAL. Only a small group of top earner knows the Truth about <market>

62. Let me show you how you can <skill> in <time>

63. My secret strategies has help many scheme their dreams of <benefit>

64. You are just few minute from learning the Most Powerful <skill>

65. You have clicked on our site because you realize the most powerful way to <niche>

66. If you would like to unclothed the Best-kept secret of <niche>

67. We are in the market long enough to show you <benefit>

68. We are in the league of our own.

69. After years in the market, we are pleased to reveal that <solution>

70. The step by step techniques used by the world most successful <niche> "gurus"

71. The single most powerful strategies in <niche> that will produce stunning result

72. The Greatest <niche> secret ever surfaced

73. This is the SINGLE amazing step you must take to avoid <problem>

74. This is the quickest way to overtake anyone else and jump start the <niche>

75. Let's tap in to the fastest-growing goldmine in the market by < take action>

76. Get instant access to our Professional guidance

77. The most important tools in your <niche > collections

78. Get the absolute most powerful <niche> you will ever discover

79. The single most successful <niche> market ever produced and what you can learn from....

80. The simplest formula anyone can jump start right away

81. This unique <niche> pioneered by < > in < > has successfully produce <result>

82. The ultimate secret of <niche> ever revealed

83. The single most popular <niche> you will ever find in market

84. Where to find the Qualified <guru> and knowing exactly what you are going to achieve?

85. This is the top-of-line product that will lead you to <success>

86. Meets the America's number one < >

87. This single secret strategies will help you more than all others combined

88. This amazing <niche> is just the best in the business

89. This is the finest <product> you can own

90. The best in the industry

91. Imitator are relying on our vision to spread head the direction in the industry

92. This second to none secret strategies...

93. This Is the Best place you can <benefit>

94. Discover the most important <niche> that will give you unfair advantages

95. A brand new discovery where anyone can use it instantly to <benefits >

96. The ONLY list anyone need to succeed in <career>

97. The Most Important thing you must know before kick start in < >

98. This Top Notch information will reveal the secret of <niche>

99. A <number> step that guaranteed your success in <niche>

100. Grab this First-Class <niche> at no frill-price

101. Ultimate <niche> secret revealed for the very First Time

102. The phenomenally success of our customer provide a glimpse of how you too can do the same.

103. We are the leader of our industry

104. We have beaten our competitor in their petty game

CHAPTER SEVEN

IF YOUR HEADLINE SUCKS, YOU'RE DONE!

AS YOU MAY ALREADY KNOW, THE PURPOSE OF YOUR HEADLINE IS TO GET THE PROSPECT'S UNDIVIDED ATTENTION.

WHAT YOU WANT YOUR READERS TO DO WHEN THEY SEE YOUR HEADLINE IS TO SAY, "WOW, I HAVE TO GET MORE INFORMATION". YOU WANT TO GET THEM TO JUMP DOWN TO THE NEXT LINE AND BE EXCITED TO READ MORE.

THAT'S WHY THERE'S A BOATLOAD OF THEM HERE FOR YOU TO ADAPT, TWEAK & ALTER THEN USE FOR YOURSELF.

CHAPTER 7: HEADLINES

1. How To <benefit> ...in Less than <timeframe>

2. Who Else Wants To <benefit> in Only <timeframe>?

3. Who Else Wants To <benefit> and <goal>?

4. <no Of Steps/tips> To <benefit>

5. To People Who Want To <benefit> -- But Can't Get Started

6. To Men Who Want To <benefit> -- But Can't Get Started

7. To Women Who Want To <benefit> -- But Can't Get Started

8. It's A Shame For You Not To <benefit> -- When These People Do It So Easily

9. Thousands Now <benefit> Who Never Thought They Could

10. Great New Discovery Helps You <benefit>

11. Great New Discovery Helps You <benefit> in Less Than <timeframe>

12. Here's A Quick Way To <benefit>

13. What Everybody Should Know... About How To <benefit>

14. Free Book... Tells You <no Of Steps/tips> To <benefit>

15. Greatest Gold-Mine Of Easy "<benefit>" Advice Ever Crammed Into One Product

16. <benefit> in As Little As <timeframe> With These <no of Steps/tips>

17. <no of Steps/tips> To <benefit>

18. <no Of Steps/tips> To <goal>

19. <no Of Steps/tips> To <benefit> in Just <timeframe>

20. Thousands Now <benefit> Who Never Thought They Could ...With These <no Of Steps/tips>

21. <no of Steps/tips> to <benefit> and <goal>

22. The Secret of <goal>

23. The Secret of <goal> in Just <timeframe>

24. Proven Advice To <benefit> -- By An Expert

25. Proven Advice To <benefit> And <goal> -- By An Expert

26. You Can Laugh At <benefit> Worries -- If You Follow This Simple Plan

27. It Seems Incredible That You Can <benefit> And <goal>

28. It Seems Incredible That You Can <benefit> In Only <timeframe>

29. How I <goal> in Less Than <timeframe>

30. How Often Do You Find Yourself Saying: "I Wish I Knew How To <benefit>"

31. How Often Do You Find Yourself Saying: "I Wish I Knew How To <goal>"

32. You Are Guaranteed To <goal> -- Or We Pay You

33. Everywhere People Are Raving About These Amazing <no Of Steps/tips> To <goal>

34. Everywhere People Are Raving About These Amazing <no Of Steps/tips> To <benefit>

35. What Everybody Ought To Know -- About How To <benefit>

36. The Truth About How To <benefit>

37. The Truth About How To <goal>

38. How To <benefit> Today Starting From Scratch

39. How To <benefit> in Only <timeframe> Starting From Scratch

40. How To <goal> Today Starting From Scratch

41. How To <goal> in Only <timeframe> Starting From Scratch

42. Dare To <benefit>

43. Dare To <goal>

44. A Startling Fact About How To <benefit>

45. A Startling Fact About How To <goal>

46. A Startling Fact About How To <goal> ...In Less Than <timeframe>

47. A Startling Fact About How To <benefit> ...In Less Than <timeframe>

48. Need To <benefit>?

49. Need To <goal>?

50. Are You Willing To Follow <no Of Steps/tips> To <benefit>

51. Are You Willing To Follow <no Of Steps/tips> To <goal>

52. It's A Shame For You Not To <goal> -- When These People Do It So Easily

53. Thousands Now <goal> Who Never Thought They Could

54. Great New Discovery Helps You <goal> In Less Than <timeframe>

55. Here's A Quick Way To <benefit> In Less Than <timeframe>

56. Here's A Quick Way To <goal> In Less Than <timeframe>

57. The Shocking Truth About How To <goal>!

58. The Shocking Truth About How To <benefit>!

59. <goal>. It's No Accident. In <timeframe>, I Can Show You How To <benefit>

60. <goal>. It's No Accident. In <timeframe>, I Can Show You How!

61. <no Of Steps/tips> To Keep Your Fears From Holding YOU Back - <benefit> Now!

62. <no Of Steps/tips> To Keep Your Fears From Holding YOU Back - <benefit> In <timeframe>

63. Would You Like To <benefit>?

64. Would You Like To <goal>?

65. Look Inside To Discover How To <goal>

66. Here's <no Of Steps/tips> To <goal>

67. Here's <no Of Steps/tips> To <benefit>

68. Look Inside To Discover How To <benefit>

69. Serious About Wanting To <benefit>? Here's How To <goal>! Guaranteed... Or Your Money Back!

70. You CAN <goal> In Only <timeframe> ...Guaranteed!

71. You CAN <goal> With These <no Of Steps/tips> ...Guaranteed!

72. Yes YOU Too Can Learn How To <benefit> With Ease!

73. Yes YOU Too Can Learn How To <goal> With Ease!

74. Yes These <no Of Steps/tips> Will Help You Learn How To <goal> With Ease!

75. Yes These <no Of Steps/tips> Will Help You Learn How To <benefit> With Ease!

76. Yes These <no Of Steps/tips> Guarantee You Will <goal>!

77. Yes These <no Of Steps/tips> Guarantee You Will <benefit>!

78. Yes These <no Of Steps/tips> Helped Me <goal> And They Will Work For YOU Too

79. Yes These <no Of Steps/tips> Helped Me <benefit> And They Will Work For YOU Too

80. Proven Tips, Tools and Tactics To <benefit>

81. Proven Tips, Tools and Tactics To <goal>

82. The Complete Guide To <goal>

83. The Complete Guide To <benefit>

84. The Complete Guide Of <no Of Steps/tips> To <benefit>

85. The Complete Guide Of <no Of Steps/tips> To <goal>

86. The Quick And Easy Way To <goal>

87. The Quick And Easy Way To <benefit>

88. The Quick And Easy Way To <goal> In Only <timeframe>

89. The Quick And Easy Way To <benefit> In Only <timeframe>

90. How To <benefit> Quickly And Easily – 100% Guaranteed!

91. How To <goal> Quickly And Easily – 100% Guaranteed!

92. Imagine... You Can <benefit> In Just <timeframe>

93. Imagine... You Can <goal> In Just <timeframe>

94. You Deserve To <benefit>!

95. Proven Techniques Help You <benefit> - Guaranteed!

96. Proven Techniques Help You <goal> - Guaranteed!

97. You Deserve To <goal>!

98. Don't Wait Another Moment! <goal> Now!

99. How To <benefit> Fast And <goal>

100. They Laughed When I Said I'd <benefit> in <duration>-- But When I <goal> They Begged Me For My Secret!

101. <no Of Steps/tips>To How To <benefit> in <duration> And <goal>

102. Want To <goal>? Here's How To <benefit> in <duration> Now!

103. FREE Report Reveals 5 Secrets To <benefit> in <duration>

104. New Discovery Reveals How To <benefit> in <duration>!

105. Who Else Wants To <benefit> in <duration> And <goal>?!

106. It's True: You Really Can <benefit> in <duration> And Here's How...

107. New <benefit> Program Helps You <goal>... Guaranteed!

108. Tests Now Show Our <benefit> Program Can Help You <goal>

109. Double Your Money Back If You Don't <benefit> in <duration> With Our Amazing System

110. Free Book Tells You <no Of Steps/tips> To <benefit> in <duration>

111. Here's A Quick Way To <benefit> in <duration>

112. To People Who Want To <benefit> in <duration> But Can't Get Started

113. Double Your Money Back If You Don't <benefit> in <duration>

114. Free Book Tells You <no Of Steps/tips>To <benefit> in <duration>

115. Here's A Quick Way To <benefit> in <duration> And <goal>

116. To People Who Want To <benefit> in <duration> But Can't Get Started

117. Moral, Ethical, & Perfectly Legal Ways To <benefit> in <duration>

118. (Your State or City) Man/Woman Reveals A Short Cut To <benefit> in <duration>

119. The Lazy Man's Way To <benefit> in <duration>

120. <benefit> in <duration> In Just <duration> - Guaranteed!

121. I Never Thought I Could <benefit> in <duration> - But I Finally Discovered The Secret! Here's How...

122. Here's The Only Way Left For Regular Guys/Gals Like You And Me To <benefit> in <duration>

123. Top (Add Title) Spills The Beans On How Industry Insiders Are Quietly <benefit> in <duration>

124. Top (Add Title) Spills The Beans On The Inside Secrets To <benefit> in <duration>

125. The Quickest Way I Know To <benefit> in <duration> And <goal>

126. A in <duration> And FUN Way To <benefit> in <duration>

127. For The First Time, New Breakthrough System Reveals How To <benefit> in <duration>

128. What You Don't Know About Is Costing You A Fortune! - Here's The Straight Scoop On How To <benefit> in <duration>

129. Ex- Executive/Insider Exposes Underground Trade-Industry Secrets To <benefit> in <duration>

130. If You Want To <benefit> in <duration> And Have All But Given Up... Here's Hope!

131. Here's The #1 Way To <benefit> in <duration> - And I'll Prove It To You!

132. Paying Too Much? Here's How To <benefit> in <duration> BETTER - For Less!

133. If You Can Follow Simple Directions, Here's How To <benefit> in <duration> In Your Spare Time - And Have Fun Doing It!

134. <benefit> in <duration> While You Sleep - Our Proven System Will Do The Work!

135. 100 Percent Guaranteed! ... <benefit> In Only in <duration> ... Or Your Money Back!

136. 100 Percent Guaranteed! ... <solve your problem> In Only in <duration> ... Or Your Money Back!

137. A Better Way To <benefit>

138. A Better Way To <solve your problem>

139. A Breakthrough in How To <benefit>

140. A Breakthrough in How To <benefit> ... In Only in <duration>!

141. A Breath of Fresh Air! ... Now You Can <benefit> In As Little As in <duration>

142. A Chance Like No Other! ... Now You Can <benefit> In As Little As in <duration>

143. A Complete Arsenal of Powerful Information on How To <benefit> - By An Expert

144. A Complete Guide To <benefit>

145. A Complete Guide To <benefit> And <solve your problem> In As Little As in <duration>!

146. A Complete and Comprehensive Blueprint On How To <benefit> - By An Expert

147. A Complete and Comprehensive Blueprint On How To <benefit> ... Guaranteed Or Your Money Back!

148. A Comprehensive Plan to <benefit> in Only in <duration> ...Guaranteed!

149. A Comprehensive Plan to <solve your problem> in Only in <duration> ...Guaranteed!

150. A Custom Designed Program Just For You On How To <benefit> in as Little As in <duration>

151. A Fresh Approach in How To <benefit> - By An Expert!

152. A Fresh Approach in How To <benefit> .. Just What You Have Been Looking For!

153. A Good Friend Of Mine Asked Me How To <benefit> ... Here's What I Told Him

154. A Guaranteed Way to <benefit> ... In <No of steps/tips/secrets>

155. A Guaranteed Way to <benefit> .. Quickly And Easily!

156. A Guaranteed Way to <solve your problem>... Quickly And Easily!

157. A New Twist in How To <benefit> and <solve your problem>... In as Little As in <duration>!

158. A Once In a Lifetime Opportunity ... Learn How To <benefit> - From An Expert!

159. A Powerful Way To <benefit>... In Only in <duration>

160. A Proven Method to <benefit> ... Quickly and Easily!

161. A Rare Opportunity to Learn From An Expert - How To <benefit> Quickly And Easily

162. A Rare Opportunity to Learn How To <benefit> - From An Expert!

163. A Startling Fact About How To <benefit>

164. A Startling Fact About How To <benefit> ...In Less Than in <duration>

165. A Startling Fact About How To <solve your problem>

166. A Startling Fact About How To <solve your problem>...In Less Than in <duration>

167. A Wonderful Way to <benefit> Quickly and Easily

168. A Wonderful Way to <solve your problem> Quickly and Easily

169. Amazing! You Can Really <benefit> in Only in <duration> ... We'll Show You How!

170. Amazing! You Can Really <benefit> in Only in <duration> ... With Our Help

171. Amazing! You Can Really <benefit> in Only in <duration> ... With These 5 of the Most Critical Steps!

172. Amazing New System Helps You <benefit> Like Crazy ... Exciting Details Below

173. Amazing New System Helps You <solve your problem> Like Crazy ... Exciting Details Below

174. An Amazing Way to <benefit> ... 100 Percent Guaranteed!

175. An Amazing Way to <benefit> in Only in <duration> ... 100 Percent Guaranteed!

176. Are You Willing To Follow <No of steps/tips/secrets>To <benefit>

177. Are You Willing To Follow <No of steps/tips/secrets>To <solve your problem>

178. Attention: Men Who Want To <benefit> ...These <No of steps/tips/secrets>Will Show You How!

179. Attention: Men Who Want To <benefit> ... You Gotta See This!

180. Attention: Men Who Want To <benefit> .. We Have the Perfect Solution!

181. Attention: Women Who Want To <benefit> ...These <No of steps/tips/secrets> Will Show You How!

182. Attention: Women Who Want To <benefit> .. . We Have The Perfect Solution!

183. Attention: Women Who Want To <benefit> ... You Gotta See This!

184. <benefit> Now! You're <No of steps/tips/secrets> Away!

185. Congratulations! .. You've Found It .. The Perfect Way to <benefit>

186. Congratulations! .. You've Found It .. The Perfect Way to <solve your problem>

187. Dare To <benefit>

188. Dare To <solve your problem>

189. Discover Mind Blowing Ways To <benefit>

190. Discover Mind Blowing Ways To <benefit> and <solve your problem>

191. Discover Mind Blowing Ways To <benefit> in As Little As in <duration>!

192. Don't Touch That Dial! ... You Can <benefit> in in <duration> .. We'll Show You How!

193. Don't Touch That Dial! ... You Can <solve your problem> in in <duration> .. We'll Show You How!

194. Don't Wait Another Moment! <solve your problem> Now!

195. Endorsed By Experts ... Our System Will Help You <benefit> Quickly and Easily .. Guaranteed!

196. Endorsed By Experts ... Our System Will Help You <solve your problem> Quickly and Easily .. Guaranteed!

197. Even the Experts Admit .. This is the Best Way to <benefit> ... Period!

198. Even the Experts Admit .. This is the Best Way to <solve your problem>... Period!

199. Everybody's Talking About It ... Now You Too Can <benefit> With These <No of steps/tips/secrets>

200. Everybody's Talking About It ... Now You Too Can <benefit> in Only in <duration>!

201. Everybody's Talking About It ... Now You Too Can <solve your problem> in Only in <duration>!

202. Everybody's Talking About It ... Now You Too Can <solve your problem> With These <No of steps/tips/secrets>

203. Everywhere People Are Raving About These Amazing <No of steps/tips/secrets> To <benefit>

204. Everywhere People Are Raving About These Amazing <No of steps/tips/secrets> To <solve your problem>

205. Expert Reveals How You Can <benefit> in Only in <duration> ...Guaranteed!

206. Expert Reveals How You Can <benefit> in Only in <duration> ...With These <No of steps/tips/secrets>

207. Expert Reveals How You Can <solve your problem> in Only in <duration> ... Guaranteed!

208. Expert Reveals How You Can <solve your problem> in Only in <duration> ...With These <No of steps/tips/secrets>

209. Experts Agree .. This is the Best Way to <benefit> ... Hands Down!

210. Experts Agree .. This is the Best Way to <solve your problem>... Hands Down!

211. Finally! A Sure-Fire Way To <benefit> At Breakneck Speed! ... I'll Personally Guarantee It!

212. Finally Revealed! How to <benefit> and <solve your problem>

213. For Those That Want to <benefit> At Breakneck Speed .. This is a No Brainer!

214. Free Book... Tells You <No of steps/tips/secrets> To <benefit>

215. Great New Discovery Helps You <benefit>

216. Great New Discovery Helps You <benefit> In Less Than in <duration>

217. Great New Discovery Helps You <solve your problem> In Less Than in <duration>

218. Greatest Gold-Mine Of Easy "<benefit>" Advice Ever Crammed Into One Product

219. Guaranteed! ... <benefit> In Only in <duration> ... Or Your Money Back!

220. Guaranteed! ... <benefit> In Only in <duration> ... With These <No of steps/tips/secrets>... Or Your Money Back!

221. Guaranteed! ... <solve your problem> In Only in <duration> ... Or Your Money Back!

222. Guaranteed! ... <solve your problem> In Only in <duration> ... With These <No of steps/tips/secrets>... Or Your Money Back!

223. Hard Hitting Facts About How To <benefit> - From An Expert

224. Hard Hitting Facts About How To <benefit> - You Don't Want To Miss This!

225. Here's A Quick Way To <benefit>

226. Here's A Quick Way To <benefit> In Less Than in <duration>

227. Here's A Quick Way To <solve your problem>In Less Than in <duration>

228. Here's <No of steps/tips/secrets> To <benefit>

229. Here's <No of steps/tips/secrets> To <solve your problem>

230. Here's An Unbeatable Offer ... I'll Personally Teach You How To <benefit> In As Little As in <duration>!

231. How Anyone Can <benefit> and <solve your problem> In Only in <duration>!

232. How I <solve your problem> In Less Than in <duration>

233. How Often Do You Find Yourself Saying: "I Wish I Knew How To <benefit>"

234. How Often Do You Find Yourself Saying: "I Wish I Knew How To <solve your problem>"

235. How To <benefit> ...In Less Than in <duration>

236. How To <benefit> In Only in <duration> Starting From Scratch

237. How To <benefit> Quickly And Easily - 100 Percent Guaranteed!

238. How To <benefit> Today Starting From Scratch

239. How To <solve your problem> In Only in <duration> Starting From Scratch

240. How To <solve your problem> Quickly And Easily - 100 Percent Guaranteed!

241. How To <solve your problem> Today Starting From Scratch

242. I Did It So Can You! ... <benefit> Now

243. I Have a Confession To Make ... It Wasn't ALWAYS This Easy to <benefit>

244. I Know Your Skeptical But You Really CAN <benefit> With These <No of steps/tips/secrets>

245. If I Can Do It So Can You! <benefit> Now!

246. If You're Like Me You Want to <benefit> Quickly And Hassle Free .. Well Now You Can!

247. Imagine... You Can <benefit> In Just in <duration>

248. Imagine... You Can <solve your problem> In Just in <duration>

249. Introducing ... A Brand New Way To <benefit> In Only in <duration> ... Or Your Money Back!

250. It's A Shame For You Not To <benefit> -- When These People Do It So Easily

251. It's A Shame For You Not To <solve your problem>-- When These People Do It So Easily

252. It Seems Incredible That You Can <benefit> And <solve your problem>

253. It Seems Incredible That You Can <benefit> In Only in <duration>

254. It's Never Been Easier to <benefit> ... If You Know How!

255. It's Never Been Easier to <benefit> .. If You Know The Secret

256. Jealously Guarded Secret Reveals The Best Way To <benefit>!

257. Keep Reading For The Most Highly Acclaimed Information on How To <benefit> Ever Assembled!

258. Late-Breaking News! ... Yes You Can <benefit> ... In Only in <duration>!

259. Late-Breaking News! ... Yes You Can <benefit> .. We'll Show You How!!

260. Late-Breaking News! ... Yes You Can <solve your problem>... In Only in <duration>!

261. Late-Breaking News! ... Yes You Can <solve your problem>... We'll Show You How!

262. Look Inside To Discover How To <benefit>

263. Look Inside To Discover How To <solve your problem>

264. Need To <benefit>?

265. Need To <benefit>? Here´s a Blueprint For Success!

266. Need To <benefit> and <solve your problem>? ... Here´s a Blueprint For Success!

267. Need To <solve your problem>?

268. Never Before Released Information on How to <benefit> In As Little As in <duration>!

269. Never Before Released Information on How to <benefit> Quickly and Easily!

270. Never Before Seen Information on How To <benefit> in as Little As in <duration>

271. News Flash! Now You <benefit> in as Little As in <duration> ...We'll Show You How!

272. News Flash! Now You <solve your problem> in as Little As in <duration> ...We'll Show You How!

273. Now! ... You Can <benefit> In Only in <duration> ... 100 Percent Guaranteed!

274. Now! ... You Can <benefit> In Only in <duration> ... Or Your Money Back!

275. Now! ... You Can <solve your problem> In Only in <duration> ... 100 Percent Guaranteed!

276. Now! ... You Can <solve your problem> In Only in <duration> ... Or Your Money Back!

277. Now You Too Can <benefit> in Only in <duration> ... Guaranteed!

278. Our System Helps You <benefit> in Only in <duration> ... Guaranteed!

279. Our System Helps You <solve your problem> in Only in <duration> ... Guaranteed!

280. <solve your problem>. It's No Accident. In in <duration>, I Can Show You How!

281. \<solve your problem\>. It's No Accident. In in \<duration\>, I Can Show You How To \<benefit\>

282. Proven Advice To \<benefit\> -- By An Expert

283. Proven Advice To \<benefit\> And \<solve your problem\>-- By An Expert

284. Proven Techniques Help You \<benefit\> - Guaranteed!

285. Proven Techniques Help You \<solve your problem\>- Guaranteed!

286. Proven Tips, Tools and Tactics To \<benefit\>

287. Proven Tips, Tools and Tactics To \<solve your problem\>

288. Revealed! A Practical Way to \<benefit\> Quickly and Easily

289. Revealed! A Practical Way to \<solve your problem\> Quickly and Easily

290. \<No of steps/tips/secrets\> To \<benefit\>

291. \<No of steps/tips/secrets\> To \<benefit\> And \<solve your problem\>

292. \<No of steps/tips/secrets\> To \<benefit\> In Just in \<duration\>

293. \<No of steps/tips/secrets\> To Keep Your Fears From Holding YOU Back - \<benefit\> In in \<duration\>

294. \<No of steps/tips/secrets\> To Keep Your Fears From Holding YOU Back - \<benefit\> Now!

295. \<No of steps/tips/secrets\> To \<solve your problem\>

296. Serious About Wanting To \<benefit\>? Here's How To \<solve your problem\>! Guaranteed... Or Your Money Back!

297. Suddenly It's Possible to <benefit> Quickly And Easily .. Stay Tuned For Details!

298. Suddenly It's Possible to <benefit> in As Little As in <duration> .. Details Below!

299. Suddenly It's Possible to <solve your problem> Quickly And Easily .. Stay Tuned For Details!

300. Suddenly It's Possible to <solve your problem> in As Little As in <duration> .. Details Below!

301. The Amazing Formula To <benefit> In Only in <duration>!

302. The Amazing Formula To <solve your problem> In Only in <duration>!

303. The Best Way To <benefit> ... In Only <solve your problem>!

304. The Complete Guide Of <No of steps/tips/secrets> To <solve your problem>

305. The Complete Guide Of <No of steps/tips/secrets> to <benefit>

306. The Complete Guide To <benefit>

307. The Complete Guide To <solve your problem>

308. The Definitive Guide on How To <benefit> - By An Expert

309. The Definitive Guide on How To <solve your problem>- By An Expert

310. The Most Highly Acclaimed Information on How To <benefit> Ever Assembled!

311. The Most Sought After Information on How to <benefit> Can Now Be Yours!

312. The Quick And Easy Way To <benefit>

313. The Quick And Easy Way To <benefit> In Only in <duration>

314. The Quick And Easy Way To <solve your problem>

315. The Quick And Easy Way To <solve your problem> In Only in <duration>

316. The Real Facts on How To <benefit> in Only in <duration> ... 100 Percent Guaranteed!

317. The Secret Of <solve your problem>

318. The Secret Of <solve your problem> In Just in <duration>

319. The Shocking Truth About How To <benefit>!

320. The Shocking Truth About How To <solve your problem>!

321. The Truth About How To <benefit>

322. The Truth About How To <solve your problem>

323. Think You Can't <benefit>? ... Think Again!

324. Think You Can't <benefit>? We've Got News For you!

325. Think You Can't <benefit>? You're In for a Pleasant Surprise!

326. Think You Can't <solve your problem>? ... Think Again!

327. Think You Can't <solve your problem>? We've Got News For You!

328. Think You Can't <solve your problem>? You're In for a Pleasant Surprise!

329. Thousands Now <benefit> Who Never Thought They Could

330. Thousands Now <benefit> Who Never Thought They Could ...With These <No of steps/tips/secrets>

331. Thousands Now <solve your problem> Who Never Thought They Could

332. To Men Who Want To <benefit> -- But Can't Get Started

333. To People Who Want To <benefit> -- But Can't Get Started

334. To Women Who Want To <benefit> -- But Can't Get Started

335. Want To <benefit>? We Got Ya Covered!

336. Want To <benefit>? You've Gotta See This!

337. Want To <solve your problem>? You're Not Gonna Believe This!

338. Want To <solve your problem>? You've Gotta See This!

339. What Everybody Ought To Know -- About How To <benefit>

340. What Everybody Should Know... About How To <benefit>

341. What The Experts Won't Tell You About How To <benefit>

342. What The Gurus Won't Tell You About How To <benefit>

343. Who Else Wants To <benefit> And <solve your problem>?

344. Who Else Wants To <benefit> In Only in <duration>?

345. Why Wouldn't You Like To <solve your problem>?

346. Would You Like To <benefit>?

347. Would You Like To <solve your problem>?

348. Yes These <No of steps/tips/secrets> Guarantee You Will <benefit>!

349. Yes These <No of steps/tips/secrets> Guarantee You Will <solve your problem>!

350. Yes These <No of steps/tips/secrets> Helped Me <benefit> And They Will Work For YOU Too

351. Yes These <No of steps/tips/secrets> Helped Me <solve your problem>And They Will Work For YOU Too

352. Yes These <No of steps/tips/secrets> Will Help You Learn How To <benefit> With Ease!

353. Yes These <No of steps/tips/secrets> Will Help You Learn How To <solve your problem> With Ease!

354. Yes YOU Too Can Learn How To <benefit> With Ease!

355. Yes YOU Too Can Learn How To <solve your problem> With Ease!

356. Yes You Can <benefit> With Our System ... It's So Easy A Child Could Do it!

357. You Are Guaranteed To <solve your problem>-- Or We Pay You

358. You CAN <solve your problem> In Only in <duration> ...Guaranteed!

359. You CAN <solve your problem> With These <No of steps/tips/secrets>...Guaranteed!

360. You Can Laugh At <benefit> Worries -- If You Follow This Simple Plan

361. You Deserve To <benefit>!

362. You Deserve To <solve your problem>!

363. You Might Be Thinking It's Really Hard to <benefit> ... Well Think Again!

364. You WILL <benefit> In Only in <duration> ... Or Your Money Back!

365. You WILL <solve your problem> In Only in <duration> ... Or Your Money Back!

CHAPTER EIGHT

WHILE THE HEADLINE HAS A PLACE OF GREAT IMPORTANCE IN
COPYWRITING, THE SUB HEADLINE OFFERS A GREAT VALUE, AS WELL.

THE SUB HEADLINE CAN BE USED TO SET OFF POINTS ABOUT THE
PRODUCT THAT CAN ENTICE THE READER TO KEEP GOING ON THEIR
WAY THROUGH THE COPY. IT CAN ALSO PROVIDE A MEANS TO MAKE
THE COPY FLOW MORE EFFICIENTLY AND READ MORE EASILY.

DON'T UNDERESTIMATE YOUR SUB-HEADLINES BECAUSE IT CAN MAKE
OR BREAK YOU.

TRY, ADAPTING, TWEAKING OR ALTERING A FEW OF THESE.

CHAPTER 8: SUB-HEADLINES

1. Follow Me as I Take a Serious, Step-by-Step, HARD Look at _____That, Combined, Produce _____... And Then See How YOU, Too, Can ____ From _____ These Untold, Little-Known, Closely-Guarded Secrets!

2. ALL The Most POWERFUL Secrets, Tips, Tricks, Tools & Techniques That Have EVER Been Written (or Spoken) on the Subject of _____& How to _____ Are Included in This LARGER-THAN-LIFE _____!

3. ____ Free Bonuses Not Available Anywhere Else - Just For _____

4. _____ Gives You the Competitive Advantage in Todays _____, and it's Practically Automatic!

5. _____ is my specialty!

6. _____: The Complete Guide to _____

7. A 100% complete package that empowers ANYONE to _____ and _____ in a few days

8. A Foolproof Way to _____

9. A Life Transforming _____

10. Absolutely no _____ required!

11. All You've Got To Do Is Get This Package, _____!

12. An Open Letter to _____ Frustrated By _____, _____, _____? And Going Nowhere!

13. And it Gets Better Your Satisfaction Is Completely Guaranteed!

14. And It's The Same Way With _____

15. Announcing A Little-Known Revolutionary Secret That Will Allow You To Finally _____ And _____!

16. Are There Any Strings Attached?

17. Are you frustrated by the lack of _____?

18. But don't make this fatal mistake:

19. But I Know What You're Thinking, You Skeptical, Negative Bugger

20. But the _____ made me drop my jaw!!

21. But, Really, It's an incredibly Easy Decision to Make?

22. By The Time You're Through Reading This Report, You'll See:

23. Catapult Your _____ To A New Level With These Inside Secrets

24. Checklist For Finding the Right _____

25. Discover how to _____, just like clockwork - as well as effectively use _____ to _____

26. Discover the _____s Little-Known Secret of _____!

27. Do you ever get stuck when you have to _____?

28. Do You Feel Frustrated With _____? If you do, then there is only one way to stop the pain: _____!

29. Grab your own _____ for a whopping _____ OFF if you act before the deadline of _____

30. Have you ever wished that you could sit down for a couple of hours with _____? And get them to _____?

31. Here Are Some Of The Other _____ That You Get:

32. Here Are The Powerful Advantages You'll Gain From _____

33. Here's How To Get Started

34. Here's How to Make Sure You Don't Miss Out?

35. Here's How To Start _____ Right Away

36. Here's My Unconditional _____ Risk Free Guarantee!

37. Here's Proof That This _____ Will Work For You

38. Here's the Bottom-line?

39. Here's the Deal?

40. Here's the definitive, step-by-step guide for _____ that will make your revenues soar! ...especially in a tough economy.

41. Here's The Difference That Makes This Program So Much More _____ Than Anything Else You've Ever Seen:

42. Here's What Makes This _____ So Different And So Much More _____ Than Anything Else You've Ever Seen

43. Here's what you get _____

44. Here's what you need to start _____

45. HOW A NEW DISCOVERY _____!

46. How Any _____ Can Save _____ In _____

47. How Can I Be Sure _____ Will Work For Me?

48. How Do I Get In?

49. How Easy Is It to Get Started?

50. How I Raised Myself From Failure To Success In _____

51. How Much?

52. How To _____ By _____

53. How to _____ in Just _ Hours!

54. I will reveal the shocking truth about _____. Once you discover the truth, you can begin to _____...

55. If You Order _____ Within the Next __ Days, You'll Get These FREE Bonuses Worth $_____!

56. If You Really Want To _____ And If You Really Want To _____, Simply _____

57. If you want to get _____, you need To Act Now!

58. If you're willing to invest _____ of your time, then you'll discover _____ that GUARANTEES your success... I'll even give you _____ - and _____

59. IMPORTANT: You can now take advantage of our _____ - it's only available for a VERY limited time. Read on to find out more.

60. In a Nutshell?

61. In Addition To This _____, Street-Smart Education – There's More Still!

62. In Fact, I'll Show You How _____ Can _____ Without You Lifting a Finger, 100% guaranteed!

63. Iron Clad 100% Money Back Guarantee

64. It Gets Better Still --Your _____ Is Completely Backed By My $___ Double Guarantee

65. It's Your Chance To _____

66. Just _____ and Let Them Start _____!

67. Just the Tip Of The Iceberg!

68. Kidnap An _____ Expert And Force _____ To Tell You ALL _____ Secrets

69. Learn how to _____ by _____.

70. Learn the _____ that can make you rich.

71. Let Me Swing Open The Concealed, Secret Door:

72. Let's Do Some _____

73. Let's see what other _____ are saying:

74. Let's take a look at _____

75. Listen to What Other People Have to Say about _____

76. My True Motive

77. No less Than a Bargain of a Lifetime!

78. Now you can _____ by _____

79. Now Let's Talk About Your FREE BONUSES!

80. Now You Can Do It Too!

81. Now is Your Chance To _____

82. Of Course, You Have A Lot More Questions?

83. Incidentally, Here Are The ____ Most Important Things To Know About Why I'm Qualified To Help You:

84. On the Other Hand

85. Once you've obtained this _____, you can:

86. Place Your _____ in Front of Millions!

87. Plus, Along with the _____ you'll also get?

88. Step-By-Step System for _____!

89. Stop Risking All Your Time, Effort And Money -- Let _____ Show You Dozens Of Proven Ways To _____!

90. Take Control Of Your _____ Starting Today!

91. Tell Me More About _____

92. The #1 that that determines success is _____!

93. The _____ Strategy That Never Wears Out, Never Loses Its Power

94. The answer to the burning question on everyone's mind, what is the best way to _____?

95. The Choice Is Yours.

96. The Components Of _____

97. The Costly Truth About _____

98. The Day _____ Arrives Is The Start Of _____

99. The Ideal Way to Turn Your _____ Into A _____

100. The Most Outrageous Guarantee Ever!

101. The New _____ Home Study Course

102. The Reason You've Been Getting _____ Is Directly Related To _____

103. There's Just One Slight Catch

104. Think About This:

105. This _____ Also Includes:

106. This _____ Is A Valuable Bonus That Isn't For Sale!

107. This _____ Is Your Ticket To Immediately Start _____!

108. This amazing _____ reveals the secrets no one else is telling you, time-tested and proven strategies that you can use right now to _____

109. This Information May Be More Important To _____ Than Anything You've Ever _____

110. This Is Not Like Anything You've Ever Seen Before Now

111. This Means If You _____ ,You Won't Have Any _____

112. This new _____ holds nothing back!

113. Want More Proof Of How Valuable This Is?

114. Well, very seriously, you have to act now. Because we _____

115. What Do You Actually Get?

116. What does it cost to get involved with _____?

117. What Kind Of Investment Is Required To _____?

118. What Makes This Discovery So Valuable?

119. What's The Best About _____?

120. Who Should Get _____?

121. Why Am I Being So Generous?

122. Would You Like To _____ More?

123. You Immediately Get _____

124. You Really Can't Afford Not To Invest In This _____!

125. You'll Even _____

126. You'll Never Find An Easier, Sure-Fire Way To _____

127. Your _____ Is Everything

128. Your Direct Route To _____

129. Your Success in _____ Is Totally Dependent On _____

130. You're cheating yourself out of all the _____

131. At last! Handle _____

132. Best-Kept Secret in _____ Revealed!

133. By This Time Next Month, You Could Have A _____.

134. Can You _____ These _____?

135. Can You Answer the _____Most Important Questions About _____?

136. Can You Pass This _____ Test?

137. Can You Really Achieve _____In Todays _____?

138. Can You Talk About _____ With The Rest Of Them?

139. Caution: Don't Let This Program Make You Too _____.

140. Conquer _____

141. Dare To Be _____

142. Depression-Proof _____

143. Did You Know That Most _____ Actually Destroys _____?

144. Discover the _____ Available To You From The

145. Discover the Unlimited Opportunities of _____

146. Discover Your Hidden _____

147. Don't Let _____

148. Don't Envy the _____ -- Be One

149. Every _____ Should Have One

150. Enhance Your Power to _____

151. Enjoy _____-And Better _____!

152. Get Out Of _____

153. Gonna _____ you Like You've never _____.

154. Have You Envied _____?

155. Have You Ever Seen A _____?

156. Here's a Quick Way to _____

157. How _____ Are Made

158. How _____ Averages $_____ Working _ Months A Year

159. How _____ Came to _____

160. How to _____ in Hard Times

161. How to _____ Overnight

162. How to _____ with a Simple Idea

163. How to _____ without _____

164. How You Can Profit From the _____

165. I Found a _____ That Works - Period

166. I Have All The _____ I Need. How About You?

167. I Help People _____!

168. I Thought I Was A Big Success Until I Talked With _____.

169. I Was Scared Out of My Wits Whenever I Used This _____ Tactic, but the _____ Was Too Good to Pass Up

170. If You _____ You'll Love Our _____

171. If You Are _____, You Can _____

172. If You Buy One _____ This Decade, This Should Be It

173. If You Can _____ - You Can _____!

174. If You Can Answer These Questions, You Don't Need This _____

175. If You Ever Wanted To _____...Now You Can

176. Is It Immoral To _____ This Easily??

177. Is Keeping Your _____ Worth ____ Cents A Day?

178. IS YOUR _____ WORTH _____ BUCKS?

179. Is Your _____ Safe against _____? Take This Test to Find Out

180. IS YOUR FUTURE WORTH _____?

181. It _____ While It _____

182. Is _____ Worse Than A Root Canal?

183. It's Easier Than You Think To _____

184. It's Easy To Cash In _____

185. It's Easy To Cash In On Your Amazing _____

186. It's Not Just What You Know about A _____ - Its _____, too.

187. It's Not What You _____...But _____

188. It's Time for You to know the _____!

189. It's True, Simply by Helping Others _____...You Can Become A_____!

190. Keeps _____ from Stealing YOUR _____

191. Keys to _____? For _____

192. Know How To _____

193. Learn From a Team of Top _____

194. Learn How _____ Can Help _____- Give You Greater _____ And Help _____!

195. Learn How and Where To _____

196. Learn To _____ in ___ Short Hours: Learn the Basics in ___ Easy Sessions

197. Learn To _____ Like A _____!

198. Let Me Count the Ways You Can _____

199. Let Me Review Your _____, _____, _____ or _____, and Receive Actionable Recommendations to Improve _____!

200. Let This _____ Work for You

201. Literally Everything You Need To _____ by _____

202. Little Known Ways to _____

203. Maybe Your Next _____ Should Be _____

204. New Concept in _____

205. New Help for Not So _____

206. Now You Can Have _____!

207. Now You Can Instantly _____!

208. Now You Can Learn The _____ Secrets That Created A _____!?For Free!

209. Old Books Discovered That Unlock the Secrets of Real _____

210. Profit from the Wisdom of Over ___ _____

211. Protect Yourself from _____

212. Say YES, And Tomorrow You'll Know How To _____

213. See How Easily You Can _____

214. See Why the Nasty Truth of Your _____ Cannot Tell A Lie!

215. Shortcuts to Creating & Maintaining _____

216. Should You _____?

217. Shouldn't You Start Your _____ Now...While Still _____?

218. Stop Wasting Valuable _____ Time!!

219. Stop wondering where your _____.

220. Super _____ at Any _____

221. The _____ Quickest Ways to Get More _____

222. The How To _____ off _____ with _____

223. The #1 _____ Secret I Learned from Interviewing Over _____ _____

224. The Amazing _____ of a _____

225. The Amazing _____ that's changing the _____

226. The Amazing Lost _____ - Secret of _____

227. The Amazing Lost Money Secret of _____

228. The Answer To _____ Is A Simple One...

229. The Art of _____

230. The Easiest Way to _____ Anything

231. The Lowdown on _____

232. The Machine That _____ While You Sit Back And Enjoy It

233. The More _____ You Get The More _____

234. The Secret Behind _____

235. The Secret of _____

236. The Secret of How _____ - And How You Can Do The Same

237. The Secrets Steps To _____ With _____

238. The Shortcut to Eliminate _____

239. The Shortest Path to _____

240. The Wrong Way and the Right Way to _____

241. There are ____ Deadly Assumptions that could wipe you out...And You're Already Making _____ Of Them!

242. There Is Still A Way You Can _____.

243. There's _____ in _____!

244. These ___ Secrets Can Help You _____

245. Thousands Now _____ Who Never Thought They Could

246. Turn Your _____ into _____

247. Turning _____ into _____

248. Unleash the Power of _____ with _____

249. Unlike Any _____ you've Ever _____.

250. Using a _____ May Be Dangerous To Your Wealth

251. We Broke The Rules? Finally a _____ without the Hassles.

252. We guarantee you'll _____ faster and better, or well refund your money

253. What Have You Got To Show For The _____?

254. What Is Your _____ Potential?

255. When _____ Feel _____ This Is What They Do

256. Who Else Wants To _____?

PART II

INFLUENCERS

CHAPTER
NINE

IF YOU'VE NEVER CONSIDERED THE POSSIBILITY OF BEING ABLE TO "RESET" A PERSON'S THINKING PATTERNS SO THEY ACCEPT AND ACT ON THE NEW IDEAS YOU "FEED" THEM...

YOU PROBABLY DON'T BELIEVE THIS CAN ACTUALLY HAPPEN.

BUT I'M GOING TO TELL YOU THAT IT CAN--BECAUSE OVER TIME WE'VE ALL BEEN SUBTLY HYPNOTIZED TO ACCEPT CERTAIN TRIGGER WORDS.

IN FACT, THE PROCESS STARTED BEFORE YOU COULD EVEN SPEAK OR WRITE A WORD.

GO AHEAD AND TRY SOME OF THESE HEADLINES AND SEE IF YOU CAN ENTICE AND INFLUENCE!

CHAPTER 9: HYPNOTIC OPENINGS

1. Here's your chance to_____

2. _____ was in trouble. Our _____ were selling like crazy. Orders were coming from everywhere. We were able to get _____, but it wasn't enough. We stopped advertising but the orders still kept coming.

3. A _____ or so from now, you could have _____. Wouldn't your friends and family be totally amazed? Wouldn't you feel fantastic about it?

4. After nearly 12 months of long hours, late nights and weekends at the office, my editors and I have collected over _____ of our biggest and best _____ secrets for _____ ? and bound them into one huge volume.

5. Allow me to introduce myself. My name is _____. Chances are you haven't heard of me before. But when you finish reading this, you'll be glad you finally did.

6. Americans are spending _____ of dollars each year on _____ and very few are getting any results! You might even be one of them.

7. Maybe you've tried the _____ or one of the other _____ out there with little success.

8. Are you caught in a constant struggle for _____?

9. Are you determined to _____? Then you have finally reached the right place to start your journey to _____ ... NOW ... Not tomorrow, Not in 12 months' time !!

10. Are you insane?

11. Are you interested in discovering how to _____ just by _____?

12. Are you letting _____ take control of your life?

13. Are you maximizing your _____ for maximum profits? If you don't already know about the simple method I'm about to reveal to you, you're missing out on a lot of potential sales !

14. Are you paying too much for _____?

15. Are you REALLY serious about taking control of _____ by developing a _____ plan?

16. Are you spending huge amounts of _____ and _____ to your _____ , only to see _____?

17. Are you struggling to write _____?

18. Are you tired of all the _____ that don't work, the latest _____ that promise success and leave you seething with frustration and disappointment?'

19. Are you tired of spending endless hours _____?

20. Are you used to spending hours, surfing the Internet, looking for a particular _____ which is suitable for _____; or just for good enough _____? If so, you are one of the many people who would benefit from using this downloadable _____.

21. As I promised. I am giving you a dollar ($1.00) and with you permission, I'll also send you the FREE GIFT I promised. (More about that later.) For now, all I ask is that you read this letter.

22. As you can see, I have attached a _____ to the top of this letter for two reasons: I have something very important to tell you and I needed some way to catch your attention. Since what I am writing about money, I thought a little financial eye catcher was appropriate.

23. As you carefully scan each and every word of this page, you will begin to discover a new revolutionary method of _____.

24. At this very moment you are competing with hundreds, thousands, maybe even millions of other _____all fighting to get your customer.

25. At your request, I shall be glad to send you one of the most talked-of little books ever written.

26. Before anything else, I want to start by giving you something that'll make you money tomorrow! But then again...I am living, breathing proof that it works...

27. Can one-third of all _____ in America be wrong?

28. Can you be ethically bribed to become a member of my

_____

29. Could you use an extra $_____ a week?

30. Did you ever dream you could _____?

31. Did you know that if you _____ incorrectly you _____ could be _____ from _____?

32. Do you ever wonder why it can be so hard to _____? You try everything out there, and nothing seems to really work.

33. Do you hate _____ that doesn't work?

34. Do you know the #1 reason people like you can _____ and _____?

35. They know exactly where to _____! Yes, it's that simple.

36. Do you think that you could increase _____ with over _____ _____ every _____?

37. Don't you wish that you could get _____, _____ or _____? You Can!!

38. Even though I'm going to be short, sweet and to the point...

39. Ever wonder how it is that others seem to just know _____? Read on, and you'll learn how to use and apply the same secret weapons of _____ that top _____ are using right now, to _____.

40. Every Monday morning, a rather unusual publication arrives at the desks of a select circle of individuals in positions of power and influence.

41. Every month I average more than $_____ in sales from just one of my websites (I have _____ of them)... and I do this with traffic I don't lay out a single penny for up front!

42. Finally, _____ and _____ can get _____ and make money from a fair, effective and profitable _____!

43. Finding time to meet new, interesting single people and develop special relationships gets more difficult every year.

44. First, three brief questions, if we may:

45. Frankly, I'm puzzled?

46. Frankly, membership in The _____ is not for everyone.

47. Get PAID to _____!

48. Good news -- this isn't a problem. It's a huge opportunity for you!

49. Hats off to _____.

50. Have you ever said: _____? Then... you'll love the way this_____ _____ while you continue to _____. You can actually _____.

51. Have you ever thought of _____?

52. Have you ever wondered why _____ are more _____ than others?

53. Have you ever wondered why some people seem to have a knack for _____?

54. Have you wondered how people can sell _____ for so cheap?

55. Hello. My name is _____ and I'm a former _____. I've recently packaged all of my years of experience in the _____ industry in such a way that will help you _____ as _____ owner or operator dramatically--a way to _____ that immediately _____!

56. Here is a wonderful new way to bring the _____ right into your own home.

57. Here is one of those specials that we let our customers and friends in on every once in a while.

58. Here's a dollar: ? Yes, it's a real dollar ? nice and clean and new. Keep if you want to, after you've read this letter, but I don't believe you will, then. Here's what it's all about:

59. Here's an amazing opportunity!

60. Here's how you can quickly and easily _____ by _____.

61. How can you earn between _____ and _____ profit per day every day in your spare time _____? You can do this! I'll prove it...

62. How many times each week do you _____ with no _____ and you end up resorting to...

63. How much _____ are you planning to spend on _____, _____ for your _____?

64. How much is one more sale worth to you?

65. How much is your _____ and your _____ worth to you?

66. How would you like _____? Sounds perfect, but too good to be true?

67. How would you like to _____ that _____ in such a mysterious way that they _____?

68. How would you like to become one of them?

69. How would you like to earn $_____ a day ….every day?

70. How would you like to get _____-like results from the _____ you buy at your _____?

71. How would you like to learn a simple formula that I developed from many years of research which can bring to you the perfect _____ and best of all _____?

72. I am excited to be able to finally write this letter to you. For many _____ I've wanted to get these powerful _____ into a format where I could help as many people as possible get their hands on them, and I've done it.

73. I am going to send you, in the next few days, _____ that are DIFFERENT, for your most particular customers.

74. I am writing to inform you about a_____

75. I am writing to urge you to take immediate and profitable advantage of the most unusual (and fleeting) _____ opportunity I've ever extended. The opportunity just became available and it's nearly 30% sold out!

76. I couldn't wait to write to you.

77. I got the message around 7 pm, and I got going at once! I knew I had to drive all night in an ancient Jeep through a steaming jungle that would scare a tenderfoot like me out of three years growth, even in the daytime. I also knew that if I could get to where I was going in time it was worth a few prickles up and down my spine during the tight spots.

78. I guess the reason you're reading this letter now is because you're having a hard time _____...

79. I have $_____ in free bonuses reserved in your name. To discover how easy it is to get all of them for FREE, read the rest of this letter. Please do it now because this is a limited time offer, so you must act quickly to take advantage of this rare value and opportunity.

80. I have a picture of you in my mind's eye.

81. I have a small secret that I've been using for quite some time now, and I felt that it's time to reveal this new _____ formula to you.

82. I have been in the _____ business for _____ years and I have found only one _____ that has enabled me to _____. That _____ is called _____.

83. I know you're busy. I know you have too much to read. Yet, that's exactly why I want to?

84. I looked at her like she was crazy.

85. I mean, some _____. And some don't. It all comes down to the _____. You either know how to _____...

86. I need your help.

87. I recently made a whopping $_____ by following some simple, yet powerful, concepts I'm about to share with you.

88. I thought I would have heard back from you by now.

89. I used to work hard. The 18-hour days. The 7-day weeks. But I didn't start making big money until I did less ? a lot less.

90. I wouldn't believe what I am about to tell you.

91. I'd like to share with you a Holiday gift idea which has long been a tradition here in _____

92. I'd like to tell you about_____

93. I'll be honest with you.

94. I'm excited about something very important, and I wanted to share it with you immediately. So, I sat down and wrote this long, but time-critical, letter. Please take a few minutes and read it now.

95. I'm really steamed up! And I'm not going to take it anymore!

96. I'm writing to you because I've heard rumblings about your company.

97. I'm writing to..

98. I'm writing you this note for a personal reason. I've rarely written notes like this in the past, but I feel that it is essential to bring this to your attention.

99. I've got to get this off my chest before I explode!

100. If I could give you a more effective marketing strategy that would outperform the selling approach you are currently using, would you be interested?

101. If I were to tell you that I will _____ for you _____ for less than $_____, I'm sure you'll tell me either that I must be kidding or that there must be no professionalism involved at that price.

102. If money was no object, would you own _____?

103. If the enclosed <Dollar Bill> pays for one minute of your time, consider yourself engaged.

104. If the idea of being able to _____ or _____ regardless of how much money you have, your educational background, your skills or the amount of equipment you own, is something that appeals to you, then you will be _____ like this...

105. If you _____, then you know the frustration of _____. It's painful isn't it?

106. If you are _____, then you need to know how to _____!

107. If you are concerned about _____, this letter is for you. STORIES:

108. If you are like most people, you have wasted countless hours on_____. Most tasks can be accomplished with only a few _____.

109. If you are looking for a good way to _____ that really works and I will prove it to you in a moment then please read this message very carefully. It will be the most important information you read all year.

110. If you are looking for a sure-fire way to _____ by _____, then this may be the most important letter you've ever read...

111. If you are ready to _____ or if you are just getting started _____, this is your chance to finally get the inside story of what it really takes to _____and achieve _____.

112. If you are thinking of buying a _____ ? Don't!

113. If you are worried about the future about increasing inflation and the factors that make for such a nervous economy, I have some ideas you should seriously consider.

114. If you care about your _____'s wellbeing - and you're sick of old, ineffective advice on _____, _____, _____, _____ and more

- this may be the most important letter you'll ever read. Here's why...

115. If you could finally have _____ quickly and on a budget you can actually afford, would you be interested?

116. If you have _____, this could be the most eye-opening letter you will ever read.

117. If you have a _____ then you simply cannot afford to leave this site

118. If you or a loved one have _____, you undoubtedly wish that you could find some magic remedy that keeps that _____ far away, forever. I know I did. But suppose that wish were the very thing that is stopping you from achieving that dream, a dream that in

119. If you own a single Dow stock, even just one big-name mutual fund or any investment tied to the market index, I have an important even urgent message for you today.

120. If you think you are spending too much time _____, it might be the time for you to take one step up and automate some of the tasks that you have been doing manually.

121. If you use _____ to _____, I have some shocking news for you. You are getting ripped off!

122. If you want _____, _____, a better _____, or just love to _____and _____ gurus, then you're going to fall in love with this website!...

123. If you want the _____ independence and _____ from _____, the satisfaction and prestige that comes from _____, and if you want to do it while you're still *young* enough to enjoy it... then this might be the most important letter you'll ever read.

124. If you want to _____ (and I mean really _____!) then this could very well be the most important website you will ever see.

125. If you want to find out why you haven't been able to get the results that you want in _____, then this letter is perhaps the most critical piece of reading to your _____ future.

126. If you want to skyrocket your _____, _____, and _____, then this is the most important letter you'll ever read.

127. If you want to _____, I can't think of a better way to do it than _____

128. If you work for yourself, and are working harder than you wish this new breakthrough will interest you.

129. If you'd like to unearth the best-kept secrets of _____, _____, and even _____, keep your eyes glued to this page. You won't find this insider information anywhere else on the Web, Why? Because the _____ industry doesn't want you to find out. If everybody

130. If you're interested in creating a huge (and immediate) cash flow for yourself or your business, this is going to be the most exciting message you will ever read.

131. If you're talking desire and commitment, we're talking big money and big success.

132. If you've ever thought about writing your own book or newsletter, or wondered what it would be like to run your own publishing company, you'll be interested in this letter.

133. If you'd like to _____ -- without having to sell your firstborn child to raise the capital -- this information may be critical to your online success.

134. If you'd like to _____, _____, and learn the secrets to _____, then this might be the most important information you'll ever read.

135. If you'd like to _____, without using _____ and you don't want to spend an arm and a leg, then this might be the most important letter you'll ever read.

136. If you'd like to finally _____, _____ and _____ without _____, then this might be the most important letter you'll ever read.

137. If you're like most of the thousands of _____, the answer is probably, yes! As a result, you're missing out on _____ and a priceless amount of _____.

138. If you're looking for a fast, easy, and legitimate way to _____, listen to this:

139. If you're not _____, then you're not making all of the money you could (and should) be making on the Internet.

140. If you're prepared to see _____... then you've come to the right place.

141. If you're sick and tired of _____, you'll thank heaven for the _____ a new _____ breakthrough.

142. If you're sick of _____ or settling for barely _____ with your _____, I have good news for you:

143. If you're sitting in traffic when you would rather be home studying, our _____ are for you. Listen to our material while you commute to work and learn _____. There is a lot of material to remember in order to _____. Use your sense of hearing to help you succeed.

144. If you've been online for any amount of time at all, you already know that, with the exception of _____ sites _____ are

THE #1 _____ online. Without question. Hands down. _____ are the top _____ on the web.

145. If you've ever struggled with _____, you're in the right place. And I'm here to help you. That's because I've developed a powerful new _____ that will make your life a lot easier.

146. I'll be real honest with you. When I first _____, one of the most difficult things that I had to overcome was _____. With little to invest and no experience at all, I faced the same _____ options that most people face when _____...

147. I'll cut to the chase. If you follow the _____ instructions, I *guarantee* you will _____.

148. I'm about to share with you, or you will ruin it for

149. I'm already taking heat from some _____ for revealing this information here. But you know what? I don't care!

150. I'm excited to reveal to you an amazing _____ system that can rapidly _____.

151. I'm going to show you the _____ _____ secrets to _____ you've always dreamed of. By using your _____, _____, or _____ and _____.

152. I'm not a _____ by any means, but I can tell you with great certainty that you probably fall into one of _____ categories...

153. I'm not going to waste a second of your time with any specially designed sales pitch that is supposed to convince you that you need what I've got.

154. Imagine a system that can _____. Imagine setting it up one-time, walking away from it...

155. Imagine having an _____ that _____ for you. _____ that _____ the hottest _____ opportunities on the Internet.

156. Imagine this. Imagine _____ today and returning tomorrow to find that it had brought in _____ for you.

157. Imagine what it would be like to quickly _____, _____, or _____with the push of a button, even if you have several _____.

158. Imagine, for a moment, that it's 6 months from today?

159. In every man's wardrobe is some particular article a tie, a shirt, or a suit that he likes best to wear, because he looks his best and feels his best in it. That's the way you'll feel about these _____ - once you've worn one of them.

160. In looking over our records I noticed that you _____

161. In the next _____ minutes I am going to show you some amazing facts about _____. By the end of this letter you will know exactly how you can _____.

162. In the time it takes you to read this letter, _____ can possibly _____.

163. Introducing _____, a wonderful _____ to _____. A simple _____ is not a good idea any more. Our _____ will _____ which is much more powerful than _____.

164. It is a fact, people DO _____! Don't believe me? Go into any _____ and look around. Nine times out of ten it is the _____ that will _____. It's at that moment _____ and the _____..... or _____!

165. It is true! There are a lot of people _____ from the comfort of their own home by _____.

166. It was a mistake. Somebody goofed and put the _____.

167. It will mean a lot to me if you close your office door to avoid interruptions for the next 10 minutes or so, to give me the opportunity to transfer my simple, proven, workable ideas that

will directly translate into money, success, power, distinct business advantages and happiness with relative ease. And very little (if any) risk.

168. It's easy to become a good _____. Surprisingly easy. You don't have to be a sitting duck for_____, _____.

169. It's hard to find high quality, timely _____ that are in your budget.

170. It's a jungle out there . . .

171. It's no secret. If you've _____ longer than one day, then you've found out one universal truth...

172. It's no secret. If you've been _____ longer than one day, then you've found out one universal truth...

173. I've recently developed an _____ formula that's so powerful, I can stop marketing today - not get another paying customer for the next _____ months - and STILL pull anywhere from $_____- $_____ a _____.

174. Let me cut right to the chase.

175. Let me get this out of the way right now. The _____ costs $_____. I'll save you some time from scrolling down to the bottom to find out the cost. There it is, up front. $_____ total. No surprises

176. Let me make a prediction?

177. Let me make your life as an _____ easier. (And _____ in the process :)

178. Let's face it

179. Let's cut to the chase, shall we?

180. Let's cut to the chase. How would you like to see a significant increase in your _____, regardless of _____?

181. Let's face it. Not all _____ are _____. In fact, very few are.

182. Let's face it...

183. Listen up, because what I have to say beats any _____ or _____ hands down, GUARANTEED. It already _____ for _____ of our members, and can do the same for you right now.

184. Looking for something to _____ when your normally hectic pace slows for a few minutes?

185. May I ask you a question...? Are you interested in _____; written in a no-nonsense style and with an outrageous humor that no other _____ would dare even publish? Yes? Good...

186. Men who know it all need go no further into this letter than this paragraph, because it is not for them. Neither is it for those who are satisfied with their present positions, and the progress they have made in life.

187. My name is _____ and I'm here to tell you about _____.

188. My name is _____, and in all my _____ years of studying the investment markets, I've never known a time so full of opportunity yet so fraught with danger.

189. My name is _____. I'm a _____. I'm not a professional ad writer. But what I have to share with you is so extraordinary and so powerful, I decided to write you myself. So bear with me a little.

190. My name is _____ and I beg you, don't wait another minute for success in your career (or in your life for that matter!).

191. Never before has the attainment of smooth, clear, beautiful complexion been as simple, as inexpensive as now.

192. No doubt about it: When you chose to buy a _____ you made a smart decision.

193. No matter who you are, where you live or how much experience you have... I'm about to teach you a 100% foolproof formula that guarantees to _____ using _____ or you don't pay a single penny.

194. NOT ANYMORE!!

195. Now there are handy guides packed with strategies to _____. You can be reading these proven _____ tips, guaranteed to teach you how to _____, in just five minutes.

196. Now you can get _____ in one fully automated and proven to work_____!

197. Now you can!

198. On a beautiful late spring afternoon, twenty-five years ago, two young men graduated from the same college. They were very much alike, these two young me. Both had been better than average students, both were personable and both as young college graduates were filled with ambitious dreams for the future.

199. On an autumn day, not too long ago, _____

200. Only once in _____ years come an improvement like this:

201. Our records show that you're one of our best customers, and that's why I'm writing. Frankly, I need your help.

202. People of culture can be recognized at once.

203. Picture yourself _____ in a day than most people do in a week. You can do it! (You'll even _____ while you _____.) You are about to discover how to _____!

204. Please accept this check and get three months of unlimited _____ a $_____ gift to you!

205. Please excuse my audacity, but I'm willing to bet $_____ your business can be a lot more profitable than it is now.

206. Please take a minute from your busy schedule and read this letter. I promise you will not regret it.

207. Regardless of what you are marketing on the internet, the _____ is the ONLY _____ you need to _____.

208. So, you've got a _____ that you want to _____. It doesn't matter whether it is an _____ that you _____. It can be any of these things...

209. Someone is going to tell you the truth.

210. Ssshhh! These, Dear Friend, are the secrets to having it all!

211. Stick it to us. Rip us off. Here's the promotion that's been verified by our vice president, our accountant and my wife. It's a promotion that's such a good deal for you, (it really is) that it's virtually guaranteed to lose us money.

212. Suppose you could instantly access all the secrets, tools and resources you need to _____. At fees much _____ than you are currently _____.

213. Suppose you were told the whole truth about _____ that could unlock the _____ gates and _____.

214. Suppose you were told the whole truth about _____ that could unlock the _____ gates and unleash _____.

215. That's why I created this website!

216. The _____ is the result of _____ from more than _____ _____ from a _____ of the industry.

217. The fact is that no matter who you are, whether you are young or old, weak or strong, rich or poor, I can prove to you readily by demonstration that you are leading an inferior life, and I

want the opportunity to show you the way in which you may completely and easily, without inconvenience or loss of time, come in possession of new life, vigor, energy, development and a higher realization of life and success.

218. The publisher of _____ asked me to make a very special subscription offer to a small, select group of advertising and marketing professionals. Your name was submitted as one who qualifies.

219. The results are in...

220. The secret is out. _____ are the best _____ to come along in a long time for your _____.

221. The world has changed. And it's going to change even more. But most poor saps don't see it coming.

222. There are numerous ways to _____. And? because there are so many different ways to do this many new _____ are totally overwhelmed with _____ information.

223. There are only two basic requirements for every _____. I believe you may already have one of them.

224. There are several million _____ in this country. _____ of them share one key secret to success. When you finish reading this letter, I think you'll want to become _____!

225. There are very, very few people who have spent as much time studying the _____ patterns of _____ as I have - and I've seen it all...

226. This exciting new _____ will BLOW YOU AWAY. You'll be amazed if not SHOCKED when you download it and discover...

227. This free site will help you _____. This automated system was designed for _____ newbie's but yet it's so powerful that even the pros are using it.

228. This is a letter that is not like any you have ever received or I have ever written.

229. This is simply incredible. A sure-fire method of _____ in less than _____ _____ of work. And it won't _____. Talk to me here - where else can you find such a deal?

230. This is unlike me. It really is. If you've read any of my sales letters from _____, then...

231. This letter is going to be short and to the point. We don't want to make big thing of it. Not yet anyway.

232. This may be the luckiest day of your life! You are one of only a few selected people to receive this personal memo.

233. This may be the most startling _____ news you have ever read.

234. This private invitation is going out to just a handful of people, yourself included. I hope you'll accept my invitation. But even if you decide not to, I want to send you a gift. Absolutely Free.

235. Those were the words I woke up to every morning in _____. It's funny, but even thinking about that now fills me with energy and makes me ready to face the day.

236. Trust me, I know how you feel...

237. Until You Read This Page!

238. Want to learn how to really (I'm not talking hype here, I mean really!) learn how to _____? Then stay with me - this short story is important... i. Warning! Do Not Attempt To _____, Or Even Think About _____

239. We all have _____ that we want to improve. Whether it is related to _____, _____, _____ or _____. And it is now possible

to _____ you have always wanted from the convenience of your own _____.

240. We can send _____visitors to your_____ -- starting immediately!

241. Would you like to have _____ looking at your _____, ready to _____? If so, then read on ...

242. Welcome to _____, where we believe in _____!

243. Welcome to _____. With over _____ years of experience, _____ is a premier provider of _____ solutions. _____ now has _____satisfied clients in _____ countries and over _____ _____ cities.

244. Welcome! You've clicked on our site because you know that the most powerful way to _____ is to _____. Plus, you've recognized that the most affordable AND powerful way to do that is to ensure your _____ achieves a _____.

245. Well, read on and I'll give you _____ proven ways of _____!

246. What is the one thing all successful _____ have in common? They _____ to _____ and to _____ fast. Just listen to _____...

247. What would you do if, in _____ _____ or less, you could easily _____ that:

248. What would YOU give for the real _____solution? Do you want to achieve more _____with YOUR online business?

249. What would you say if I told you that you could _____ -- plus, keep _____?! You can even start in about _____ minutes!!

250. When a man steps from a $_____ a month job as a _____ to a position that pays him $_____the very first month is it luck?

251. Whether you love em or hate em, you just can't deny that _____ produce _____.

252. Who else wants to _____? Ask that question in any group, and everyone will jump up shouting, I do, I do, I do.

253. Why did you request this information be sent to you? Or did a friend request this information be sent to you? This is the second and final time we can contact you. Following this mailing, your name will be removed from our mailing list.

254. Why is it that some _____ and _____ prosper while others encounter only frustration and obscurity?

255. Why is it that there are so few _____ in the world who have a truly _____?

256. Will do me a favor?

257. Will you accept a _____? In return for a little favor I want you to do?

258. Will you examine _____? If we send you a set at our own expense for a week's examination?

259. Will you give me a little information about yourself? just your_____?

260. Will you try this experiment?

261. With the amount of _____ you've got to do, it probably seems impossible to keep up with today's _____.

262. Within just a few minutes YOU can have _____...

263. Within the next few days, I want to send you, with my compliments, a _____.

264. Without finding out how you can...

265. Would you be good enough to do me a favor? I promise not to ask too much.

266. Would you be pleased if you made _____% on your portfolio every _____ months?

267. Would you do us a favor? You have been specially selected to participate in an important survey.

268. Would you like to _____... while _____... and never _____?

269. Would you like to _____? How about _____? Learn from someone who has had over _____ years of experience in the _____ business. Honest straight forward techniques to get you started easily. Learn the _____ trade secrets needed to _____ in this dynamic industry.

270. Would you like to discover, once and for all, how to _____ every single _____?

271. Would you like to get more _____ and _____ coming to you who want to _____ now?

272. Would you like to greatly improve your _____, _____, _____, but feel that some important ingredient is missing?

273. Yes, it's absolutely crazy, but true!

274. Yes, its' true

275. You already know that deciphering the rules of the _____ game can be a confusing and costly chore. Fortunately, the hidden secrets of _____ guides you through the fastest, most accurate way_____ and _____ in _____ _____ flat!

276. You are among a very small group of _____ invited to use the Gift Certificate we've enclosed.

277. You probably wish your _____ could _____ among the _____ on the _____.

278. You will never _____ again! My friends and I can show you how to_____ which will give you everything you need to _____. We will show you how to do it all with NO EXPERIENCE and right from the comfort of your own home.

279. You --Yes --You Can _____... with my _____. This is how it felt when it happened to me.

280. You've got enough people trying to waste your time with things you don't really want or need. I'm not one of those people.

281. Your _____ is complete. You've _____. You're ready to _____! But is it enough?

282. You're going to love this.

283. You're sick of _____ and _____ right? You'd like _____, correct? You don't want to waste a lot of time trying to _____ and you don't want to spend your life savings trying to _____ Am I on the right page, here?

CHAPTER TEN

DON'T UNDERESTIMATE THE POWER OF ASKING A GOOD QUESTION.

ASKING CUSTOMERS QUESTIONS IS A TECHNIQUE COMMON TO ALL SUCCESSFUL SALES. IT ISN'T, HOWEVER, QUITE AS STRAIGHTFORWARD AS ONE MIGHT BELIEVE.

THIS CHAPTER IS REALLY EASY TO USE, JUST INJECT RELEVANT ANSWERS TO THE <>'S AND YOU'LL INSTANTLY HAVE VERY POWERFUL AND ENGAGING QUESTIONS.

CHAPTER 10: ENGAGING QUESTIONS

1. Do you want to learn to <benefit> right away?

2. Do you want to learn to <goal> and <benefit> right now?

3. Are you willing to do whatever it takes to <benefit>?

4. Are you willing to do whatever it takes to get rid of <problem> instantly?

5. So is it wonderful to <benefit> with minimum risks?

6. Why do you think you should take up this offer?

7. Is it possible for me to learn this within <number of days>?

8. Thinking of how you can solve <problem>?

9. Thinking of how you can <benefit> and <goal> within the next month?

10. What you need to know about <benefit>?

11. Troubled? <benefit> will show you the way out

12. Feeling great? Here are more <benefit>

13. Did I just hear <benefit> coming out from your mouth?

14. Did I just hear <problem>keep repeating in your mind? Interested to eliminate them?

15. Thinking this might be a scam?

16. To the men, isn't it awesome to <benefit> right away?

17. To the ladies, isn't it awesome to <benefit> right away?

18. A newbie in this area? Let me show you how you can become pro instantly.

19. Too old to learn <benefit>? Would you change your mind if I tell you the secret to <goal> in just <timeframe>?

20. Who else want to <benefit> in 1 week?

21. Who else want to be <goal> in 1 week?

22. Who else want to solve <problem> and achieve <goal> and <benefit> at the same time?

23. You really love to have <benefit> right? So keep focusing now.

24. You really love to have <goal> with minimum risks? Pay attention to what is below.

25. Want to learn more about <benefit>?

26. Want to learn more about <goal> and how you can do it immediately?

27. Why only certain people can <benefit>? Learn the secret now

28. Why only certain people know the <problem>? Learn the secret now

29. Experience <problem> and still thinking of solution? Check <benefit> out!

30. Are you ready to reap <benefit> now? 31. Are you ready to experience <goal> now?

32. Are you ready to solve <problem> now?

33. <problem> is why people cannot do it. Want to learn why?

34. Are you hungry for <benefit>?

35. Looking for a way to <benefit>?

36. Looking for a way to <goal>? Just read on

37. See how a college student can do with <benefit>. You want to do the same?

38. Want to learn to start <goal> with just $100

39. Hope to beat your procrastination with <benefit> straight away?

40. Interested in <benefit> but don't know where to start?

41. Interested in <goal> but don't know where to start?

42. Interested in solving <problem> but don't know where to start?

43. If I were to reveal the hidden secrets of <benefit>, would you be interested?

44. If I were to reveal the hidden secrets of <problem> and solutions to them, would you be interested?

45. Are you in for the unique experience to <goal>

46. Are you in for the unique experience to <benefit>

47. Do you want to reap the <benefit> ahead of the rest?

48. Want to know the tricks to <goal> without going school again?

49. Want to know the tricks to <benefit> without going school again?

50. Confuse about <goal> and want to achieve it right away?

51. Confuse about <benefit> and want to achieve it right away?

52. Confuse about <problem> and want to solve it right away?

53. Have you wondered how to <goal>?

54. Have you wondered how to <benefit> and <goal> with ease?

55. Have you wondered if you can <benefit> and <goal> in <timeframe>?

56. Isn't it time for you to realize your <goal>?

57. Isn't it time for you to reap <benefit> and move towards your <goal>?

58. Isn't it time for you to turn your <problem> to <goal>?

59. Did you know that you can learn <benefit> in the next minute?

60. Did you know that you can achieve <goal> and <benefit> in <timeframe>?

61. Did you know the secret to your <problem>?

62. Are you curious about <benefit> and how it will change your life?

63. Are you curious about the methods you can use to reach <goal> right now?

64. Are you curious how you can solve <problem> in <timeframe>?

65. Are you curious the way you can <benefit> and <goal> in <timeframe>?

66. Are you still interested in <benefit> and <goal>?

67. Are you aware that you can learn to <benefit> and <goal> in <timeframe>?

68. Will you be ready for the <number> powerful ways to <benefit>?

69. Will you be ready to learn <number> powerful methods to <goal> and <benefit>?

70. Will you be ready to become <goal> and learn <benefit> instantly?

71. Did you ever ask yourself the <problem> you faced every day?

72. Did you ever ask yourself how to <goal> with just 3 simple steps?

73. Have you ever think about the simple way to <goal>?

74. Have you ever think about the solutions to <problem>?

75. Have you ever think about the way you can <benefit> and <goal> with least effort?

76. Have you ever think about you can just <goal> and <benefit> in <timeframe>?

77. Sick of the same old <problem> you have and want to <benefit> instantly?

78. Don't you wish you can <benefit> right away?

79. Don't you wish you can <goal> and <benefit> in <timeframe>

80. Don't you wish you can <goal> and solve <problem> at the same time?

81. Don't you wish you can <benefit> with just <number of steps>

82. Would you like to <benefit> and <goal> with no risk and minimum effort?

83. Would you like to <benefit> and <goal> in just <timeframe>?

84. Would you like to know the insider secret to <goal> in the next minute?

85. Would you like to find out <benefit> instantly?

86. Wouldn't you like to learn <benefit> in just <number of steps>?

87. Wouldn't you like to find out <number> powerful guides to <problem>?

88. Don't you need to know the easiest way to <benefit> and <goal>?

89. Don't you need to know <number of steps> to <benefit> and <goal> in <timeframe>

90. Have you ever experience sleepless nights figuring out <problem>?

91. Do you ever stayed up late night thinking about <problem> and <goal>?

92. Do you have a fire in your belly to <goal> and <benefit>?

93. Do you have a fire in you to <goal> and <benefit> in simply <timeframe>?

94. Do you have a burning desire to eliminate <problem>?

95. Do you have a burning desire to be <goal> and <benefit>?

96. Do you have a burning desire to reach <goal> and <benefit> with only <timeframe>?

97. You must be thinking "how did I achieve <benefit> and at only <timeframe>?"

98. You must be thinking "how did I achieve <benefit> and <goal> by <age>?"

99. You must be thinking "how did I eliminate <problem> and learn <benefit> in <timeframe>?"

100. Are you suffering with <problem> and interested to find out solutions **immediately?**

CHAPTER ELEVEN

A GREAT NEW IDEA IS LIKE STRIKING GOLD.

HOWEVER, MANY PEOPLE HAVE TROUBLE CONVEYING THEIR IDEAS AND GENERATING EXCITEMENT AROUND THEM. THAT'S WHAT MAKES THIS BOOK IS A GOLD MINE!

INSIDE THIS CHAPTER, YOU WILL NOT BE AT A LOSS FOR WORDS WHEN YOU WANT TO PASS YOUR KILLER IDEA TO YOUR AUDIENCE.

CHAPTER 11: GETTING AN IDEA ACROSS

1. What if your product is the next ___ in the <market>?

2. What if you can make <benefit> right after you know the unusual secret?

3. What if your tomorrow will never be the same as yesterday anymore?

4. What if you can solve your long-entangled problem in the next hour?

5. What if you can buy your dream house and ride you could ever dream of ?

6. What if you can impress your <enemy/friend> immediately after you know the Real Truth!

7. What if you can double your <benefit> in your next <encounter>?

8. What if your profit soar through the roof in your next <encounter>?

9. What if next you're the One laugh your way to the bank and no others?

10. What if you can achieve your <goal> much earlier than anyone ever expected?

11. What if we are shouldering the risk of your purchase for the next 60 days?

12. This breakthrough product can help you achieve your <goal> much faster than you could imagine.

13. The <niche\product> allow you to go on vacation anytime you want

14. This secret skill will allow you to buy anything you want without looking at the price tag

15. Taking part in the <niche> will allow you to spend more time with family

16. This <niche> will allow you to be part of the Elite Group and dominate the <market>

17. Thinking about all the <benefit> you will get with our <product>

18. This will allow you to save big bucks by getting it all in one place for one low price

19. This investment will pay off continuously for many years to come

20. Get rid of your <problem> with a click of the mouse

21. You will be able to dazzle people with hypnotic < skill> that make them < >

22. This proven secret will turn your life around immediately

23. Learn the ultimate secret to <action > the <problem>

24. What if you too can out your testimony in this page

25. If you don't <benefit> within 8 weeks we will buy the product back from you

26. Please don't put this off, every minute passing by will render your slot taken by someone else

27. Give me 5 days and you might make $....

28. Remember, our <product> can make you <benefit> today, not in 30 days.

29. You are moment away from having a powerful amazing <benefit> right from the comfort of your home

30. Once you have it, you can <benefit>. It is as easy as 1 2 3.

31. As a bonus incentive you will get <benefit> in just < price>

32. We will reward you with <benefit> if you take action now

33. You will also get <benefit> if you take action within <time>

34. For the next 72 hours you will get 95% off

35. The proven blueprint can help you <benefit>

36. This Amazing secret will skyrocket your <profit > in <time>

37. Taking action now can eliminate unnecessary cost and fast forward your <benefit>

38. This specialize <niche> will allow you to work anywhere, and anytime you want

39. With my 4 weeks course you will definitely <benefit>

40. With this ultra-class < product> sure you will <benefit>

41. You will be able to <benefit> after knowing the unprecedented Truth

42. If you take action now I guarantee you will <benefit>

43. Let us help you <benefit> and enjoy the life of your dream

44. Take action now and you will retire earlier, drive a brand new car, and own your home

45. Click now to discover the unprecedented truth of <niche>

46. What if you can possess the power of this <product> in your hand against all odds

47. You only need to know fifth grade math and all you do is collect your cash at the end

48. I want you to have complete confidence and peace of mind in <niche> tomorrow

49. Do you want to have an average <benefit> all of your life? Or get <real benefit> starting tomorrow

50. You can take control of how much more profitable and pleasurable your <niche> in less than <time>

51. You can take full advantage of <niche> right now before it is too late

52. You will snap on <benefit> once you have this once in a life time killer <product>

53. What if you can unleash the most powerful secret weapon now and thanking me for years to come

54. Within <time> of ordering you will receive <benefit>

55. Let's test drive the <product> and you will <benefit>

56. You will receive all this <benefit> :

57. This special <skill> will make you wonder how will you manage without it

58. After knowing the truth you will wonder why you waited

59. What if you can make the turning point of your life after a click of the mouse

60. What if you can Double your saving after knowing <niche>

61. What if you can take an extra 50% off the ticketed price when you take action right now

62. What if <benefit> is yours Free just for saying "yes" to

63. This <product> will show you why you have no obligation to buy anything ever

64. This simple <product > will help you <benefit> in 2 weeks

65. This awesome <skill> will make you <benefit> others could ever envy with

66. Within 10 days from today you could be <benefit>

67. What if knowing <niche> will help you take a giant step in <progress>

68. This will help you learn about <niche> in 10 minutes

69. Knowing <skill> will make you <benefit> and surprise you with unexpected pleasure

70. Knowing <skill> will allow you to experience the wonder of....

71. Mastering <skill> will equip you an edge in <market>

72. A sip of the truth of <benefit> and you will never remember how the old days were.

73. This will allow you to learn the astonishing truth in <time>

74. Knowing the spine-tingling truth of <benefit> will enable you to <progress>

75. Revealing the ancient blueprint of <benefit> will make you <growth> in <time>

76. Master the <niche> will unleash your ultimate taken and imagination

77. This will lead you to the kind of <life> you have only dreamed of

78. Knowing <skill> will make you feel brand new

79. <time> after knowing will allow you to indulge in <benefit>

80. Mastering <skill> will alter your perception towards all your previous <problem>

81. Mastering <niche> will open dozens of money-making opportunities

82. This special offer will allow you to get rich without going to work

83. This ultimate product will put you in your fast track to wealth

84. This ancient secret will Triple your <benefit> in <time>

85. This amazing product will make you successful in <market>

86. This unrevealing truth will earn you <benefit> in your spare time

87. This unprecedented product will help you generate <benefit> in first 3 months

88. If I don't show you a proven path to <benefit> you owe me nothing

89. Let me show you how you can accomplish something better in <market>

90. Let me show you how you can <benefit> with my proven path

91. Let me show you how to <benefit> in < recession/ bad time>

92. Knowing <skill> will allow you to identify your passion and make them into wealth

93. Unlock the <product> code will allow you to <benefit> in an incredible inexpensive, fast and easy way

94. You will learn the secret that most people will never know about after Unlocking the <product > code

95. Once you first identify <benefit> you will success in <market>

96. What if you can learn how to parley as few as 4 hours a week into a full time income without interfering you current career

97. What if your entire career can be automated, and fool-proof in just 10 minutes

98. What if you manage to copy my <niche> blueprint and rake your income to 5 figure in 6 months

99. Discover how you can learn <skill> with no business knowledge or computer skill

100. What if you have master the revolution of <niche> and make others green with envy

CHAPTER TWELVE

CREATING SOCIAL PROOF USING WRITTEN COMPARISONS IS A UNIQUE TALENT.

HAVING SOCIAL PROOF LIKE THIS HAS MORE IMPORTANCE NOW THAN EVER BECAUSE CUSTOMERS ARE BECOMING MORE INFORMED ALL THE TIME.

NEEDLESS TO SAY, IT'S IN YOUR BEST INTEREST TO DISTINGUISH YOURSELF AGAINST THE REST AND EFFECTIVELY UTILIZE THIS CHAPTER SO YOU CAN KEEP A PROSPECT ON YOUR PAGE INSTEAD OF LOOKING FOR SOMETHING OR SOMEONE ELSE.

IT'S EVEN MORE POWERFUL WHEN YOU USE IT WHEN CUSTOMERS ARE GETTING CLOSER TO MAKING A PURCHASE.

CHAPTER 12: COMPARISONS

1. We are giving you extra information on \<benefit\> than any other source

2. We are giving you extra information on \<problem\> than any other source

3. We are giving you extra information on \<goal\> than any other source

4. Do not leave your hard-earned money on your ignorance

5. Do not simply waste your hard-earned money on information that is unnecessary

6. Don't be taken in by the cheap price, quality matters

7. Don't be taken in by the cheap price offered, we prove them wrong

8. No one has ever come close to giving this much of information

9. No one has ever come close to guarantee this

10. No other internet marketers give you more quality than this

11. No other internet marketers give you more insights than this

12. Do not judge a product by its price

13. Do not judge a product with purely instinct

14. This is not a second rate product

15. This is going to be the best you will ever experience

16. You will not see this price elsewhere

17. You will never see this bonus elsewhere

18. You will not see this amount of information elsewhere

19. Go for the best, not the second best

20. No one has such many credits for this product

21. This is not a copy of other similar products with just a change of cover

22. Don't be seduced by the flowery words to purchase a product

23. Don't be seduced by the incredibly low price, look at the content

24. We offer the extra bits of <benefit> at no cost

25. We offer the extra bits of solution to <problem> at no cost

26. We take great responsibility in our product

27. We take great responsibility in our research

28. Despite of what you may have come across, you can be assured this is the best

29. Isn't is better to pay slightly more now and gain unlimited times in the future

30. You can be confident that it will save you more money in the years ahead

31. You can be confident that it will gain you more money in the years ahead

32. You are definitely guarantee that you are paying for the highest quality

33. Consider all the extraordinary benefits you can get with our products

34. Nobody can match our prices

35. <number of %> cheaper than our closest rival

36. We provide 100% of the information you need

37. Everything you need to know about <subject> is presented clearly in here

38. This is an all-in-one package of information that you no longer need from others

39. Everything you wanted to find out from basic to advance are all in here

40. Do you want to settle for less?

41. Do you want to settle for second best?

42. Don't settle for a less reputable product

43. Do you want to settle for lower quality?

44. Do you want to give in for an inferior product?

45. Do you want to waste your money on a less quality product?

46. Do you want to maximize your hard-earned money on the best product?

47. Do you want to settle for something that is not essential?

48. Do you want to settle for a lower quality product?

49. If you're planning to get average product, please get other less quality products from our competitors

50. Don't ever compare with our rivals, because you'll love our product even more

51. Don't ever compare with our competitors, in the end you will know we are the best

52. Don't ever compare with our competitors, because you will end up finding no one close to our standard

53. You will never see a more complete package than the one we are offering

54. There is no comparison for this, because we accept no substitutes

55. This is no imitations of any other similar products you can find

56. This is not any ordinary _____; we take pride in our commitment to create the best product

57. You are simply paying for the top-notch quality of information here.

58. Do you really want to continue with mediocre products?

59. If you are not fully committed and determined to change your life, you can get other lower quality products from our rivals

60. We only believe in 100% authentic

61. Who you buy from is as important as what you buy, quality is definitely important.

62. You are the one who benefits and do not settle for less quality product

63. We only demand for excellence and do not give in for imitations

64. We don't play games with our customers and we are dedicated to serve them till perfection.

65. You will not have to look for further details with our guarantee products

66. Choose only the one you are committed to and bear in mind of the quality served.

67. You will find out how easy and simple to understand our guide compared with the rest

68. We are professionals in this field and you can be assured with the highest standard we are providing.

69. We are confident that this is the right stuff for you with the excellence we demanded

70. We have first-hand experience for what's in the guide and you can rest assured that it is complete

71. We expose the myths about the subject in the guide so you will be aware

72. We are offering the cold hard facts

73. We are confident to offer you an extraordinary learning experience

74. Our products will open up new directions of information to you so you will have a greater scope of what you are learning

75. Our products exceed standards and possess the highest quality

76. This is going to be a lifetime of satisfaction and don't you settle for inferior quality

77. Compare the products for yourself; you will know we are offering the best

78. When you explore other similar products out there, you'll see no one even comes close

79. Go find out what are in there for other similar products, no one will provide better information

80. You will never lose sleep again looking for more information with our full package

81. This will let you have a competitive edge over others with the knowledge you are going to have

82. You will be keeping ahead in the game with our trusted products

83. You will find out you won't settle for anything less than the one we provided

84. We are giving the best in the business and you can expect more from it

85. Our products can only be compared with more than all others combined

86. We always provide something new and different in our products to keep the excellence we have

87. Nobody else is going to give you more detailed information than us

88. We are in a class by itself so no one will even be near our standard

89. Before you decide to make payment, find out what standard the product has to offer

90. We are all ready to prove everything we provide

91. You can never find a more complete package of information than this

92. It may be slightly expensive but it is going to worth more

93. You may find imitations from our but it will never be exactly the same

94. This is the one and only full package of information you ever need

95. You will know this is the best when you come across other similar product from others

96. We offer the most in-depth and extensive information you can ever find with least price

97. We have all the specifications you would have expect

98. Our products are designed to be clearly and simply explained

99. We developed the products to be the best and only the best

100. This can be the first and the last product that you can get for best result

CHAPTER THIRTEEN

WHY BULLET POINTS?

LIKE IT OR NOT, BULLET POINTS KEEP PEOPLE READING YOUR BLOG POSTS, PAGES, ARTICLES, AND COPY LIKE NOTHING ELSE...

BULLETS SIMPLY ACT AS YOUR LITTLE HEADLINES.

THEY SHOULD CONTAIN THE BENEFIT THE CUSTOMER WOULD RECEIVE FROM YOUR PRODUCT OR SERVICE.

I'VE FOUND YOU SHOULD ALWAYS HAVE 5 TO 8 BULLETS THAT ARE BENEFIT DRIVEN AND EXPLAIN TO THE CUSTOMER WHY THEY NEED TO TAKE ACTION.

YOU ARE ALWAYS WELCOME TO ADAPT, TWEAK & ALTER THESE.

CHAPTER 13: HIGH CONVERTING BULLET POINTS

1. The _____ of _____ - all of which you can adapt to your own _____. Discover the easiest and most guaranteed way that you can _____ for your_____ - enjoy a lifetime of _____!

2. The one skill that propelled me from losing $10,000 to now pulling in up to $2000 in a single day -- without ____.

3. A complete, no holds barred, step-by-step guide at putting together _ in the least amount of time. I'll show you what to do, how to do it, and when to do it.

4. A complete _____ hindsight view at throwing together _____, keeping _____, and _____ in the least amount of time. I'll show you what to do, how to do it, and when to do it. Think how much

5. _____this alone could _____.

6. A list of powerful no-cost or low-costs tools to practically put your income generating efforts on auto-pilot! No need for super expensive or fancy software needed to start building your own _!

7. The truth about ____, weekly, etc. whether your goal ____ or ____.

8. Why _, and _ have almost nothing to do with getting ____ and ____.

9. How you've been working like clockwork for 5, 10, 20, even 30 years making ____ BUT ____.

10. Revolutionary new _____that you can use to easily generate _____of _____ in your sleep, and where you can get _____.

11. How to _____on the web astonishingly fast – and _____

12. Why you could just be one pay check away from financial disaster!

13. 5 steps you can take right now to _!

14. Zero in on the most lucrative _ in minutes.

15. Declare Your Independence From Programmers as You Discover How You Can Set Up Your Own _ In Minutes And Update _ In A Flash.

16. You'll discover how to use 'Upwork" to attract huge numbers of clients in record time and which FIVE techniques will allow you to stand out from the crowd and successfully swipe all the business from under the noses of the cheap offshore SEO companies.

17. How to decide _____ for your _____. I'll show you how I _____ in a _____ period with a _____than I would have done for _____ -- with the same _____!

18. Slip these _____ before your _____ -- and people will feel compelled to do exactly what you say. Master _____ emotional triggers that will arouse your _____ inner _____.

19. Where you can get a juicy slice of many $800,000 niche markets almost nobody knows about...

20. How to Effortlessly Create _ Applications Even if You Have NO Programming Skills

21. Let's say you're just starting out, you have $150 a month spare to put into your business. Which route are you going to go with?

22. Dominate your_____ with_____ that surround _____ with an invisible field of magnetism that very few people can resist.

23. Learn the greatest hypnotic secret ever revealed – this is _____ that is absolutely indispensable as you embark on your _____

24. Brainstorming niches -- and a list of 17 "desperate buyer" words to use when you use Google to do your research...Using the automated method I have developed you simply pick how much revenue you want to earn, copy and paste a few things, and sit back and relax.

25. Why You Should Almost Never Use Joint Tenancy To Own Your Assets!

26. Own _____seductive _____ that will pull _____ directly into your _____.

27. _____ hidden commands that are so good, _____won't even realize you are secretly commanding them.

28. The Amazingly Simple Steps You Must Take Now To Avoid Wasting Thousands of Dollars In

29. Needless _ Later On!

30. 78% Of The TOP _ Shared The EXACT Same Values!

31. You don't need to create your own _...

32. You don't need to create a _!

33. How to get _____ of other people _____for you in just a matter of _____ without spending one red cent!

34. An easy-to-setup, _____ for _____to draw _____like honey attracts flies.

35. Learn _____unforeseen _____ that will mysteriously _____without your prospects realizing it.

36. You don't need to build a list of customers...

37. There is ABSOLUTELY NO _ involved!

38. Why it PAYS to lose money in order to acquire _... and how you can control _ - and why you might even have to _!

39. How to use _____, _____ or a combination of several psychological triggers to double _____of your existing _____

40. How to boost _ by up to 30-50%!

41. The _ THAT ALWAYS proves to be the missing piece of the puzzle for struggling _____

42. Just imagine the size of opt-in mailing lists you could build in _ when you can rank you're _ at the top of the hottest in your niche...

43. The quickest way to overtake everyone else and jump straight in to the #1 _before your competition even knows what's happening.

44. Need more money? Fancy _? Just optimize _, and sit back as the revenue comes pouring in. This is money on demand!

45. How to eliminate _ without the use of _.

46. Unleash your body's natural ability to _ from _!

47. Enjoy more free time by knowing _, so you know exactly _.

48. Tap into the goldmine of _ by viewing Google data in over a dozen countries... all with a click of a button!

49. Slam your opposition in _ and start earning your _ profits in just a few short weeks as you discover the secrets of successful on-page SEO.

50. Feel the pleasure of seeing your bank balance rise literally while you sleep by learning how you can line up a whole years' worth of content and then just let it run itself!

51. If you want to make more income, work less, and have an enjoyable retirement, you must start creating income streams that DO NOT require your direct involvement.

52. Get instant access to ____ that are proven to work

53. Earn 100% of the profits and keep 100% of the customer list you generate

54. Never have to worry about _, _, _ or anything like that, ever again.

55. Which _ site drove over 400,000 unique visitors to a website within just 3 hours?

56. Exposed! The exact _ that took her only five minutes to do, that brought in the _

57. 15 baby sleep tricks you haven't tried yet

58. How you can tell he's ____

59. Automatically _____ all of your _____!

60. 20 beauty cheapies for under $10

61. Plain women who attract _ -- what have they got?

62. The two most important goals of _! (Not one person in 1000 in this country even has a clue how to "_!)

63. Get happy! Ditch the five things that _

64. Trying for _? A _? How _ can help

65. How to permanently lock your _ into "_"... so you'll never be _

66. You don't know it, but you are probably _____ (right now!) ten ways from Sunday - right under your very nose. Learn the _____ biggest _____. They are

67. Not what you think. Chances are you are_____ this very moment by not knowing this critical information.

68. How to "read" the signs of _ who are dying to get you right now! (They think they're being obvious, but I'll bet you're blind to the signals. Just learning this one secret how to "read" _-- will boost your "_ potential" through the roof!)

69. 185 cool _

70. Bad _? Can't _? It's not your fault -- here's why, page XX

71. How to decide _____ for your _____. I'll show you how I _____ in a _____ period with a _____than I would have done for _____ -- with the same _____!

72. The secret weight-loss spice

73. How to avoid the really dumb mistakes _ (and nearly all _) make with their _- and how to turn "loser" or marginal _ into blockbuster moneymakers!

74. Broken _ -- the new _

75. 44 things _ should do before they _

76. The very best way to _

77. A smart way to _

78. What _won't tell you

79. How to find -- without spending a red cent

80. How the three basic _ (multimillion dollar) _ can also be used to increase the _

81. How to skillfully enter the _____ of your _____ so that they will _____.

82. How to make room in your life for _____. How to transform any _____ or _____ into _____ in your life

83. How to automatically _____ day after day without even trying! THE best way to create _____ on the internet month after month!

84. How anyone can _____ to _____.

85. ___ secret… how to legally _, _, and various _without having to pay money for _!

86. The _____ that will get you _____. _____ quick and easy ways to get the word out about your

87. How to _____, without _____ or _____. Using this _____, several entrepreneurs _____. And some of them didn't even have _____!

88. How to approach any _ - and know exactly what to say to get them to _ without 'paying a dime'.

89. How to secretly _____ and fill it with your _____

90. Get the absolute most powerful form of _____ you've ever discovered.

91. A _____ for earning _____ - _____ more from _____ by _____!

92. The most successful sales letter ever written (close to a billion copies have been mailed) and what you can learn from it to make millions of dollars selling cars.

93. How to get _____ busting their guts trying to promote your _____.

94. How To _____ By _____

95. Are your _ healthy? Know your risk

96. How to Maximize Your Successful Submissions & Guarantee HORDES of Easy Traffic

97. The _____ you MUST include in your _____to make certain folks don't _____.

98. The simple _ formula anyone can use to create a _ that will get the job done.

99. How to structure an irresistible _. (A great _ with average copy will outsell a bad offer with great copy!)

100. How to _____ Right Now With _____ Make ANY _____ effortlessly become _____

101. How to take _____ of _____just like the professionals do!

102. Utilize an AMAZING secret that when used properly will result in _____.

103. A unique strategy pioneered by a car dealer in New Zealand that is 10 times more effective than "expensive" billboard advertising... and 100 times cheaper!!!

104. Discover how to _____ (and why it will help you make breakthroughs you've never thought possible!) Get rid of _____, such as _____

105. Harness the secret _____ for _____.

106. We'll reveal a _ to contact whose _ have the potential to generate $10,000's of dollars of _. It's so obvious but hardly anyone ever thinks of it.

107. How to guarantee your _____ gets noticed among the gazillion different _____ being offered on the Internet today!

108. A system for expanding _____ day after day for _____, _____, and _____ Why most people are_____in their very own _____ and why it's _____! Find out how you can avoid _____ and learn to work smarter, not harder!

109. Learn the _____to manifesting _____

110. Two "shoe-string budget" _ that allow you to "steal" once-faithful-_ from your biggest competitor. (These techniques are 100% legal... but just barely!)

111. How to instill in your _____ a visceral need they can feel at the gut level – and create a desire for a resolution that only your _____ or _____ can satisfy

112. How to turn _____ into _____

113. _____and _____your way to _____. How to put your _____ on _____

114. What "Marketing Incest" is, and how it is just as sickening to you as real incest!

115. Find out _____, plus _____ others people who will want to _____ _____ undercover techniques for discovering what your _____ REALLY want in a _____. Successfully _____ every _____ using a special _____

116. After you are finished with the automated method, you are only minutes away from making a steady flow of money every week.

117. The _____ most popular types of _ deals. You probably haven't even thought of some of these. Use _____ that will condition your _ to persuade themselves to buy.

118. Where to find qualified and targeted _____- and how to know exactly what they want from you. _____ kinds of articles that anyone can write, regardless of their writing experience or

ability, beginning today! Seriously, anyone who can follow simple instructions can get these done right.

119. How to turn any _ in any _into a "_" where you can _ without _!

120. How to SUCCEED beyond your wildest dreams in _ in just five easy steps –

121. We already talked about why _____ (or even being accused) is a recipe for disaster.

122. How to evaluate a _____ candidate to make sure they can help you. The power of _____ and how you can get it now!

123. The little-known secret to _____! This includes our _____ formula, a special _____, and the one thing you must _____ on the _____ that could make the difference between _____ or _____!

124. Plus, we reveal a secret way of _____ in _____ days or less! (Less than _____% of _____ even know about this secret tactic!)

125. What to write on a cheap little postcard that will make people _!

126. The biggest mistakes almost every _____ makes and how it instantly KILLS any chances you had for_____!

127. How to create winning _____ in any business and create massive profits

128. Get _____ _____ that will _____. These can be altered for any _____. The #1 key to _____… an absolute must for any _____… especially you!

129. Learn the ultimate secret to _____– this is a diabolical principle of _____ that _____

130. Get Extremely High Traffic Domain Names With This FREE Simple Tool _ Don't Want You To Know About!

131. How to stay extremely _____ at all times…no matter what!

132. The #1 myth in _____ today…and how to protect your _____ by applying this strategy today!

133. Use these amazing techniques with ANY _____. Small, medium or _____ - it doesn't matter!

134. Whether you're _____ or _____... these techniques will _____ that is absolutely guaranteed.

135. Where to find _____, _____ and _____ for you to _____– this will get _____.

136. Discover Tools and Step-By-Step Guides To Help You Find The Right _ And _ In Only 120 Minutes Or LESS!

137. 9/10 _ completely overlook.

138. Automate your _____ building_____ in _____at _____! (This alone will save you hours of time and _____!)

139. Effective use of _____for _____.

140. A trick I learned at the _____ that made me a little over $6000 in 2 months the very first time I put it to use.

141. How to _____without _____.

142. Discover the secret _____for _____.

143. 2 FREE services that can triple _.

144. How to _____ with _____. Using _____to _____.

145. Plus how to _____ to start _____ with _____.

146. How to fail fast and win BIG. (One reason most people don't succeed is simply they don't _.)

147. The "parrot" rule and how it can help you succeed no matter how many times you've failed before.

148. How to build_____ among _____ to keep them_____.

149. How to quickly _____online!

150. The TWO SECRETS everyone has to know before they can succeed as _

151. Where to get FREE insider information on _ – These secrets are sure to send your _ skyrocketing!

152. Find out how to _____. Discover _____ and _____that _____. How to _____and _____to your advantage, just like _____. How to _____ and _____on every page. Techniques for _____, _____and _____.

153. Discover Tools And Step-By-Step Guides To Help You Find The Right _ And _ In Only 120 Minutes Or LESS!

154. How to _____ without lifting a finger.

155. How to become a magnet that attracts_____ who will trust you and _____ you.

156. The 5 simple steps to a profitable _ AND the order to do them in -- most people are doing at least 1 of the steps in the complete wrong order and it severely hurts their chances of _.

157. The best places to _____ and _____ -- and _____. I'll recommend my most _____ strategies and resources.

158. How to immediately transform your _____ into a powerful _____– a _____ that consistently attracts _____ to your _____

159. Leverage the _ of popular _ and channel them right to your _. It'll be like funneling water into your farmland without ever spending a cent!

160. Turn _ of popular _ into your number one raving fans. This crazy method is so simple that any ten-year-old kid can do it!

161. What 1 thing you can do to unlock a massive flow of _____ from your _____. _____ System for_____ within you to bring in even more _____ into your _____.

162. Discover the most important _____ that can give your _an unfair advantage. Use these to the hilt before your competitor's catch -The brain-dead simple way to quickly expand your _ without adding mind-numbing complexity.

163. How to position _____ in the eyes of your_____ so that it will be virtually effortless for you to attract _____ – and there'll be very little _____ on your part because _____ would have already been _____

164. A brand new discovery (just approved by _) which any man can use to instantly (and safely) boost _! (Note: This will not only improve _... but also... _.)

165. The two almost unknown secrets (one _, one _) men need to know to have _... at any age! (These are crucial secrets to improving _.)

166. How to create instant _____ at the drop of a hat.

167. How to use your _____ to _____ draw _____ like a powerful magnet

168. Do you want to go back to school? If so there is a good chance the _ will send you _ every month to help you do just that.

169. What both men AND women need to know about _... and... how this knowledge will solve almost all problems caused by _!

170. The _____secrets that you can quickly and easily master to become _____.

171. Learn how to saturate your _____ with intense, emotion-provoking _____ that _____

172. Flirting secrets used by all _ that 95% of _ don't even recognize... and... how a _ life instantly gets ten times more exciting... when _ understand these little known secrets!

173. How to use a _____ to place your _____ in a trance, and force them to _____... and then let them thank you for it!

174. How to multiply _____ exponentially via _____. It's not nearly as difficult as you think. _____ not only makes it look easy, but also gives you simple, but surefire _____ to make _____.

175. How to _____ from *passive* _____ who barely even try to _____.

176. How to get into a deep, soul-pleasing rapport with your lover... and... stay there forever! (You will never feel alone again.)

177. The only list anyone can trust about what really makes a _ attractive to _! (Why can this list be trusted? Simply because... it was compiled by thousands of _.)

178. How to get the exact name and address of thousands of people who would love to send you _! (See page XX)

179. How to skillfully enter the _____ of your _____ so that they will _____.

180. The most important thing you should do before _____. Miss this _____ and you'll join the _____.

181. The hidden truth about _____ and _____ & how to effortlessly create _____

182. How to take advantage of the highly-targeted traffic from _____! (I don't even bother _____ anymore. It's too much work! I'll show you an easier way to _____!)

183. How to _____ with ZERO _____ - no _____, no _____, no _____, no _____ at all.

184. The startling truth about _____ ... and the inside information you must know before you embark on any _____ campaign

185. 9/10 _ owners completely overlook.

186. The brain-dead simple way to quickly expand your "one day" _ without adding mind numbing complexity.

187. Master _____ emotional triggers that will arouse your _____ inner _____.

188. How to dazzle people with hypnotic _____that make them

_____

189. The "20 minute secret" that can turn your _ around immediately! (It's so simple; you'll kick yourself for not having thought of it.)

190. Seven "very specific" secrets a _ can use to take a _ "over the top" and... why, with this fabulous _technique... some _ will literally "_" (safely)... from _!

191. Learn the ultimate secret to controlling _ – this is a diabolical principle of _____that creates _____ outside of _

192. You've got a BIG _____staring you right in the face inside your _____...learn what it is and _____ ways to use it!

CHAPTER FOURTEEN

BENEFITS AND FEATURES ARE TWO ENTIRELY SEPARATE THINGS.

BENEFITS ANSWER THE QUESTION: "WHAT'S IN IT FOR YOU?"

THEY CONNECT TO YOUR CUSTOMER'S DESIRES, SUCH AS SAVING TIME; REDUCING COSTS; MAKING MORE MONEY; BECOMING HAPPIER, HEALTHIER, MORE RELAXED, OR MORE PRODUCTIVE.

BOTTOM LINE: BENEFITS SEDUCE PEOPLE TO PURCHASE PEACE OF MIND.

ADAPT, TWEAK & ALTER THESE TO SUIT YOUR NEEDS.

CHAPTER 14: 102 BENEFITS

1. Never Released Before

2. Newly Launched

3. The Latest _____

4. Hot!

5. Smoking Hot!

6. _____ of the year

7. One of a kind

8. Not rehashed or recycled from anywhere else

9. The first of its kind

10. Why pay more?

11. More for less

12. Secure your copy today for only $_____

13. Act now while it's still at its lowest price Blowout Sale! Explode your _____

14. Boost Your profits

15. Reduce your _____

16. Double / Triple / Quadruple your profits

17. Skyrocket your sales count!

18. See your profit margin soar through the roof!

19. Can an extra $1000 a month help improve your lifestyle?

20. Become a _____ machine

21. Add new income streams instantly

22. Boost your _____ by tonight

23. Step-by-step formula to making your _____

24. Get paid to _____

25. _____ freedom

26. _____ on pure autopilot

27. Line your pockets with …

28. Affordable

29. Low-cost

30. Get everything for the price of one

31. More value for money

32. Save time on _____

33. I respect your time so I'll cut the chase and go straight to the point

34. This one's on the house

35. Zero-cost

36. Free of Charge

37. Here's a gift for you, simply for _____

38. As a bonus incentive, you get _____ just for _____

39. This is valued at $_____ bit it's yours FREE

40. I would have easily sold this for $_____ but for a limited time only, it's yours FREE

41. Bonus!

42. I'm giving away _____

43. At no extra cost

44. No additional charge

45. I'm also throwing in _____

46. If you act now, you also get _____

47. But that's not all. You also get _____

48. I'm saving the best for the last 49. Say goodbye to frustrating _____

50. Let us do all the work for you so you don't have to

51. Fire your boss

52. Pay your bills on time

53. Work anytime and anywhere you want

54. If _____ is not a problem, what do you want to do?

55. In a blink of an eye

56. Instantly

57. Faster than you can say _____

58. Starting this second, you can _____

59. As easy as pie

60. You don't have to be a rocket scientist

61. _____ in just seconds / minutes

62. It's a whole lot easier than you think

63. _____ just got easier

64. Even if you don't know anything about _____

65. You probably wouldn't have guessed it was that easy

66. Even if you are a newbie

67. In an instant

68. Immense

69. Massive

70. Collection of _____

71. Time Tested

72. Proven

73. Thoroughly tested

74. _____ resistant

75. Exciting

76. Mind Boggling

77. Sizzling Hot

78. Premium

79. We used only the best _____

80. Widely recognized _____

81. Join the ranks of _____

82. Renowned

83. Only for a select few

84. You are the reason why we're in business

85. Why even "beginners" are able to use_____

86. How to use the secret of _____ to_____

87. The one basic secret of _____

88. How to easily pull off _____

89. Why it's actually more simple (and profitable) to _____

90. How to get better (and faster) results than_____

91. A dirt-cheap, simple do-it-yourself _____that gives you _____

92. How to avoid the embarrassing mistakes even experienced _____ make when_____

93. A "lazy man's" _____ way to _____

94. Secret "2-minute" _____ techniques (that's all it takes!) that

95. New (and simple) _____ that actually _____

96. Exactly how and what to _____

97. Detailed strategies to _____

98. Little-known secrets that can steer you to tremendous _____

99. 6 too-simple-to-pass-up ways to _____

100. 3 "no brainer" ways to _____

101. 6 too-simple-to-pass-up ways to _____

102. 3 "no brainer" ways to _____

CHAPTER FIFTEEN

BONUSES INCREASE YOUR SALES.

WHY?

BECAUSE, PEOPLE ABSOLUTELY LOVE FREE STUFF!

JUST ADDING ONE MEASLY BONUS TO WHATEVER YOU ARE OFFERING MIGHT MEAN THE DIFFERENCE BETWEEN SOMEONE KICKING THE TIRES, AND CONVERTING THAT TIRE-KICKER INTO A CUSTOMER.

SCAN THROUGH THIS CHAPTER TO GET AN IDEA FOR YOUR NEXT BONUS.

CHAPTER 15: BONUSES

1. If you BUY now, I'll be sending you another mystery bonus as a token of appreciation.

2. You won't find these bonuses anywhere!

3. These bonuses is going to compliment your progress towards _____

4. We know you won't settle for less, so we are going to offer you an irresistible bonus!

5. Who else wants these bonuses worth $10,000?

6. I'm selling this for $197 but you're getting it for FREE Today!

7. You'll get these amazing bonuses when you purchase this by midnight!

8. Announcing a special bonus offer for the first 5 customers!

9. I've just added $300 bonuses for 30 customers only!

10. If you buy from our competitors, you're going to miss out these great bonuses

11. Great bargain with these killer bonuses!

12. Hurry, only 3 bonuses left! Don't miss out!

13. This is your last chance to grab these eye-popping bonuses

14. Trust me, these bonuses is going to turn you ON!

15. I know you won't miss out on our bonus offer!

16. Say "YES" to our bonuses ☺

17. If you're seriously interested to purchase our product, I'm giving away this $200 bonus to you.

18. Important! This is offer is valid for 24 hours only!

19. This is your last chance to grab our bonus

20. Hurry in for these bonuses

21. Good news! We have decided to throw in these bonuses

22. Is there anyone who would like to download these massive bonuses?

23. No one offers such a huge bonus package like we do

24. Everyone is so excited with our fantastic bonus offer

25. Awesome bonus for awesome customers like you!

26. You should be paying extra $500 for these bonuses! But it's FREE today!

27. Get this fabulous bonus bargain when you sign up our premium membership

28. I'm giving away my best selling product for absolutely zero cost

29. We are offering extra value to our customers with this gigantic bonus offer!

30. We want to make sure you get more for your dollar; hence we added this extensive bonus package!

31. With great product, comes a great bonus! ORDER NOW!

32. That's not all! You're getting an extra $____ worth of bonus when you ORDER today!

33. If that's not enough, we are giving away this incredible bonus to you.

34. There you have it: A time limited bonus offer which expires in 24 hours!

35. To make your life easier, we have included this ready-made _____ as a bonus!

36. If you prefer to buy this product without our crazy bonuses, please buy it from our competitors!

37. You can download these bonuses instantly when you join us now!

38. Would you be interested if I add in extra 5 bonuses?

39. This is not another crappy bonus package! You're getting REAL value from this offer!

40. This one's on the house

41. At no extra charge

42. Yours FREE…

43. We're giving away…

44. All yours to keep

45. A gift for you for signing up

46. Zero-cost

47. Free of Charge

48. Here's a gift for you, simply for _____

49. As a bonus incentive, you get _____ just for _____

50. This is valued at $_____ but it's yours FREE

51. I would have easily sold this for $_____ but for a limited time only, it's yours   FREE

52. Bonus!

53. This one's on us!

54. It's yours FREE just for saying "yes" to....

55. Keep it, use it, enjoy it!

56. At no charge

57. I'm giving away _____

58. I'm also throwing in _____

59. It's our way of saying "thank you"

60. If you act now, you also get _____

61. But that's not all. You also get _____

62. I'm saving the best for the last

63. Included in the package is _____

64. $0.00

65. It's yours FREE

66. Giving away

67. If you act now, you will also get

68. At no extra cost

69. No additional charge

70. Here are your bonuses

71. I'll reward you with _____ for taking action now

72. You'll also get

73. Inside the member's area I have also included

74. Here's everything you'll be getting...

75. This would have cost you $_____ if you attempt to _____

76. At only $_____ that's a steal and you will also be getting _____ for FREE

77. I have no intention of charging you $_____ today

78. You'll Also Receive 3 Incredible Resources Worth over a Hundred Dollars... Yours FREE!

79. ORDER NOW and you'll also receive the following 4 FREE bonuses worth more in money terms than my e-book itself!

80. But Wait... There's More!

81. WAIT !! HUGE BONUS...

82. For a VERY SHORT TIME, I'm going to do something CRAZY!! I'm going to give you a FREE copy of my ...

83. Yours today FREE when you purchase _____

84. You're getting ALL THIS.... and it's not even Christmas Yet!!

85. The $_____ Bonus Pack

86. This _____ includes 2 bonuses to get you started taking action

87. Your Special BONUS...

88. Here are your special BONUSES...

89. But just to sweeten the deal, I'd like to ethically bribe you with these... (Note: You DON'T need these bonuses to make the method work!)

90. Time Limited Bonus...

91. Unannounced Bonus...

92. A Free Unannounced Bonus That's Going to Be Its Own course Shortly Is Yours at NO Cost.

93. The Bonus is worth the price of the entire program in my opinion

94. HUGE SAVINGS while taking advantage of all these added bonuses...

95. 4 Bonuses - Total Value = $____

96. Bonus From <name>

97. FREE $___ Bonus

98. You get all these Bonuses just for taking action today.....

99. I offer bonuses of REAL VALUE! If you are drinking something right now, DO NOT read any further until you swallow, because you just might spit it out if you do!

100. Unannounced Goodies…

CHAPTER SIXTEEN

A PERSUASIVE GUARANTEE IS THE SUREST WAY TO MAKE YOUR RESPONSE SOAR.

IT ABSOLUTELY WILL BECAUSE YOU ARE PRETTY MUCH TELLING THEM NOT TO WORRY AND PUTTING THEIR FEARS TO REST

THEY ARE NOT TAKING THE RISKS, YOU ARE.

IN MANY CASES, THE MORE OUTRAGEOUS YOU MAKE YOUR PERSUASIVE GUARANTEE; THE BETTER YOUR RESULTS WILL BE!

GO THROUGH THIS CHAPTER TO GET AN IDEA FOR YOUR NEXT OUTRAGEOUS GUARANTEE.

CHAPTER 16: PERSUASIVE GUARANTEES

1. You're getting my 100% no risk guarantee because I'm completely confident that _____ is what you exactly need to achieve_____. In fact, I'm so confident it'll work for you and I'm prepared to let you try it risk free for an entire 60 days.

2. I'm so confident that you will be happy with your purchase that you get my 100% Money back Guarantee. If you don't like the sound of me, what I have to say, what I write about, or you plain think it stinks - I will send you your money back in full and without delay. All I ask is that you spend __ days trying out my _____.

3. You see, I don't have to worry that you're at all unhappy, because if you decide _____ isn't the right system for you, get a full refund at any time during the 60 days. So you're free to download the whole thing, and try it out.

4. There's absolutely no risk to you with my 100% Money back guarantee. To prove everything I have promised is absolutely true, here is my offer to you: Use the information and techniques in my _____ for a full __ months and If the _____ isn't everything I say it is, if you aren't absolutely thrilled, if you are dissatisfied in any way shape or form and if you fail to earn at least __ times your money on the _____ price within __ months of purchasing it, I'll give you a prompt courteous refund. No questions asked... and keep the free bonuses. You are legally 100% protected - what could be fairer than that'

5. I'm never satisfied unless you are more than satisfied, so here's my simple 'No Small Print' guarantee...Claim your _____ today and put it through the ringer. Use each of the tools as many times as you like for 60 days. You be the judge.

6. If you don't get the results or not as good as you thought, or just don't like_____, no problems at all! You'll get every last cent refunded to you. No question asked. This is completely no risk purchase.

7. You can try everything, risk free for a full 60 days. Because the only way to be 100% certain _____ works as well as I say it does. And that is exactly what you can do today. I only ask you to give _____a fair run to prove itself to you.

8. SEND NO MONEY. If at the end of __ days, you decide not to keep the book, simply return it without obligation.

9. If you decide to subscribe' And I bet you will, once you see how genuinely informative, useful and valuable _____ proves to be' you'll get a full year for only $___ (a $__ discount off the regular price for home delivery). But if not, just return our bill marked' Cancel' and pay nothing. You can't lose. Any risk is mine.

10. This is a win-win situation for you. And, as is the policy of all the products we sell in our company, my _____ carry an unconditional, money-back guarantee. If my _____ are not everything that I have said they are and you are not in fact overly satisfied, you will receive every cent of your money back, no questions asked.

11. If you haven't seen the results in the first week, I want you to return it right away for a full refund.

12. Subscribe today. If you think your first issue' Or any issue ever' doesn't deliver at least $__ worth of ideas and information,

you can tell us to take a hike. We will cancel your subscription and send you a prompt refund for all un-mailed issues, no questions asked. We won't be happy to know we failed your value test, but that will be our problem, not yours.

13. A shamelessly irresistible, doubly better than risk-free proposition: If you decide to cancel your attendance anytime up to ___pm on Day _ of the live event (which, quite frankly, is highly unlikely), I want you to keep the $_____ as my gift for signing up in the first place.

14. There is absolutely no way that you can lose' except by not taking me up on a free 30-day examination of _____. I personally guarantee that you've never heard anything like it. If you aren't _____ within __ days after receiving the program, simply return it and owe nothing.

15. When you claim your copy of _____, you will have a full 60 days to review your membership and ensure your satisfaction. I am 100% confident you will be absolutely thrilled with everything you are about to discover...

16. You are fully covered by my iron clad, no quibbles satisfaction policy, which means if you are not totally delighted with ____, you will get a prompt and courteous refund.

17. If for any reason within 60 days I didn't feel it was worth 10x the price you'll give me 100% of my money back.

18. If you decide to keep it, well bill you in four easy installments of just $__ each. That's a total of only $__ not even a drop in the bucket considering that the _____ secret on page __alone will save you thousands of dollars a year immediately.

19. You risk nothing. You have the right to a prompt and full refund at any time' even after you've read the _____ or received all the issues of your subscription. Fair enough'

20. My _____ comes with a no-question, no-quibbles, One-Year money back guarantee. If for any reason, you find that my course isn't perfect for you, just send it back any time within ONE FULL YEAR, and I'll buy it back from you at the full purchase price. You have up to a full year to use and profit from my _____ without any obligation to keep it' to make sure that it is everything I say and more.

21. If you're not completely convinced that _____ can help you foresee the changes that will affect your life and money in the years ahead' Or if you decide _____ can't help you _____ in the months to come' Just let us know after reading the first issue and the bonus reports. We'll refund every penny you've paid. And the reports are yours to keep and profit from.

22. Try _____ at my expense for __ days. You pay nothing until you've tried and applied the specific, immediately useable _____ tactics that _____ teaches. If the program hasn't paid for itself many times over by the time the __ days are up, pay nothing and return it. Only if the program makes a significant contribution to your bottom line after __ days we will bill you only $__ (regularly $__), plus shipping, handling and applicable sales tax.

23. My 100% money-back guarantee is yours for the term you select. So take the bigger savings and the extra FREE bonuses you get with two-years of my service. Because I'll return your money ' and you get to keep everything I send you ' Even if you wait until the next-to-the last month of membership to tell me, sorry _____, I'm not happy with your service.

24. You're fully protected by our iron-clad money-back guarantee: If you decide that your _____ membership and _____ aren't for you, just let us know at any time during your membership period. We'll send you a prompt 100% refund' every penny you paid. That's a full refund, not partial or pro-rated. All

the issues and the bonuses are yours to keep' Even if you cancel. Could any offer be fairer than that'

25. If you're not absolutely thrilled with your order from _____' For any reason at all' we'll cheerfully replace your order or refund your money, whichever you prefer.

26. I absolutely guarantee if you stick with me the full 12 months and take action on _____ you'll make at least 10 times your investment. If you don't, you'll get every red cent you paid me refunded to you, no questions asked. All I ask is you prove to me you made a' Good faith' Effort to take action on my advice.

27. If you don't agree that this is the most impactful, eye-opening, and profitable seminar you have ever attended, simply tell me and I'll issue you a 100% refund on the spot plus I'll give you an extra $100 for your trouble.

28. If you decide to keep the _____, you can pay for it in a few easy installments. If not, sent it back (at our expense), and you'll owe nothing. Either way, I'd like to send you a free gift just for giving it a try.

29. If, after reading your three free issues, your verdict is' No thanks, that's okay, too. It really is. Just write' Cancel' on our invoice and pay nothing, owe nothing.

30. Here's the best guarantee you've ever seen! Ask for a refund at any time and a check is on its way to you 'for the full amount 'even if you cancel on the very last day of your subscription. Keep everything I send you. Every _____. It's all yours FREE forever! I can't be any fairer than that. Re-read the above paragraph for loopholes if you like. You won't find any. My money-back guarantee is absolute. That's how sure I am you'll profit like crazy from _____. See if I'm right.

31. Once you receive your free issue, the next move is up to you. You can continue with _____ at the special low rate of $___ for _____ (__ more issues). Or simply write 'Cancel' across your bill, send it back and owe nothing. The free issue is yours to keep with my thanks for giving _____ a try!

32. As you know, I will never consider your purchase binding until you've had time to preview all of this material and put it into action. So, use what you learn for __ days. Then, if it doesn't have a significant tangible impact on your advertising results, just return it for a full refund, no questions asked! Frankly, there's really no reason not to order your _____ today. Just _____ all risk is lifted from your shoulders and placed squarely on mine. Join today.

33. If _____ is not absolutely everything I claim it to be...send me an immediate email and I will not only give you a prompt, no-hassle, no-questions asked 100% refund, but I will even let you keep _____ plus all the bonuses as my way of saying ""thank you for trying _____.

34. I am so completely convinced that this is the best investment you could ever make for your _____ that I am going to take all the risk away from you, at this very moment. I will even go so far as to say that if you are not 120% satisfied with _____ within _____ days... I want you to immediately return the _____ for a full refund of your entire purchase price. You can even keep every one of the added bonuses as my way of saying ""thank you"" for just trying _____! How's THAT For A 120% Risk-Free Guarantee'

35. GUARANTEE: If the _____ is not everything that we say it is and you are not completely satisfied with it, then we will refund every penny of your money with no questions asked. That's more than a guarantee, that's a promise.

36. Here is how it works: Order _____, and use them as if you owned them. If for no reason at all, you aren't completely satisfied after __ entire months (by which time I had _____) - just send back the _____, in any condition, and Ill personally guarantee you get a complete refund of your purchase price by return mail, No questions asked. No hassles or forms to fill out. No problems at all.

37. _____, at your own pace, in your own home, and learn everything he has' for a full 3 months without risk. Treat the _____ as hard as you like – they're yours for the entire __ months. If, at the end of that time, you aren't 100% convinced you've just been _____ you could ever have, simple return the _____ and _____ will see that you get an immediate refund of the purchase price. No questions asked. No nonsense... and _____ will still consider you a friend. He respects you enough to let you decide for yourself.

38. Don't even decide today. Start using the _____ right now for a full 60 days – on me.

39. There are no catches to this offer. There is no fine print. Simply order the _____, learn from them for __ months' and send _____ back in any shape, for a complete refund if you aren't utterly blown away by them. No questions asked. No hassles. You control everything!

40. In case you're wondering, we also want to give you the peace of mind you deserve. _____ comes with an unconditional 60 days money back guarantee.

41. I personally guarantee that you will be absolutely delighted with your new ""_____"". In fact, I'll give you a __ day ""free peek"" at this blockbuster material. Take __ days to examine the "_____"". If you feel that I fell short in any way on delivering everything I promised in this letter just return ""_____"" and I'll

be happy to give you a full refund, issued the very same day we get the _____ back. No hassles and no questions asked!

42. I personally guarantee if you make a diligent effort to use just a few of the techniques in this course, you'll _____ in the next __ months. That's right, _____. If you don't, Ill refund the entire cost of the _____ to you. Actually, you get double protection. Here's how. At any time during the __ months, if you sincerely fell I fell short in any way on delivering everything I promised, I'll be happy to give you a complete refund. Even if it's on the last day of the _____ month!

43. You get my double money-back guarantee! If you're not happy with this program for any reason, I want to buy it back. Period. No questions asked. If, at the end of one full year, you haven't earned at least 10 times what you paid for it, I'll give you your money back! You cannot lose with my double guarantee.

44. Of course your investment is 100% guaranteed. In fact, if you are _____, and this _____ doesn't change your mind about _____, I insist you return it for a full and complete refund.

45. You have our absolute guarantee that once you've tried and applied the concepts, if they Don't work for you within __ months' and not only work, but give you tools to quadruple your _____, then you need only send it back for a complete and immediate refund.

46. All _____ are guaranteed to last you a lifetime. In fact, if you're unhappy with any _____ you buy from _____ for any reason whatsoever -- including breakage -- simply return it and well cheerfully send a 100% refund of every penny you've paid. No questions asked. No hard feelings either. What could be fairer than that?'

47. I know my _____ is everything, I say and more. But of course you don't know that yet, and why should you believe me'

so, just to erase any doubts you may still have, I offer you my personal unconditional ___ day money back guarantee. If at any time within ___ days after receiving my _____, you want to return it for any reason -- Do It! I'll send you a complete refund immediately - no questions asked any hassles!

48. Still not convinced _____ is the best deal on the market' don't Decide Now! Buy it, try it for a few days and if you still don't think _____ is worth every penny, well buy it back!

49. If for any reason whatsoever, you are not completely convinced and delighted, just let me know and your membership will be cancelled, and your fee fully refunded.

50. I personally guarantee that, if you follow the _____ exactly as outline in the _____, you will _____. And, I'll give you _____ to try it out. If within a year you aren't 100% completely satisfied, let me know and Ill issue you an immediate, no hassle, no questions asked refund right on the spot.

51. If you do not get the _____ you want, or if for any reason you don't feel that this is the most impactful, eye-opening, _____ book you've ever read, simply tell me and I'll issue you a 100% refund immediately.

52. I personally guarantee that if you make an honest effort to try just a few of these proven secrets for yourself, you'll make at least 100 times your investment back in spend able cash flow within the next _____ to _____ _____. Plus, you'll also at least DOUBLE your free, spare time to spend however you choose during the next _____ months. That's right, 100 times your investment back plus double the freedom and spare time. You've got full _____ months to prove to yourself that these secrets are for real. But if you aren't 100% satisfied, let me know and I'll give you an immediate, no questions asked, no hassle refund on the spot.

53. When you get _____, you get a 100% money-back guarantee. That means that you can learn how to _____, and get _____ free bonuses but if you are dissatisfied for any reason whatsoever, then simply tell us, and you will be issued a prompt and courteous refund.

54. You can't lose with our 100%, ironclad, money-back guarantee if for any reason, you aren't thrilled and satisfied with your purchase, just contact us within _____ days and well refund 100% of your purchase price. What we're saying is don't decide now if _____ is right for you. Try it out for _____ - risk free.

55. Our guarantee is simple: Try _____ out for yourself. If you don't agree that _____ can substantially _____, _____, _____, and _____, just drop us an e-mail within 60 days and well refund your money - no questions asked.

56. 100% Money-Back Guarantee I insist that you order _____ entirely at my risk. That's why this collection comes with a Risk-Free, 100% Money-Back Guarantee. There's absolutely NO RISK on your part.

57. _____ is everything you need and is designed to get quick results, however you can take your time if you prefer as you've got a full 60 days to try out my course.

58. You can't lose with my 100%, my word is my bond, money-back guarantee your satisfaction is assured through my no risk, you-can't-lose, 100%, no questions-asked, my word is my bond money-back guarantee. If for any reason, you aren't thrilled and satisfied with your purchase, just contact me within _____ days and Ill refund 100% of your purchase price.

59. Of course I wouldn't expect you to take any risks at all… That's why I'm personally giving you a 60 day Full Money Back Guarantee. I want you to feel safe and secure knowing you have

cutting edge tools… That do EXACTLY what they say they will. I'm 100% confident you're going to LOVE this…

60. We're so sure this is exactly what you need to get into profit that we're giving you two whole months to try it out… See if you like it…see if you can use it to get the freedom you want… And if you can't use it, or just don't like it, no hard feelings. We'll personally refund every penny of your cash with a smile on our face and no questions asked.

61. So here are my TWO ""RISK FREE"" and ""THE RISKS ON ME"" Guarantees: 1) A Flat-Out, Unconditional, NO-RISK, Iron Clad, 90 Day, No Questions-Asked, Money-Back Guarantee, Period I just flat out know that the material you're going to get from my _____ is SO GOOD, that once you've read and see what I'm talking about you're going to be blown away!

62. I want you to have absolutely NO RISK involved in this decision. You'll get an UNHEARD of -- the ""RISKS ON ME"" -- if my material doesn't enable you to _____, I'll give you ALL your money back, plus _____ for taking the time to ""check me out.""

63. 30 Day - 100% MONEY BACK GUARANTEE If you buy the _____ and within 30 days don't feel it lives up to its promises, your money back, no questions asked.

64. While I don't believe this _____ needs to be guaranteed - after all, the value you will receive from this knowledge far outweighs the low investment you will make now… you are welcome to take a full 30 days to examine the information. If, during that time you are not entirely convinced that this _____ has _____… if for any reason it does not live up to your expectations or deliver what I say it will, simply contact me and tell me why… and I will gladly enable a full refund of your investment. You get to keep the free _____. I can't make it any better than that!

65. Your ""No Questions Asked, Full Money Back"" __ Day Guarantee If this _____ does not provide you with _____ to your utmost satisfaction I will personally provide a full no questions asked money back guarantee. What's more I will give you 90 days from the date you purchase _____ to get your money back. If you are not satisfied just let me know.

66. That's right! Try _____ for a full __ days, RISK-FREE. If you feel that you didn't get your money's worth, even with all the _____, I will give you a full refund PLUS Ill allow you to keep the product and most of the bonuses.

67. What I Guarantee I won't guarantee this _____ will win you a Pulitzer or Nobel Prize. But, I do promise that if you follow the steps and advice, you WILL _____. In fact, I'm so confident that you can succeed in _____, that I will return your money, IN FULL, for ___ months

68. You see, we're so sure that _____will blow you away that we're happy to give you a no-strings guarantee...You're not going to find a guarantee like this with just any product...So if you want access to this amazing system at zero risk, you need to get in right now!

69. I give you my honest word that when you order _____, and if you apply the power into your _____, you will _____, or your money back...guaranteed.

70. Our ""love it or shove it"" money back guarantee' the policy is simple. If you want a refund for _____, just email _____ and well process an instant refund and stop any future charges. This refund is valid for the entire life of your membership. And you don't need to give us any reasons either. Just say ""Hey, cancel my charge"" and we will. Just let us know before the next billing period, and well stop any future charges. This totally reinforces

our zero-risk policy. When you join this site, you have no risk! It really is as simple as that.

71. And of course, what would a _____ be without someone to stand behind it. There is a guarantee. This one is simple: If you don't like it you have __ days to ask for a refund no questions asked

72. I'm still going to give you 60 days to try it out, if you don't see results, no stress, just ask for a refund.

73. Try it at my risk for 60 days, if you don't like it, send it back and ask for our money back guarantee.

74. Within 60 days, if you feel this is not for you or whatever reason it could be. You can get a full no questions asked refund.

75. I know_____ works because I use it every day and I personally guarantee that it will deliver on what I've promised. In fact, I'm so confident in my product that I'll back it up with a 60 days 100% "no quibble" guarantees.

76. I personally guarantee that _____ will work for you or you get your money back. That's right. Follow my step-by-step formula for a full 60 days… if it doesn't deliver everything that I've promised then I want you to get your money back. All the risk is on me.

77. You'll never have to worry about a refund. Once you start using the ____ and see the no results or progress, just drop me a note and I'll give you 100% refund.

78. 60 days steel and iron clad guarantee! Yes you read that RIGHT! Your satisfaction is assured through our no risk, you-can't-lose, 100%, no questions asked, iron-clad money-back guarantee.

79. Grab the _____ today. Take it out for a test drive... and just follow the couldn't-be-simpler step-by-step instructions... and keep an eye on your results. Because if by day 59 sales aren't hammering your inbox like a tropical hailstorm....then I don't want your money. You can ask for a refund at any time during the first sixty days... for any reason or no reason at all.

80. The _____ results from using the tips and ideas in this book have been attested to by _____. This makes it possible to offer you a no questions asked money-back guarantee. After __ days, if you are not satisfied with the return on your investment, send me an e-mail or call me at _____ and you will receive a prompt and courteous refund.

81. Your satisfaction is assured through my no risk, no-questions-asked, money back guarantee. If you aren't satisfied, contact me within _____ days and Ill refund 100% of the purchase price.

82. GUARANTEE: If you are not satisfied with _____ for any reason, then simply contact me and I will issue you a prompt refund. No questions asked. No hassles. That's more than a guarantee, that's a promise.

83. Each purchase is backed by _____ "love it or shove it" 100% money back guarantee ... you MUST be satisfied!

84. GUARANTEE: If _____ is not everything that we say it is and you are not completely satisfied with it, then we will refund every penny of your money with no questions asked. That's more than a guarantee, that's a promise.

85. Get the _____ today and if you decide any time in the next __ days that you don't want, like, need, rate what I sold you – just let me know and I'll give you a full refund. No quibble, no questions, I'll just do it.

86. 100% money-back guarantees if you are not honestly happy with our _____. Take __ days to decide if you like. If, for any reason or for no reason at all, you aren't completely satisfied during that first __ day's trial, just email me with your request for a refund. Ill personally guarantee a full credit of the entire purchase price. That's more than a guarantee, that's a promise! How can I offer this? Because I know you will be satisfied)

87. Your order is protected by my fully unconditional and completely risk-free, 60 day money-back guarantee... If for any reason whatsoever, you are not completely convinced and delighted, just let me know and your fee fully refunded.

88. If you're not absolutely thrilled with the money you're making with _____, all you have to do is shoot me a quick email at the address you'll find on the download page and I'll refund every penny you paid on the spot.

89. I want to ensure you are fully protected, which is why I am offering you a full 60 days guarantee.

90. We're so confident that you'll love the ___you get with ____that we'll stand behind it like this...If you don't see your results within 60 days after you start taking action - we'll buy it back from you.

91. Just a promise from us that if you aren't 100% happy and confident with your purchase today, you get 100% of your money back instantly.

92. If our _____ don't do everything we've said they will, simply contact us and we'll refund every penny of your purchase. But we're convinced that once you try them, you'll be astounded at just how easy it is to _____ in less time!

93. So, at any time, if you decide to upgrade your satisfaction is GUARANTEED. If you're not completely satisfied with _____ --

anytime within 60 days -- you'll receive a refund. And, of course, there are NO questions asked. NO catches. NO fine print.

94. 4 weeks Risk-Free Trial. Don't decide now if _____ is right for you. Take 4 Weeks to put us to the test! If _____ doesn't show you exactly how to _____, we'll give your money back ... no questions asked!

95. You either love _____ like everyone else, or you get 100% of your investment back.

96. To Remove The Risk Completely... Here's The No-Questions Asked Money Back Guarantee. So, if you're not completely thrilled with the ___ after going through it, then I'll give you your money back, instantly and with a big smile.

97. That's Right, I said You'll Get Your Money Back! Once you are onboard, take 60 days to test drive the _____. If you're not _____ and or not satisfied, just ask for a refund.

98. Take a full 60 days to decide if it's for you. You can actually use it first, ONLY then, make your final decision. You must be absolutely convinced that _____ will deliver your expected outcome and I'll rush you a full refund – no questions asked.

99. Become a member today and see if this isn't the best way to _____ on the planet. If you're not seeing massive _____ by then (whatever "massive" means to you), I'll promptly return every penny you gave me. I don't want it.

100. 2 Months of unconditional guarantee. That's 60 days exactly … If at any time, for any reason at all, you decide you want your money back, just send us an email and we will process a full refund, no questions asked, no hard feelings, stay friends style.

PART III
DEAL
SEALERS

CHAPTER SEVENTEEN

IT'S VERY EASY FOR PEOPLE TO FEEL OVERWHELMED WHEN IT COMES TO MAKING DECISIONS, SO YOU MIGHT WANT TO ETHICALLY HELP MOVE YOUR POTENTIAL CUSTOMER TO MAKE THE BUYING DECISION.

THIS CHAPTER WILL GIVE YOU PHRASES, LINES, AND SENTENCES YOU CAN EASILY USE TO URGE THEM OFF THE FENCE AND MARCH THEM TO BUY RIGHT NOW.

CHAPTER 17: QUICK DECISION MAKERS

1. Before its gone forever

2. Seats will be sold out anytime soon

3. Only limited copies available

4. Rare copies

5. Flying off the shelf

6. Selling out fast

7. This happens once in a lifetime!

8. When the counter reaches 0, this page will be gone forever

9. Your competitors will be reading this too

10. Secure your copy before time runs out

11. After that, this offer will be removed forever

12. For the next 72 hours only

13. This offer ends in 72 hours

14. For a limited time only

15. 90(stroked out). 76 copies left

16. Get it now before it's too late

17. It won't be up for long

18. Selling fast

19. It's now or never

20. Time waits for no man

21. Time is a factor

22. This won't last forever

23. Don't wait anymore

24. I don't know if I can put this up much longer

25. Running out of time

26. This is scarce

27. Once in a blue moon

28. Never gonna happen again

29. Hard to come by

30. You'll never see it again

31. Remember, your purchase is 100% guaranteed.

32. If you don't like what you see or if you don't feel my package will help you _____, then I want you to request a refund.

33. When I did private consulting, my clients paid me $500 an hour to learn these secrets. And my clients often paid me over a span of 12 weeks. But here's what's important to you: You won't pay $1,000, $500, $197, or even $97 to own _____!

34. Satisfaction 100% Guaranteed. Remember our Bullet-Proof, No- Questions Asked, 90-Day, Money-Back Guarantee.

35. I am so confident that _____ will more than pay for itself, that I'm offering a 90-Day, money back guarantee.

36. I don't care what the reason is, if you aren't 100% excited and satisfied with the purchase of this _____, I don't want your

money! Just let me know within 90Days and I'll refund every penny.

37. At _____, we want you to be a happy long-term customer. We always operate honestly and openly. That's why we _____, and we always welcome any questions or concerns you may have.

38. If within the first _____ days, you want a refund for your purchase, we will happily oblige.

39. Your opportunity is NOW and it is handed over to you on a silver platter.

40. Imagine how much opportunity and money you would lose if you do not invest now

41. What if you were to miss out on <benefit>?

42. Don't regret over your decision if you do not take action now

43. There are only <number> copies left so it's now or never.

44. Just imagine

45. Think about all the _____ you can get with our _____

46. Look at the big picture

47. You don't have to say a YES or NUMBER Just MAYBE.

48. Don't think. Don't wonder. Just try us out.

49. 100% satisfaction… or your money back

50. Test drive _____ for the next 90 days after your purchase

51. You have absolutely nothing to lose

52. What have you got to lose, except a chance to try it out?

53. Give us a chance to help you out

54. It's your success or your money back

55. We understand you might think it's risky, that's why we're giving you a chance to try us

56. I'll let others tell you why

57. If they can do it, so can you

58. We hope to see your testimonial in this page too.

59. Get everything you need for one price.

60. It would have cost you more if you …

61. As you are looking at this page, thousands of other people are reading too

62. When the counter reaches 0 this page will be removed permanently

63. Only you and 299 other people can have the privilege

64. There's nothing else out there quite like _____

65. Massive _____.

66. Get that _____, snatch it up, run the thing and start collecting cash!

67. Over-worked... over-tired... over-stressed... under-happy... with just enough money to get by.

68. And this new robot had to combine MINIMAL RISK with HUGE, CONSISTENT profits.

69. Constant cash-siphoning mixed with low risk and the LOWEST possible drawdowns!

70. Keep your dreams alive. Understand to achieve anything requires faith and belief in yourself, vision, hard work, determination, and dedication. Remember all things are possible for those who believe.

71. What if you hit it big next week? Or next month? How would you feel with an extra $50,000 in your account? What about an extra $100,000? ...or why not $1 Mil?

72. I'm So Sure My _____ Strategy Will work for you I'll let you try it for free.

73. "Give Us 3 Days and We'll Teach You How to Easily Crush the <niche>!"

74. Today Information Is King

75. Let Me Explain How All of this Works, Who I Am and More Importantly, Why You Should Listen To What I Have To Say

76. You Will Now Be Able To Build A Brand New Business, Which Enables You To Create Your Own Schedule, Be Your Own Boss, Have More Freedom And Most Importantly Help Others Achieve their Dreams By Providing the Sought After Information that they Need To Be

77. Successful!

78. This Business can be Managed in 15 Minutes a Day.

79. What I Teach You Will BLOW AWAY Any Of the Info I Learned From those Seminars!

80. I Decided To Make One Very Lucky Person Wealthy...

81. PROVEN Results - Even In Troubled Times

82. An Automatic Wealth-Creating System - Yours For Only $77

83. Try This Profitable Way To Make Money For A Full 60 Days Without Risking A Single Penny!

84. No Special Education...No Experience... No Skills...Almost No Money, And Lock Into A... Guaranteed Income Every Month!

85. I will Show You A Rock Solid <niche> System that Literally Requires A Few Minutes A Day.

86. You Need Step-By-Step Details Spelled Out Quickly! ...By A Team that Can Teach You the Ropes!

87. My three most valuable tips how to increase your profits quickly and effectively DRAMATICALLY

88. The exact steps, how the strategy can be tested immediately without risk

89. This is an "evergreen" business. Even as the markets shifts, and the economy changes... my system will always work!

90. Once you know the system, this business can be managed in 15 minutes a day.

91. So, if you're fed up with just getting by, having no money left at the end of the month, or even tired of the daily grind and commuting... then you need to take a look at this... and here's why...

92. My _____ course is an effective, expert guide that will show you how to become a respected _____ professional with your own lucrative _____business and the freedom to set your own hours...

93. IMPORTANT: 347 Internet Marketers In Pondicherry. Are Already Using this Tool To Reap An Unfair Advantage On their Websites ....Don't Get Left Behind!

94. Get Your Prospect To Pay More Attention, And You'll INSTANTLY Increase Your Conversion Rates!

95. The Truth Of the Matter Is that Million-Dollar Corporations Have Been Using this Simple Tactic To Rake In Tens Of thousands Of Dollars In EXTRA Profits Year After Year... And Now It's Your Turn!

96. No more, no less! this book is the best available resource currently online, and you can have it now!

97. You will have more free time every day

98. This Is Your One Chance To Do Something Really Very Special For Yourself...

99. Will these Secrets Really Make a Difference and Work for Me?
100. I have no problem making this iron-clad guarantee because I've personally used many of these strategies and techniques so I know they work. Fair enough?

CHAPTER EIGHTEEN

THIS IS ONE OF THE MOST IMPORTANT PARTS:

CLOSING THE DEAL BY GAINING AGREEMENT FOR THE SALE.

MANY TIMES YOU WANT TO BE VERY DETAILED IN WHAT YOU WANT THEM TO DO.

DON'T BEAT AROUND THE BUSH.

I HAVE EVEN BEEN SO BOLD AS TO SAY:

"FOLKS, HERE'S WHAT I WANT YOU TO DO RIGHT NOW, PUT YOUR HAND ON YOUR WALLET OR GO GRAB YOUR PURSE. PULL OUT YOUR CREDIT CARD AND THEN SEE THAT LINK BELOW, I WANT YOU TO CLICK ON IT AND THEN GO FILL IN ALL YOUR INFORMATION AND PUT IT RIGHT THERE."

YOU WANT TO HAVE A STRONG CLOSE BECAUSE PEOPLE WILL LISTEN.

CHAPTER 18: CALL TO ACTION CLOSERS

1. We are offering _____ for just $___, for a limited time only!

2. Make a difference today

3. You can access the downloads instantly after purchasing online via our secure server

4. Get it now risk free

5. Get rid of your problems now in an instant

6. We are here to help you

7. We want to be part of your success story

8. We will hold you by the hand

9. Talk to us and we'll help you make a decision

10. Lock your spot at $90 off

11. For the next 48 hours, you can get 90% off

12. Secure your copy now for _____

13. Act now while it's at its lowest price

14. Rebate

15. Only through this link

16. Huge savings when we cut our prices

17. Blowout sale

18. Why pay more

19. More for less

20. Its new, big, innovative, saves time and it works! So grab your spots now!

21. And as if that weren't enough, here is __ phone number that you can call to listen to the webinar recordings right now and get all of your questions answered:

22. I didn't think we'd see anything truly innovative in the _____ market until next year, but I guess these guys were saving the best for last!

23. Make sure you secure a copy of this system before it is too late.

24. Secure your copy right now while there are still some available (if it's already sold out, please accept my apologies):

25. I'm very confident that _____ will help you start making real money in the _____ market.

26. Remember, you can try the system for 60 days with absolutely no risk. If at any time you don't feel the system is worth the money, you can return it back for a full refund.

27. If you haven't made a profit within 8 weeks, I will refund 100% of your membership fee. Period! How many _____ will make that kind of guarantee for their services? None. I am willing to make a statement like that, and more than willing to back it up

28. With my 8 week guarantee there is absolutely nothing to lose. If for some reason I'm wrong about this, you've risked absolutely nothing. But if I'm right, you risk everything by not taking action today.

29. With an 8 week, 100% money-back guarantee, I have completely taken the risk out of the equation. Now you just have to act. I hope to see you on the other side.

30. Ask yourself what's the downside? There isn't any; you have zero risk! Think about it: could we possibly offer this type of guarantee if our system doesn't work?

31. Order now and I guarantee you'll be thrilled.

32. Please don't take this opportunity lightly and let it slip through your fingers. Reserve your spot now...!!

33. Whatever your decision is, I wish you best of luck in whatever you do in life.

34. Do you want to start seeing hundreds and thousands of dollars commissions, without having to work yourself silly or pay through the nose to get it? If so, _____ is for you. Order Now and get started in minutes.

35. If you leave this page I guarantee someone else will take your spot ... forcing you to work at your dead end job for not enough money for the rest of your life. Reply now, and let your coach help you make money tomorrow and enjoy the life of your dreams!

36. Download now. Then go pillage and plunder the stock market! Watch while your bank account becomes bloated and inflated like you've only dreamed of.

37. Someone told me a few years ago that I'd retire in my thirties, drive a brand new car and own my home outright - I'd think they were drunk, or completely off their rocker.

38. You see, people all over the world are making an absolute FORTUNE using this system... isn't it time you did, too?

39. I've shared with you my personal story... shown you a video on how easy it is to start... and included testimonials from people who are making money with this system right now, even as you read this... and I've even offered this system to you 100% RISK-

FREE FOR TWO FULL MONTHS. The only thing left to do is click on the order button and start building your future - today.

40. Make a choice... either keep doing what you are doing and buy all the rehashed garbage out there that gets you nowhere but broke and confused or make the choice to win with a proven system with real proof, and real results. Change starts right here from making a decision just like this one

41. All I ask is that you take action FAST. Why? Because this is a strictly limited offer.

42. I've taken great care to keep this under wraps… Nobody else has a system that works anything like this one…There's simply nothing else out there that operates in the same way. Click here to know more

43. Now you have to ask yourself how badly you really want that in your life.

44. The "Add to Cart" button is below.

45. Click it now before someone else takes your spot and this offer shuts down for good.

46. You need to act now though… before the fast-action bonuses disappear or I get too many emails from my JV partners complaining about my lazy job at pricing this thing and they pressure me into hiking it up.

47. Imagine having the power of this software in your hands against all odds?? And we'll even walk you through the whole process of sniper targeting them so in the end, all you do is collect your cash. Don't wait any longer!

48. And don't forget ... you'll also get access to the _____ too. I'm adding that FREE to the package but ONLY if you take action today. TAKE ACTION NOW!!

49. If you delay any further, your chances of securing BOTH _____, will be ZERO!!

50. Well don't take my word for it! You can check it out for yourself here! It's the deal of the year!

51. Act now before this deal is gone for good!

52. I want you to have complete confidence and peace of mind in doing business with my company.

53. Here is my 100% Risk-Free, Money-Back Guarantee: You have a full 56 days to use my Amazing _____ risk free. If for some strange reason you feel it does not deliver on everything you want and expect, or you are not thrilled with your purchase in every possible way, I want to know about it. Simply write an email stating you'd like your money back. I'll issue you a refund right on the spot.

54. Do you want to have _____ all of your life? No, you don't. Finally, there is a method that is guaranteed to work for you, or your money back! You can change your life starting from today...

55. Now that I've shown you this no-risk way to increase the response of every marketing piece you use in your business... And pull more profit with all your marketing... the next move is up to YOU.

56. Seriously, if you've read this far, you know that you have a strong interest in making your copy produce the kind of response and results you really deserve. All that's left is to take the action to do it.

57. You owe it to yourself to take full advantage of this very limited, risk free offer right now before it's too late, as I will be removing some of the bonuses and increasing my membership fees very soon.

58. (I recently did, and memberships are still skyrocketing!)

59. So do yourself and your business a favor. Join today, won't you? Major credit cards and e-checking are accepted. I also accept PayPal. Don't delay any further. Every moment that passes by may be another lost sale.

60. So, what are you waiting for? You're only SECONDS away! Once your order is processed through our secure server, you'll be able to immediately download and access '_____'!

61. Please take action today. _____ is only going to be offered at this low introductory price for a limited time period. And, the only way I can guarantee you the _____ free bonuses is if you order before _____.

62. Finally, let me repeat what I explained at the top of this page. You aren't going to find this information anywhere else on the internet! Some _____ companies (mentioning no names) have actually told me that I "reveal too much". Which is why they won't publish my offer, or sell my _____ from their sites – even though I offered to split the profits with them. So don't waste your time searching for this information elsewhere; I guarantee you won't find it.

63. Will you take advantage of this once-in-a-lifetime killer opportunity now and receive _____ plus all the bonuses for only $_____, or will you test my word, wait it out and suddenly find yourself completely out of luck when I raise it to $_____? I will let you decide, but I would highly encourage you to order right now and save yourself the agony of defeat.

64. So you see, I've given you every conceivable reason to make _____ generate all the money you want online without any risk on your part. Unleash the Internet's most powerful secret weapon now, and you'll be thanking me for years to come.

65. Think about it. Where will you be a year from now? Will you still be struggling to make online marketing work, while competitors who are web marketing savvy steal business from you? Or will you be enjoying the exhilarating feeling of selling your products and services online, automatically, while you sleep?

66. The experts have gone through the pain. Now you don't have to. As many as 14 world-class experts give you authentic advice on how to make your online business the success you dreamed it could be. Don't pass up an opportunity of a life-time. You have absolutely nothing to lose and everything to gain.

67. Imagine, for a moment, that it's a year from today. How well is your _____ doing? Remember – if you continue to _____ the same way, you're going to get the same results. A year will pass by in a flash. I think your choice is clear.

68. Within _____ _____ of ordering the _____, you will receive instant access to a password-protected site so you can _____. Take the _____ for a test drive, and I guarantee that you'll start laughing all the way to the bank.

69. I have one more thing to tell you... I will be promoting this site very hard, so keep in mind that in a few hours your competitor might be reading this exact same page - and there is a very good chance that he will take action and try to leave *you* in the dust... and to top things off, he will be getting _____ that should have belonged to you in the first place.

70. Act within 24 hours – and _____ is yours not for the regular price of $79.95 but for only $39.95!!! (That's a one-time charge!) But hurry, once 24 hours passes we can't guarantee the reduced price!

71. Order now. It's easy and simple. Just click on the link below and you'll be taken to the 100% secure payment page. Once

you're order has been received, you'll get instant access to the private area where you can _____.

72. I'm not going to use a script to tell you that this offer is going to expire at midnight on _____, - that isn't how I do business. But this is a limited time offer that I can only hold for a few _____, so please order now to avoid disappointment.

73. It's a limited-time offer I may withdraw at any time, so don't miss the boat! ORDER Here Now and Get _____ Instantly With a _____ Month Money-back Guarantee!

74. I want to give you a GREAT OFFER so I'm definitely NOT going to charge you anywhere near $97(strike through) not even half the price: $47(strike through). Take action today and you'll gain instant-access to _____ + the 2 amazing bonuses for a low 1 time fee.

75. So the first 100 smart investors can get _____ with lifetime updates for only $99. With 60 day money back Guarantee.

76. Get instant access to the _____ and use it all you want for 30 days. If for any reason you are unsatisfied with your purchase, you will receive a full, hassle-free refund.

77. A copy of _____ can be ordered anytime! Even if it is 2 a.m. on Christmas day, you will still be able to receive instant access to members area where you can read or print our all the information. 100% satisfaction money back guarantee! Get 8 Weeks to Try it Out!

78. We use the most advanced SSL protection that means your transaction is 100% safe. Moreover, the transaction is made through Clickbank.com, one of the largest and trusted online retailers.

79. The _____ is a one-time investment of $97.00 With, No Monthly Fees. -Download & Install immediately after purchase.

80. Regular Price $_____ Total Value $_____ Only $_____ Special Limited Time Marketing Test Price! Might Not Appear Again! Just 1 payment with nothing more to pay... ever! You'll Get INSTANT ACCESS To EVERYTHING!

81. Instantly download _____ for only $57! It is only a onetime fee and there are no other costs to use _____. Retail value of $167. Order today for this amazing opportunity! Free premium customer support. 100% 60 day money back guarantee.

82. For Fast, Immediate and Secure Online Orders: CLICK HERE NOW

83. Secure Order Form. I fully understand that _____ is absolutely risk-free and I have a 100%, iron-clad, no-questions-asked, 60-day-money-back guarantee. I also understand that I will probably never again find a system as simple, easy to <benefit 1> and <benefit 2> as _____ for just $27!

84. I am aware that I will probably never encounter a Forex system as simple, easy and profitable as Lazy Larry Forex ever again. I understand that Lazy Larry Forex is absolutely RISK-FREE and comes with an iron-clad, 100% no questions-asked, money-back guarantee. I also understand that I will have instant access to the Lazy Larry Forex system and can be downloading it just minutes from now for just $27!

85. 60-DAY MONEY BACK GUARANTEE. If these forms aren't exactly as described, we'll refund your money, no questions asked.

86. One Time Payment... Just $97

87. For today only, our _____ is on a special 50% discount with the price of $29.99. Normally $59.98, this new system has been reduced for the next 12 hours. If you want to get rid of the _____, there is no other solution which works as well as this in the fastest time.

88. For the investment of $29.99, you'll get an instant download of our software solution & guide, allowing you to fix the <problem> within seconds of purchase:

89. Click on the Add to Cart button below, you will be taken to our payment processors and after payment of just $27 you will be taken straight to the download page. You can be using this great _____ in just minutes.

90. Your _____ journey starts here... just click on the order button below. Get _____ for $39.95.

91. Not sure this system is for you? Try it and if you're not happy, I'll give you your money back and you keep the book. BUY NOW Money back guaranteed no questions. Instant delivery & awesomeness.

92. $27 (One Time Payment), LIMITED TIME OFFER, INSTANT ACCESS! 60 DAY MONEY BACK GUARANTEE

93. Let Me Download it Now!

94. Get it instantly!

95. YES! I want instant access to the "_____" and the free online bonuses. I understand that if I order today, I will pay the limited time On Sale price of just $29.97 and my satisfaction is 100% guaranteed. Click to Order Now:

96. You can watch the videos right now, nothing to ship or download. Within minutes you'll be learning exactly what you need to know to build your _____ TODAY!

97. Yes <name>! I want "_____" and all fast action bonuses. Please give me INSTANT access to your 10 years plus knowledge in overclocking now.

98. INSTANT ACCESS to the same tried and tested techniques that have not only proven effective for <name> but for thousands of other people who have also used his system with great success.

99. If you order immediately without delay, "_____", the 7 free bonuses (worth over $142.89) are available for a risk free, bargain basement price of: ONLY $29.97

100. Own this Book Now! Special September Discount: Normally $27, now $17 until October 1, 20**!

CHAPTER NINETEEN

IT HAS BEEN PROVEN THAT THE P.S. IS THE SECOND MOST IMPORTANT THING BEHIND THE HEADLINE.

THERE HAVE BEEN STUDIES THAT SHOW THAT WHEN PEOPLE READ EMAILS, BLOGS AND SALES LETTERS, THEY READ THE TOP THEN SCROLL ALL THE WAY DOWN TO THE BOTTOM.

P.S OR POST SCRIPTS WORK REALLY WELL BECAUSE BEFORE PEOPLE BUY THEY WILL USUALLY HAVE A FINAL LINE OF DEFENSE WHICH PREVENTS THEM FROM MAKING THE PURCHASE. IF YOU HAVE A COUPLE OF POST SCRIPTS READY, YOU CAN GIVE THEM THAT FINAL NUDGE TO MOVE FORWARD WITH A PURCHASE.

SIMPLY ADAPT, TWEAK & ALTER ONE OF THESE OR USE THEM FOR IDEAS.

CHAPTER 19: POWERFUL POST SCRIPTS

1. Don't forget to check out the……

2. <name> is releasing only 723 copies and this is not a scarcity trick here, trust me. You can see the live counter on the page and it is going down pretty fast. Once it reaches zero the SOLD OUT sign will appear.

3. The response about _____ has been overwhelming and extremely positive. There are over 743 comments on the blog already! For those of you that haven't jumped on, this is one train you don't want to miss. You can still get a copy today.

4. This offer will be available at this special promotion price for a limited time only. I reserve the right to increase the sale price at any time without warning or notice.

5. Remember there is absolutely no reason for you to leave empty handed. You can take advantage of my 100% Risk Free Offer and begin _____ today!

6. If you are not earning profits within 8 weeks of _____, I will return 100% of your membership fee no questions asked.

7. Please don't put this off; every minute that passes drastically increases the chance of your slot being taken by another individual.

8. Because once the limited number of positions are filled, it's over and you've missed out. Period!

9. Test drive _____ today while there's still time!

10. I have no idea when I'll pull this from the market, but I do know it won't last forever. If you want it, please don't wait. Click the 'Add To Cart' button now.

11. There's zero risk to you if you want to give my system a try. That's all I ask. Grab a copy and start using it to make real, spendable cash. Opportunities like this are rare, so jump on this one while you have a chance! Click the 'Add To Cart' button now to order...

12. I changed my life completely by using this system. Please ... do yourself a favor and try it out. I know you'll be amazed! A six figure income is here for you too. Click Here Now!

13. I know you will make the smart decision.

14. I KNOW you can do this! I KNOW you can be making an amazing 6- figure income this year just like I do now. BUT YOU NEED TO ACT NOW! The available spots are going fast. Because people are hearing about this amazing work-at-home opportunity! I'm so excited for you! Let's go!

15. Give me 5 Days And You Might Make $300 - Or Your Money Back. Simply fill in the blanks... and you're done in under an hour, without entering any

16. Confusing code or mind numbing research – even if you've never used a computer for anything more than email.

17. If you aren't 100% sure this powerful system can work for you, grab this 100% risk-free test-drive to get you started...

18. One more thing... our script can make you money today, not in 30 days, not in 4 weeks, but now. as in A.S.A.P.

19. Remember… this isn't about the same old 'techniques' or 'instructions' you've read about so many times before… you've

just seen me PROVE this software INSTANTLY generates tons of genuine traffic that stuffs your accounts with profits.

20. Don't forget. Your new recurring income stream can be profitable as early as today…And of course, if it doesn't work out for any reason, you pay nothing!

21. It's impossible to lose here…unless you walk away empty handed.

22. Still here? I guess you just like to read… but you'd be much better off reading the first steps of the _____ course right now… and being that much closer to your first $3,000 month.

23. The bottom line is… you're at an important crossroads here… and you really have just two choices if you're at all serious about "making it" in _____ this year. Still didn't click? Did I mention that <benefit> for you too?

24. There's also a proof of income that I'd like to show you on the website with glowing testimonials from our members. You owe it to yourself to at least check it out.

25. They're so sure that this will slash your power bill, that they're even offering an unconditional 60 day money back guarantee!!

26. P.S. You can start _____ right after you order because you will receive instant access to _____!

27. All it takes is a few clicks and you are on your way to _____. Get in while you can!

28. PS - Don't wait any longer! _____ and _____ is just around the corner. _____ before your competitors do!

29. P.S. If you've never bought _____ before, don't worry, it's easy. The _____ is simply _____.

30. Once you have it, you can _____. We provide very straight forward and explicit directions on how to do this, and if you have any trouble at all in the process, we will help you through it!

31. P.S. You could search the Internet, read articles, scour bookstores and do your best to find and speak with _____. Or you can download everything you need, right now, today.

32. Click the button below now to place your order and get started.

33. P.S. How much is it worth to you to have a proven system that works...including a complete _____? Where else will you find someone who was willing to stand up and PROVE their system worked...in front of a crowd of people? Sure, anyone can claim they know how to _____ while they hide behind their _____. It's another story to prove it live.

34. Take action today and you can be on your way to _____ success by applying the _____.

35. P.S. Remember, we guarantee at least _____ in the first _____ days after using our service. Make sure to have your _____ ready - so we can prove to you that our service actually works!

36. P.S. EXTRA BONUS: Order now and I'll also include my special list of "_____"! If you want to _____, then this information is "Must Read" info! (This info will be included on the Confirmation Page - once you've ordered.)

37. P.S. Remember this is a TIME SENSITIVE OFFER. I can only *guarantee* you'll get these special bonuses and reduced price of only $_____ if you order by _____.

38. P.S. EXTRA BONUS: In addition to getting the _____, you will also get the _____ that has never seen the light of day until now. This _____ will totally change the way you _____.

39. P.S: And the Best is yet to come: As a _____, you can _____, for the lowest rates anywhere on the Internet ... Guaranteed!!

40. P.S: I will never ask you to judge us on our own words; You might find all your answers by checking what others say about our _____ in the TESTIMONIALS page ... You will be delighted!!

41. P.S. - If you're done struggling with _____ and agree that the simple way is the BEST way, _____ is ready to make your fantasies of easy, auto-pilot profits come true.

42. P.P.S - Remember, you can start profiting in _____ today with completely no risk. Use the software however you like for 30 days and if you realize it's not for you, I'll gladly give you a FULL refund.

43. P.P.P.S - To secure a copy of _____ for the exclusive pre-launch price of $99, you must order now.

44. P.S. If you're serious about _____, you need _____! Especially if you _____. Nothing out there comes close to bringing in a flood of <benefit>.

45. With _____, you could quite possibly start as soon as this afternoon.

46. P.P.S. Don't forget... you have a full 60 day money back guarantee, if you're not completely satisfied with your _____, return it for a complete refund, and keep the advanced educational trading videos as a free gift from us. A $199.00 value!

47. P.S.- You could attempt to learn this by trial and error on your own, but I assure you it will be a MUCH more costly "education" than the one I'm offering you today for a very reasonable price. It cost me years of frustration, bad trades, and huge financial losses before I figured out the "secret" system. I've watched too many smart yet "uneducated" people lose their shirts in the _____ market, and I don't want to see that happen to you.

48. P.S.- Just have a look at the picture below and tell me that you haven't dreamt at least once to one of these cars.... You can have everything you desire if you choose to play the lottery wisely:

49. P.P.S. I'm protecting you today with such a granite-strong 100% Money-Back guarantee. And I insist you get started by <benefit> in my course 100% risk-free. That way, before you invest a single real dollar in <niche>, you can see for yourself that my course come through with profits many more times than not.

50. You must be 100% thrilled by your decision to join, or I insist you write me to get every cent you invest today safely back in your pocket, no questions asked. That's why you've got absolutely nothing to lose by joining others in the _____ team right now. Okay, <Name> I'm Ready To Join.

51. P.P.P.S. Don't forget I showed you <benefit>. So what are you waiting for? Sign Me Up <Name>! I'm Ready To Join

52. PS : Remember, you have nothing to lose and everything to gain because not only are you saving a ton of money on the program, but you also have a full 60 days to decide whether or not you want to keep it.

53. P.S. Yes this really can work for you....even if you are pretty much "clueless" about the <niche>! :-)

54. P.S. As mentioned above, refunds for the training program are no problem up to 60 days after your purchase. Just contact us.

55. P.S. Give me 5 Days And You Might Make $300 - Or Your Money Back. Simply fill in the blanks... and you're done in under an hour, without entering any confusing code or mind numbing research - even if you've never used a computer for anything more than email.

56. P.P.S. If you aren't 100% sure this powerful system can work for you, grab this 100% risk-free test-drive to get you started...

57. P.S. You can start using the complete kit right away with no special education or skills. You can use this kit to make money and It doesn't matter where you live. You can be any age. Man or Woman and you can do this in your spare time.

58. I appreciate your business. So... Download the kit right now and see for yourself. If you can follow simple instructions and you take action, then I guarantee...you will get your investment back many times over from just one part-time account. What else can I do to convince you? Remember, it's completely risk free. If you're not happy, I will send you back your money.

59. P.S. Remember, with my "Money Back Guarantee", you have nothing to lose and everything to gain by putting my 8 years of experience to work for you risk free!

60. P.P.S. As soon as you complete your purchase you'll be directed to create your account giving immediate access to the resources you need to success with _____ like so many others are already doing every day!

61. P.P.P.S If you're going to, <niche> with <product> it simply doesn't pay to <niche> with anything less than the best settings available.

62. P.S. Remember, if you don't like it, you get your money back. Just ask. And, I'll give you 30 days to make up your mind. Go ahead . . . Order Now! It's Risk Free!

63. P.S.S. My time normally sells for $200 an hour, and my clients invest $20,000 to $30,000 each and every month for the advice I've put into this valuable, easy-to-read-and-use guides and templates. You get some of the most valuable pieces of what I do for my clients in this project management document set. Give it a look. All the Risk Is On Me. Order Now!

64. P.S.S.S. Without using our project templates you could continue to waste valuable time reinventing products. Now's the time to work smart, so you can leave the office early!

65. PS: Listen closely: we will NOT keep the doors open after the 10,000 copies have been sold! You're either in for a ton of money, thousands of effortlessly earned dollars (literally wake up every morning and see new, fresh money in your account!) or left behind, head-butting the wall after reading about the enormous gains other people are making, gains that you could have been enjoying as well.

66. I have explained extensively throughout this letter why we MUST limit the number of copies of _____ that we sell. You need to understand why we have to do this. We have learned from the past and we will not take any risks that might harm the money making potential of our "Golden Goose" so take action now!

67. PPS: Remember, the risk here is totally on us. A 60-day money back guarantee protects you fully, so there is no excuse for not giving it a try, even if you're still skeptical. Either I deliver on my claims and set you on your way to financial freedom within those 60 days or I don't and you get a Full, no questions asked refund. Either way you cannot lose.

68. PS I am offering you the chance to access this unique <niche> system absolutely RISK-FREE with my 100%, bullet-proof, no-question-asked 60-day money-back guarantee!... get your copy now for just $27!

69. P.S.==> Your search to find the most profitable, yet easiest to succeed <niche> industry business is over - let these industry experts show you how to fulfil your dream of earning a great living working with <niche>.

70. P.S.S.==> Let's Be Blunt: If you pass on this offer, will you have a plan to turn your passion for <niche> into significant profits? Probably not! By taking action right now you can start down the path of become a "<niche> professional" - you will love the journey!

71. PS: The strategy is tried and tested and you do not need any previous experience or special skills. All you need is explained step by step EXACTLY. In addition, I show you an effective way you can test your strategy without risk to heart and kidney.

72. PPS: I would like to prevent that the eBook is sold at many times and then lands on software piracy sites, it will only be available for a short time at this low price. Try the eBook therefore best today!

73. PPPS: And do not forget my unlimited 60-day money-back guarantee , I stand behind 100%! So you have more than enough time to test my techniques at rest, then go no risks.

74. PS Remember, _____ is unlike any system you have ever tried and comes with a bullet-proof, 100% risk-free, iron-clad, money-back guarantee!

75. PPS You are also getting _____ for the crazy, knock-down price of just $27!!

76. P.S.- You could attempt to learn this by trial and error on your own, but I assure you it will be a MUCH more costly "education" than the one I'm offering you today for a very reasonable price.

77. P.S. You're just one click away, and a few minutes away, from discovering how to make more money than you ever believed possible. And what's more, this isn't going to cost you hundreds to find out if this is for you or not!! I am assuming ALL of the risk...

78. P.P.S. If you order right now, I will include with Module 1 of my Automated Income Stream Home Study Course... my FREE Bonus DVD - showing you how I got started online, and my FREE Bonus Consultation - to help you get started as fast as possible... As well as ALL of the FAST ACTION BONUSES detailed above!

79. P.P.P.S. Remember, you have absolutely NOTHING TO LOSE from this TRIAL...

80. P.S. As long as the $97 is still listed on this site, you can lock in your lifetime membership at that introductory price. But I DO plan on raising the price soon. So, order now before the introductory price expires! After I raise the price to $147, I don't want to get any emails begging me to make an exception. I'll be busy training my first class of <niche> students. And to be fair to them, you've been warned.

81. P.P.S. Remember, even if you're simply curious, go ahead and order _____ today. You have 60 days to improve your <niche> skills. If you're not 100% satisfied with your new <niche> super-powers, then I'll refund your money with no questions asked. What could be fairer?

82. P.S. I am offering this at this low price to a few select audiences, so, if you are at the least bit interested, I'd encourage you to get it now while the price is still low. I'd hate to see you miss out on getting such a low price for this whip smart tool. Click here to get started before I come to my senses.

83. P.S.S. You have absolutely nothing to lose. The risk is all on me. Get my _____ now, start using it every day and start getting more <benefit> every day. I think you'll be astonished at the results. Just go here to pick up your copy today.

84. P.S.S.S. Getting more <benefit> isn't magic. You can start today getting more subscribers, and, yes, even more visitors with

some of our new viral features like our subscriber referral system that we just added.

85. P.S. Remember, the experts agree I could easily charge $129 per membership for everything my software has to offer. But I want you to have no excuse NOT to protect your family. Take advantage of my insane offer.

86. P.P.P.S You also have my 60 DAY RISK FREE TRIAL GUARANTEE! If for any reason my software doesn't live up to every claim I've made on this website, just let me know and I'll instantly refund every cent of your purchase price!

87. P.S. - The price will never be less than it is today... Increase your social proof and catapult your conversions by 25.9% OR MORE with a one minute tweak to your website... Click here to download _____ instantly.

88. P.P.S. - There's no risk if you take action right now... I'm giving you 60 days to try out _____ on as many sites as you like. If you don't make your tiny investment back and then some, simply email me, and I'll return every penny. Don't wait until the price goes up!

89. P.S: You really don't want to miss this opportunity. The quality of the information found in the book is well above anything you will find on the market today. Normally, you wouldn't be able to buy this book at this price, but I want to help you save time and learn how to use your <niche> fast and easy, and I wanted to make this affordable for everyone.

90. P.P.S: Keep in mind that if you're not happy with this book and you don't get the result you wanted, I will fully refund you through my 60 day money back guarantee. Simply send an email if you're not happy with the results and you will get a refund without a hassle.

91. P.S. Honestly... I've done all the foot work, saving you time, effort and of course any future deadly mistakes. All you have to do is follow my simple step by step formula that I've laid out for you and I guarantee you will have a faster performing PC that will shame any other computer in the same price range as yours with incredible ease. "Seriously... I couldn't have made it easier if I tried"

92. P.P.S. The price will be going up soon... Very soon. And believe me when I say this is not some empty threat. I add new content almost every month, just to keep it the most up-to-date <niche> Bible on the net. So when I think it justifies a price rise, I will do so. But when you order today, not only will you get the *exact system* the pros secretly use... But if you're one of the lucky 50 43 26 11 6 3 to take advantage of this truly great offer today, you'll also get instant access to $121 worth of software, taking you further down the rabbit hole of <niche> than you ever thought possible. So Click Here Now to get started and lock in your bonuses right away before somebody else takes the intuitive and grabs them before you do...

93. P.P.P.S. And with my 365 Money back guarantee, you have nothing to lose. Try it out for the full 12 months and if for whatever reason you're not completely satisfied or you don't think you're getting the results I promised. Simply email me and I'll gladly refund you the difference.

94. P.S.: With your purchase, in addition to the <product> Book with over <benefit>, you will automatically get the <bonus1> and the <bonus2> for free. That's a $34 value on its own, but today you don't pay a single penny for it.

95. P.P.S.: The _____ and bonuses are a downloadable eBook. No physical products will be shipped and you will get INSTANT ACCESS to the entire package to be viewed immediately on your

PC, Mac or iPhone. The handy PDF format can be viewed on any device.

96. P.P.P.S.: You get a full 60-day money back guarantee. So if for some reason you're not happy, just let me know and I'll give you a full refund.

97. P.S. These all-time mouth-watering bonuses worth over $100 may not be available the next time you visit this page so order now to avoid disappointment! You'll get our complete secret recipes with nothing held back!

98. P.P.S. Your privacy is guaranteed! All orders are processed by ClickBank for added security.

99. P.S. What excuse could you possibly have for waiting? Claim your copy of the _____ today by clicking on the secure orange order button below.

100. P.P.S. Remember, there is No Risk to your purchase as I am providing you a 3 month, 100% money back satisfaction guarantee if you purchase today. If within this period you are not <benefit>, I will refund you in full!

101. PS: Even if you take me up on the "100% money back" offer, the _____ are yours to keep. I want to make it as easy and risk free as I can for you to get started.

102. PPS: With my free lifetime upgrade offer, you will not need to spend any more time and money looking for _____. Order today and start enjoying!

103. P.P.S. - Remember, you are 100% protected with a 60-Day, Unconditional, Money Back Guarantee. So if you for ANY REASON find the guide and bonuses not to your satisfaction, you get a FULL refund (no questions asked), and even get to keep the Complete _____, and anything else you try out as my gifts to you. Join us NOW!

104. P.S. Act today and you'll get the exclusive _____ no-time limit guarantee. I insist that every customer be a satisfied customer, so I'll thank you to return the book for a full refund should you ever become dissatisfied. This is the way I've done business for over __ years, so you can be assured that I'll stand behind this guarantee.

105. P.S. All the free bonuses, including the _____, are yours to keep even if you take advantage of our no-risk 100% money-back guarantee.

106. P.S. Altogether there are more than __ ways you can _____ in this new program. Don't you owe it to your _____ to make sure that you're aware of them all' Discover and examine all of these _____ tactics free for __ days.

107. P.S. As our 'thank you' for giving _____ a 30-day free trial, we'll also send you two valuable gifts you can keep no matter what you decide. The first is _____. And your second free gift is _____.

108. P.S. By the way, I've just been authorized by my higher ups to let you know that they've created a space for you in the exclusive_____... allowing you to get the catbird seat to position yourself and your products for unlimited success... but the space being held just for you will only be available for __ hours and then it'll be gone forever... if you snooze, you lose and your major chance for marketing success and profits may be gone forever... here's your once-in-a-lifetime opportunity to leave the bumpy and difficult back road of marketing and product development struggle and cruise on up to the gold-plated superhighway of marketing success and financial freedom... time is ticking, you only have __ hours to respond... don't delay, apply now!

109. P.S. Call us on our toll-free line, you'll be able to use our 24-hour hotline immediately! We'll give you your private access code right over the phone.

110. P.S. Don't forget this is a tax deductible business expense. If you register early at $__, your real cost after your tax credit is approximately $__.

111. P.S. Extra free bonus book! Just for trying _____, you'll also receive _____

112. P.S. Hear real people talk about making real money: 'Eavesdrop' on conversations with my _____ by calling xxx-xxx-xxxx (24 hours). _____

113. P.S. I can't tell you how much your _____, so I sure hope you'll take part. Just return the gift certificate, and I'll see to it that you receive your free book and __ free issues. And thanks again!

114. P.S. I mentioned the report, _____, was a 'bonus for promptness.' Please respond to this offer within __ days to be sure of getting your FREE copy.

115. P.S. If purchased separately, _____costs $__ the _____ $__, and an annual subscription to _____ $___. That's a total of $___. Our current subscribers can all three for $_____, a savings of $__. But I'm offering you an even better deal: As a new subscriber, take 12 monthly issues of the newsletter and the _____and the _____ for just $___. You save $__!

116. P.S. If you accept my invitation immediately, I'll rush you one additional special report. It's called _____.

117. P.S. If you act now, we'll also send you _____ ' FREE!

118. P.S. If you are not totally convinced this offer is for you, please read the enclosed comments from subscribers to _____.

119. P.S. If you continue to work out the same way, you're going to get the same results. What I'm offering you is the easiest, most risk-free way to try the _____ so you can see for yourself how our scientifically developed exercises and conditioning routines can help you increase your strength, improve your stamina, and help you achieve the more muscled look you have always wanted.

_____

120. P.S. If you would like the names of a few individuals that are using _____ we'd be glad to give them to you when you call, so you can talk to them in person.

121. P.S. If you'd like an even better deal ' and another free report' sign on for two years of _____. You'll save __%'I'll send you a FREE copy of _____ plus a FREE copy of _____ and you'll get __ months of what's been called the most exciting _____available today.

122. P.S. It's important to note that the _____ subscription price may be tax deductible. Ask your tax advisor.

123. P.S. One more thing I almost forgot to mention ' this _____ includes the best, most unique learning tool there is ' A REAL PERSON. You get your own _____ to call with any questions you may have. As often as you need. Any time. Eight hours a day. Five days a week.

124. P.S. Our unique new guarantee reflects our confidence in _____ ability to work for you. If you don't save at least __ times your subscription cost, you get all your money back. At any time during your subscription ' right up to the very last day.

125. P.S. Please remember, your free no-risk trial is exactly that 'totally free to you and without any risk whatever. In fact, the only way you could incur any risk at all is by not accepting this invitation, and thus depriving yourself of the greatest success advantage that you might ever have the opportunity to discover.

126. P.S. Please reply promptly, because your first free issue is almost ready for mailing, and we do need your OK to send it to you.

127. P.S. Quick-response bonus! Reply within __ days and you'll also receive _____. If you liked the opportunities I outlined in the letter, you'll love this exclusive special report.

128. P.S. Remember, only __ companies will be accepted to participate in this _____. Since this is the only program I have planned for _____, this may be your only chance to take advantage of this fantastic opportunity. Don't delay ' call xxx-xxx-xxxx ext x, and speak to _____ today!

129. P.S. Remember, we ship all orders within __ hours, too!

130. P.S. Supplies of the _____ are limited and usually sell out quickly. Orders will be filled on a first-come, first-served basis. Avoid disappointment, order your copy today.

131. P.S. Thanks so much for reading my letter, and, please, I need your answer within __ days.

132. P.S. There's just one thing. This offer is good for a limited time only, and expires with the date on the check ' so please don't delay. Deposit the check now, while it's still valid

133. P.S. This is the one and only time you can qualify to attend this program at this price with such affordable payment terms ' for just _____ down you can review all of my pre-attendance materials and make the committed decision to attend. The choice

is yours ' so don't delay, your registration must be accepted by
_____to be eligible for this special offer!

134. P.S. This will be the only notification you receive and we will
not be expanding enrolment beyond the level I've set in this letter.
If you wait, you'll lose this opportunity. Don't let that happen to
you. Please call xxx-xxx-xxxx and register now while this is fresh
in your mind. Call me now ' before someone grabs your slot.

135. P.S. Will all this information make you wealthy' I have to be
frank with you: I don't know how rich you'll get once you read,
absorb and begin to use the secrets in this big package. I'm selling
you a hammer. Whether you build a doghouse or a castle is none
of my business. My suggestion: Think BIG! Isn't it time'

136. P.S. You can lose a lot of money with the wrong newsletter.
But you can't lose when you accept this no-risk offer. If you're
disappointed with your first issue of _____ for any reason, just
let us know and we'll refund your subscription payment in FULL.

137. P.S. You'll be amazed at how simple and easy it is to apply all
of these techniques. Your FREE bonus, _____ will allow you
to begin immediately ' even before you listen to the program!)

138. P.S. What other _____ can you start with so little cash
and minimal risk' I think you should not pass this opportunity to
examine this _____ in your home without any risk to you.
Send for your copy today.

139. P.S. Remember, act within the __ days and I'll give you
unlimited _____ for life. Not at any regular rate of $___ per
hour. But free! Now you have a _____ who knows this
business inside out. Ready to help you when you need it. But only
if you act now.

140. P.S. Cash In on the _____. If you're struggling a little,
then you really Do need this ""_____"" Besides, if aren't

100% satisfied, I'll send someone to pick it up for a complete refund - at my full expense! You don't have to do a darn thing - expect _____. How's that for an offer you can't refuse' Order now!"

141. P.S. Enclosed you will find a letter find a letter from _____ praising the book, recommendations from other _____, a list of valuable things you will learn from the _____, and other goodies, If can read through this stuff and not buy the buy the book, you deserve some kind of medal.

142. P.S. Don't forget, not only is my _____ doubly guaranteed, but you get to keep the free gift just for giving me the chance to prove everything I've said. The free gift alone can be worth _____ times the cost of the _____!

143. P.S. In case you haven't already noticed, I'd like to point out that the offer I've made you is better than without risk. The worst that can happen is that you will come out $_____ ahead. You see if the _____ doesn't work exactly as I've said it will I'll rush you a full and complete refund. But the $_____ worth of free bonuses are yours to keep as my way of thanking you for trying the plan. That's how much faith I have in _____ . You have everything to gain and nothing to lose. So if you're ready to take a step that can change your life, don't delay.

144. P.S. Your __% discount offer expires in just __ days, so I urge you to order today, and increase your _____.

145. P.S. ACT NOW. An exciting world of _____ is waiting' and so is a Free Gift!

146. P.S. My closet associates tell me, "" _____, you don't need the money and you don't need the trouble. Forget all this."" But

_____

147. P.S. This offer isn't available to everyone. It isn't transferable. But if you decide and _____, we can understand you might want to share the news of your ""_____"" with a special friend or two. In that event, ask them to _____.

148. P.S. I'd appreciate an early reply from you and I'll include a free bonus gift when you _____.

149. P.S. Go directly to _____ . If you order within 12 days, I'll pledge to send you, absolutely free, a special gift! I think you're really going to like it. Plus, I'll also give you a no time limit guarantee of complete satisfaction!

150. P.S. One more thing. It may be important. Your ability to _____ is crucial to your success. Here is an opportunity to learn directly from _____. Six months from now, this will very probably be one of the most talked about _____ ever produced. Moreover, every _____ who subscribes will have an almost unfair advantage over _____. Shouldn't that be you'

151. P.S. There are very few _____ that you can do without _____. This _____ offers you an opportunity to _____ without. You can examine the _____ without risking anything. If you don't like what you see or if you don't _____, simply return the full and complete refund.

152. P.S. Important UPDATE: Due to the overwhelming response to this offer, it could end as early as tomorrow. Don't delay! To get your _____ Click on the Button Below NOW. Remember, you have a full 1 year, money back guarantee with no questions asked!

153. P. S. _____ for you _____ are out there right now, _____, ready to hear about you. They're like fireflies in the night - dim sparks to you now, but capable of _____ once you draw them in. Catch lightning in a bottle - order _____ right now.

154. P.S. Remember, this offer is going to go very quickly and if you wait you may be out of luck to receive this _____ at such an ultra-low price. You have a full _____ days to _____, or your money back. Act now, or you could be the one left behind in the dust.

155. P.S. Remember - You also get _____! Along with my other powerful_____. So you can _____ just as quickly as I discover new ways of _____!

156. P.S. Let us remind you that this _____ is backed by our rock-solid 100% no risk money back guarantee. You have absolutely nothing to lose. Act now before this offer ends.

157. P.S. - Remember, there are only _____ guaranteed membership places. I usually generate between _____ and _____ orders for every email message I zap out to my opt-in list so they'll go fast when my customers catch on. Don't miss out!

158. P.S. - Some of the techniques you'll learn are so powerful and hard hitting that they have to be kept under padlock and key. Only members get access to my inner vault of _____ secrets. Try us out risk-free for _____ days for just $_____ and you'll instantly discover what I mean -- this stuff is red hot!

159. P.S. Also remember, if you want _____ YOU have to _____. I've made it as easy as I possibly can. There's just NO reason not to order now. Don't let yourself miss out on this incredible offer.

160. P.S. You do not want to put this off because this chance to _____ might only be available for the next _____ _____' after that you may only get this kind of information _____!

161. P.S. Stop and consider for a minute just how much _____ can be worth to your _____. All you have to do is ask anyone that has one, or many. They'll tell you that _____ for a _____ can be worth literally _____ of dollars in _____ each and every _____.

$_____ is a small price to pay for the knowledge that will help you achieve _____.

162. P.S. If you don't claim your copy of _____ now - and we decide to stop selling it altogether -- how will you _____'

163. P.S. - If you're unsure about _____, click here for reasons why you must right now.

164. P.S. And remember, if you're not 100% convinced that _____ will_____, then simply tell us and we will issue a prompt and courteous refund --no questions asked -- and you may still keep the _____ gifts at no cost to you. Take advantage of this risk-free trial offer immediately, while there's still time.

165. P.S. One more point. It's important: A year from today, you could be struggling to _____' or you could be _____. I thought this information was so good that I paid over $_____ for it -- but now you can experience the same benefits that only a select few have been privileged enough to discover for only $_____. It's a pretty fantastic deal when you consider how high this _____ can _____.

166. P.S. What kind of a life can you provide for your family if you _____' Imagine the look on your loved one's face when you bring home that surprise gift they've always wanted.

167. P.S. You'll be amazed at how simple and easy it is to apply all of _____ techniques. '_____' will allow you to begin immediately even as soon as _____ from now.

168. P.S. One more thing. Click Here to find out how you can _____ for FREE!

169. P.S. You can lose a lot of _____ with the wrong _____. But you can't lose when you accept this no-risk offer. If, after _____, you are not convinced that this is going to take _____ to the highest level, I'll refund your money immediately.

170. P.S. If you're not 100% convinced that this _____ will help you _____ in _____ _____ or less, then simply tell us, and you will be issued a prompt and courteous refund. But make sure that you take advantage of this risk-free trial offer immediately, while there's still time. And remember, if you decide to ask for a refund, you can keep the _____ free bonuses.

171. P.S. Remember: To take advantage of this unbeatable deal of getting both _____ and _____, as well as the _____ free bonuses ' you must order no later than _____.

172. P.S. Whilst it's impossible for me to guarantee your results (how could I' I know nothing about you nor your skills and experience), let me say this: If you don't feel that this _____ generates enough _____ for you at any stage over the next _____, just let me know and I will refund your purchase price - absolutely no questions asked. I sincerely mean it.

173. P.S. Altogether there are hundreds of ways you can _____ and _____. Don't you owe it to your _____ to learn the most powerful and inexpensive _____ strategies that can dramatically impact the growth of your _____' Discover all of _____ secrets and watch your _____ take off!

174. P.S. The special offer ends _____. Order now at the special price of only $_____ for a lifetime membership including _____ and _____. You'll never view _____ in the same way again!

175. P.S. And remember, if you're not 100% convinced that _____ will show you how to _____, then simply tell us, and we will issue a prompt and courteous refund. Take advantage of this risk-free trial offer immediately, while there's still time.

176. P.S. I don't know how long I can offer _____. If you want to ensure you get _____ and all the bonuses you need to order today!

255

177. P.S. Remember; You have nothing to lose, everything's on my shoulders. If for any reason you don't like _____ simply ask for a refund! It's that simple!

178. P.S. When you order TODAY I'll also include ""_____"" absolutely FREE!

179. P.S. Let's be blunt: Does your _____ look like a ghost town' Unless you take drastic action right now nothing is going to change. You need ""_____"" because it will show you exactly how to _____! Your satisfaction is guaranteed - get your copy right now. Click Here To Order Now!

180. P.S. After all this, if there is still even the least little doubt in your mind as to whether or not you should order ""_____"", read this quote from _____:

181. P.S. If you don't order _____ right now, how will you ever learn all of the tweaks and tricks to _____, not to mention how much money you're going to save

182. P.S. Order now to take advantage of our _____% discount. You won't have to pay the regular price ($_____), instead you get instant access to _____ -- incredible ideas that have taken me _____and _____ to develop -- for just $_____.

183. P.S. Will doubt about _____ overwhelm you the next time you _____' Will you be wondering how much better it would have been if you had _____' It doesn't have to be that way! The _____ will make YOU a success. Order NOW!

184. P.S. Now just for a second, forget about how much _____ you're going to save. Just picture yourself when you realized _____. Do you remember all the frustration and anger you felt' Now let me ask you a question. How much is it worth to you, to be able to finally _____' How good will it feel next _____ when you have _____ -- legally

185. P.S. Owning this _____ will change your _____ life forever. For the very first time you'll be armed with a powerful arsenal of professional _____ tips, information, advice, and practical tools that will make your _____ look like a real pro did it! And you can order it here and get started right away!

186. P.S. You've got lots to gain and nothing to lose with my _____-_____ Risk Free Money Back Guarantee. Besides, what's your time worth' If this _____ saves you even one-half hour of _____ time, you'll already have the cost of the _____ covered. So do yourself a favor and order it now before the price goes up!

187. P.S. If you've ever wondered what it would be like to _____, then take advantage of the current price of $_____ and all of the great bonuses right away to guarantee you get your copy.

188. P.S. There is absolutely no risk at all with ordering right now! If you are not completely satisfied I will refund your money, and you can keep _____!

189. P.S. How will you know how to be truly successful with _____ unless you have this information' How will you know if you have just missed out on the best _____ opportunity around, bar none' How will you avoid the mistakes that most _____ make' Find out then facts you should know about _____. A _____ guide for _____. A real opportunity!!

190. PS: Imagine being able to not only _____ whenever you want, but getting _____ every single month - without paying a cent to any_____ ever again! That's what _____ will teach you to do faster than any other _____ out there.

191. PS: The current low price of $_____ will not be valid forever. I've already had to increase the price _____ due to the sheer volume of new _____, _____ and _____ I _____ regularly.

192. P.S. Remember, there is ZERO risk on your part. If you follow the steps and don't succeed, I'll refund every penny you spent for up to _____ full months.

193. P.S. Remember that by taking action right now, you could easily_____ with the included _____! Please don't wait any longer to get started _____.

194. P.S. I look forward to hearing about your success after reading my book. Will you make $_____ a month or maybe $_____ a month' Maybe someday I'll be bragging about YOUR success right here! Order the key to _____.

195. P.S. Also - don't forget that as a customer, you'll have access to the ""_____."" This is something no one else offers. You get to _____, so all your information is constantly up to date and fresh. And, as a special bonus, you'll have the opportunity to get your very own copy of my special report ""_____"" for only $_____. (It's normally $_____)

196. P.S. Take action and order now. If you just sit there and do nothing, that's all you'll get in return...nothing. Take charge and start _____. You can start _____ right away!

197. P.S. The reduced price of $_____ may end after _____, so get _____ before it's too late. Order Now.

198. P.S. Please Don't Order this product unless you are looking for a high quality, comprehensive guide so you can _____.

199. P.S. We honestly can't tell you how long the price will stay so low, it really depends on how well it sells, and knowing _____,this will be picked up

200. VERY quickly. _____ will very soon be worth at least $_____, and with this e-book, it's just like _____.No holds barred! All secrets revealed!! It's called doing the math!

201. P.S. Due to the enormous demand for this _____, We're not sure how long _____ will be available for, and the offer could terminate at any time.

202. P.S. If you're ready to discover how to _____...this is a MUST HAVE for your _____. With our incredible guarantee, what have you got to lose'

203. P.S. We will not be offering _____ for long - order right now and don't miss out.

204. P.S. _____ used to sell _____ for $_____. For a limited time, you can have _____ for just $_____. We reserve the rights to raise the price at any time.

205. P.S. Remember the message from _____ and Grab YOUR Piece of that$_____!

206. P.S. Remember, you receive _____ if you order before _____!

207. P.S. Take action now! Don't wait a second longer. You'll soon have access to the information and tools you need to _____. Imagine enjoying all the benefits of _____. None of that will become a reality unless you take control and order now.

208. P.S. Remember, only you can determine if you have what it takes to _____. We think you can. . .do you' Order _____ today, and you can _____tonight.

209. P.S. Don't Order this product if you're looking for the ""same old same old."" Not just a treatise of ""re-hashed"" material, what you will get is _____. Don't delay!

210. P.S. Please Don't Order this product if you're looking for a big fat book full of fluff and filler. What you'll get is _____ full of high quality information to put right next to your _____, so you can _____.

211. P.S. Remember' you get the ""_____"" _____ plus all the bonuses that come with it, at the limited-time, low introductory price!

212. P.S. You also get _____ to test this product out. If you're not satisfied for any reason, you get a complete refund of your purchase price. Even if you never use the information, you'll still get a kick out of _____.

213. P.S. No matter what you decide at the end, you still get to _____! It's a totally risk-free offer and a win-win situation for you!

214. P.S. Order now and you get _____ and _____ is yours today for only a fraction of what it's really worth to you in _____ results.

215. P.S. Remember, your purchase is backed by our ""_____"" guarantee within _____ days of purchase - so you've got _____ full months to see if the _____ helps you _____!

216. P.S. Get your copy now and I'll also give you _____! Order Now!

217. P.S. Order your copy today and you'll also receive _____! What is it' Click Here to find out!

218. P.S. Last minute BONUS - to make it easier for _____ to _____, I've included an easy to use ""_____"". Use it, _____ it, _____! Just _____ ... so you will _____!

219. P.S. Another BONUS! Never seen before anywhere ... a complete _____ is included with _____ to start _____ quickly! Just _____, and start _____! It couldn't be easier. You'll even find a _____that _____, using _____!

220. P.S. Remember that by taking action right now, you could easily_____ with _____! Don't wait any longer and _____.

221. P.S. That is all there is to it…You will receive _____, the _____ free _____ and the free _____ at no risk to you. Satisfaction Guaranteed!

222. P.S. If you need more information then look at _____. You will be amazed at the amount of _____ covered.

223. P.S. Just think! You'll never have to suffer through the pain and hassle of trying to _____' now you'll have a proven guide that shows you how to do it 'step by step. Order Now!

224. P.S. Still have questions' Check out our Frequently Asked Questions page - FAQ Page and our Testimonials Page from people just like you who are using this breakthrough _____ right now!

225. P.S. Are you a _____' I_____ comes with _____ so you can start _____ today. Just _____ and you're ready to _____!

226. P.S. There is absolutely no risk to you. You have nothing to lose and _____ to gain! It's time to learn what it takes to _____.

227. P.S. This _____ can be adapted to _____ to _____. It is all up to you on how much you would like to _____.

228. P.S. This offer is only guaranteed for a limited time, so be sure to lock in your special price of only $_____ now.

229. P.S. If you are procrastinating right now, just remember my GUARANTEE, which makes it as if you purchased this _____ for FREE!

230. P.S. You don't really know what you are missing if you don't act today! Give my _____ a try and see for yourself why others are helped by this new _____!

231. P.S. If you're still not sure about ordering check out _____ or try out the _____.

232. P.S. Please don't miss out on those free bonuses. Order on or before _____.

233. P.S. You can start _____ right after you order because you will receive instant access to _____! All it takes is a few clicks and you are on your way to _____. Get in while you can!

234. P.S. Remember, we guarantee at least _____ in the first _____ days after using our service. Make sure to have your _____ ready so we can prove to you that our service actually works!

235. P.S. Remember this is a TIME SENSITIVE OFFER. I can only *guarantee* you'll get these special bonuses and reduced price of only $_____ if you order by _____.

236. P.S. EXTRA BONUS: In addition to getting the _____, you will also get the _____ that has never seen the light of day until now. This _____ will totally change the way you _____.

237. P.S. I will never ask you to judge us on our own words; You might find all your answers by checking what others say about our _____ in the TESTIMONIALS page ... You will be delighted!!

238. P.S. By acting right now you get a great price, all the materials you need to _____, and the special bonus report. But only if you order within the next __ days.

239. P.S. To get the Free Bonuses worth $_____, you must order within the next __ days. Otherwise, the bonuses will not be included. So go _____.

240. P.S. By acting right now, you get substantial savings, a wealth of bonuses, and all with a __ month guarantee. This _____ is only good for only __ days - and will not be repeated.

241. P.S. Accompanying this letter are comments from people who _____.

242. P.S. Your satisfaction is completely guaranteed! Use the _____ for ___. If you're not totally satisfied with the course for any reason within the next __ months, return it for a full 100% refund issued the very same day we get the _____ back.

243. P.S. Everything you need to instantly be a _____ is included in this _____. This _____ is the key to the vault.

244. P.S. Remember, we guarantee that you'll love your _____. If not, you'll promptly get every penny of your money back - no hassles, no questions asked.

245. P.S. I urge you to seriously consider my offer. Either way, you win big. After all, the worst thing that happens is you get $_____ bonus gift package to keep for FREE. Of course, the best thing that happens is that you _____. Sounds pretty good no matter how you slice it!

246. P.S. If you are not planning to invest in _____, then please ask yourself this question: ""_____"". If you can't answer that, you must _____.

247. P.S. In case you're wondering, this is completely new information, not revealed anywhere else at any time. You won't find the techniques we teach in any book, video, or seminar' and there's nobody who has made a commitment to _____.

248. P.S. There's more. You've already seen how quickly these strategies and techniques can _____. But I'm not done yet. _____. They're yours free when you place an order for the _____ within the next __ days. Don't miss out.

249. P.S. My system has been used by people around the country. People just like you. Here are a few comments about my system,:

250. P.S. Could you get excited about _____'. Are you looking forward to being _____' Well, doesn't it make sense to do something now before it's too late and discover the _____.

251. P.S. You know as well as I do that if you don't change what you're doing, then your results aren't going to change either. You know you could have made better decisions in the past about _____. We'll let this be the one decision you get right in your immediate future.

252. P.S. You must order within __ days of receiving this letter to qualify for your __ bonuses Valued at $__- after that I am sorry, but they will not be included as they are reserved for people who are serious about getting ahead.

253. P.S. You can't go wrong with my __ month guarantee' If you don't make at least __ times your investment back simple send the package back and you will get a complete refund'

254. P.S. Many people have purchased this _____ are now well on the way to _____ and there is no reason you can't follow in their footsteps and mine'

255. P.S. If you order in the next __ days only, you'll receive a Free __ day trial where you can check it out at absolutely no cost. And if it isn't everything I've promised you here, just send it back no charge. How can you lose')

CHAPTER TWENTY

MANY PEOPLE DON'T MAKE THE MONEY THEY WANT SIMPLY BECAUSE THERE TOO LAZY TO FOLLOW-UP!

AS THE OLD SAYING GOES, FORTUNE IS IN THE FOLLOW UP.

HERE YOU WILL FIND SOME FOLLOW UPS AND FOLLOW THROUGHS THAT WOULD NOT JUST MAKE YOU MORE MONEY BUT MAKE YOUR CUSTOMERS AND/OR POTENTIAL CUSTOMERS HAPPIER THAN THE MORNING SUN

CHAPTER 20: FOLLOW UPS AND FOLLOW THROUGHS

1. As a valued subscriber of mine, I would like to .....

2. Click on the link below...then come back again to talk on action

3. Here is your Internet success:

4. Dear <prospect>, do you know that you can...

5. Just in case you missed out, this is...

6. Not many people know this, but....

7. Have you tried hard enough at your <skill>

8. Do you need expert assistance in...

9. Don't you think you need <assist>

10. In case you need professional assist in...

11. I was supposed to let you know....

12. I suppose this might interest you.

13. Have you received my <Free gift Title>

14. This will give you <benefit>

15. I was suppose to tell you more about <benefits>

16. Just before I missed out, this is your <benefit >

17. Don't miss out...

18. Still haven't made your <action>?

19. Have you started your <plan>?

20. You might have been <benefit> have you not miss <my offer>

21. you might miss out <something> but it is never too late to <purchase>

22. Are you still struggling with...

23. Have you waited long enough?

24. In case you're asking,...

25. This might stir your interest.

26. Just too kindly remind you that <offer>

27. Just in case you might have forgotten, <offer>

28. we would like to remind you that our <offer> ends <date>

29. Do you know that you can < remind benefit>

30. Just in case you think it's over-priced, our <guarantee>....

31. Before the chance is gone:

32. Hi <name>, Welcome to the most important lesson of <skill>

33. What if I told you that you can <benefit>

34. On <date> you have received the <benefit>

35. I hope you have enjoyed <benefit>

36. We want you to <success>, so we have a special offer for you.

37. How would you want to <benefit>

38. This offer is only valid until <date>

39. In order to see your success, we would like to ...

40. As you know, <skill> is one of the most important asset

41. Don't miss this chance

42. Don't miss it <prospect name>

43. Don't miss the golden opportunity

44. Never miss the offer of <product>

45. It pays to be early.

46. Just to make sure you don't miss this...

47. Just to make sure you are aware of the offer

48. In case you wonder, this time limited offer...

49. The last time this was released, it was...

50. If <he/she> can success, so can you

51. So have you decided living the kind of life you dream of?

52. By the way, this might help you <benefit>

53. By the way why don't you try out this <product>

54. If you have been thinking of getting started, don't miss out...

55. Are you feeling overwhelmed?

56. Do you sometimes feel discourage?

57. Let me show you how you can <achieve dream>

58. Thank you for your subscription

59. For <hour>...50% off the <product>

60. This is the last <email/promo> on <product>

61. Attention <prospect> this is your last chance

62. Master the <skill> (72 hours coupon expires)

63. In about 12 hours. It's over my friend! Hurry.

64. Last chance to save <amount> on the <product>

65. You will get it all for <amount> but only until midnight tonight. Hurry!

66. This is absolutely crazy offer at this price point.

67. The coupon will not work even a minute after midnight tonight.

68. You have till midnight to get <product> for <price>

69. This coupon is unlike anything I have offered before

70. Oops I forgot to add the notes to your sample, if you truly want to master <skill>

71. Oops I forgot to attach the article, here is your <gift>

72. As a bonus I will also show you <benefit>

73. This <gift> is just part of the bonus.

74. Are you satisfied with the <gift> you received?

75. I believe you have digested the material I have sent to you, here is <more>

76. Test Drive <gift/product> while there is still time.

77. I have pleasant surprise for you.

78. This is our way of saying Thanks!

79. It's my gift to you.

80. We owe a big thanks to you for

81. We appreciate your interest in our <product>,

82. Extra Bonus! Order now and I will include my special offer of <gift> for free!

83. Last call for <product>!

84. Secure your copy before you run out of time.

85. This is once in a life time offer

86. I'm not sure if I can put this up any longer

87. It's now or never. Secure your order at <price>

88. <number> copies left. What are you waiting for?

89. I wish I have more time for this, but the <promo> expires in <time>

90. For <hours> left to get it all at <price>

91. I can't make you do anything you don't want to, but you can't ignore this...

92. Yesterday I gave you <gift>,

93. This is a small sample of the kind of information you are going to get out of this.

94. I hope you make the right decision because in <hours> you will <benefit>

95. You have <days> left to join us at <price>

96. We would like to show you our appreciation by offering you < percent> discount.

97. Apart from the <gift>, we would like to show you how you can <benefit>

98. Before it's gone forever, here is your test drive.

99. Just to let you know that this is a Time Sensitive offer.

100. The best has yet to come. Introducing <product> at much reduced price.

101. LAST Chance to get all <number> report for FREE

102. Don't overlooked this time limited offer,

103. I guess by now you must be wondering...

104. This special gift could have you making <benefits>

105. You were supposed to be told the whole truth about

CHAPTER TWENTY ONE

11,076 POWER WORDS AND PHRASES THAT SELL

YOU HEAR AND SEE THEM EVERYWHERE...

RADIO, TV, IN PRINT, AND ONLINE.

ANYWHERE PRODUCTS ARE BEING PITCHED AND SOLD, POWER WORDS ARE BEING USED AS A "SECRET WEAPON" TO BOOST SALES.

DON'T UNDERESTIMATE THE POWER OF THESE WORDS. THESE ARE THE WORD THAT THE MIND HEARS AND SUBLIMINALLY CREATES DESIRED EMOTION, ACTIONS, AND REACTIONS.

NOW YOU TOO CAN USE THESE PROVEN WORDS AND PHRASES (HEARD ROUND THE WORLD) IN YOUR MARKETING TO GIVE YOUR SALES A BOOST.

CHAPTER 21: 11,076 POWERFUL WORDS AND PHRASES THAT SELL

$ A month or more

$ A year or more

$ Every single month

$ From my bedroom

$ Grand

$ In free advertising

$ In free publicity

$ Worth of

$ Worth of bonuses

$ Worth of merchandise

"$xxx" per click through

"$xxx" per lead

"$xxx" per sale

"Product name" includes

"Product" contains

"Source" felt

"Source" has/have proven

"Source" heard

"Source" said it look like

"Source" saw

"Source" says

"Source" says it sounds

"Source" stated

"Source" studies show

"Source" surveys show

"Source" tests show

"Source" thinks

"Source" told me

"X" easy payments

"X" years' experience

"X"% money-back guarantee

100% of every sale

100% original information

100% pure traffic

100% royalty free resell rights

2 tier

24 hours a day, 7 days a week

24/7 affiliate support

24/7 presence

24/7 service

24/7 support

50-50 proposition

6 figure income

6 figures each year

9 to 5

A "year" classic

An absolute must

A balanced life

A blueprint for

A booming business

A breath of fresh air

A breeze

A brief list of

A brief summary of what's

A chance like no other

A child could do it

A cinch

A collection of

A complete

A complete arsenal of

A complete package

A copy of my deposit

A couple hours a week

A custom designed

A cut above

A cut above the rest

A date with destiny

A detailed

A diamond in the rough

A dime a dozen

A dirt cheap way

A drop in the bucket

A few of the features

A few success stories

A fortune this year

A free & easy way to

A fresh approach

A full archive of

A full x day guarantee

A glimpse of my sales

A gold mine of information

A good friend of mine

A great addition

A guaranteed gain

A guide to

A high degree of

A huge collection of

A letter from a client

A list of

A list of all

A long shot

A long story made short

A long time coming

A lot of people feel that

A massive collection of

A must read

A must!

A new lease on life

A new perspective

A new twist

A no brainer

A non-stop salesman

A novel twist

A numbers game

A partial list of what

A place you can go

A pleasant experience

A pretty penny

A professional image

A proven blueprint

A quick fix

A revised and expanded

A rich source

A secret that

A secret weapon

A short list of our clients

A short list of what

A sign of the times

A simple

A simple technique that

A simple test to

A small list of

A small portion of

A snap

A special arrangement

A step forward

A study conducted by

A summary of everything included

A sure thing

A valuable reference

A way to get

A wealth of information

A winning offer

An x minute

Able minded

Abnormal

Above and beyond

Above average income

Above ground

Above normal

Abreast of changing regulations

Abridged version

Abrupt ending

Absolute

Absolute fact

Absolute influence

Absolute necessity

Absolute power

Absolute reason

Absolute standards

Absolutely

Absolutely no obligation

Absorbable

Absorbing

Absorbing story

Abstracted from

Abundant in

Abuse

Academic background in

Academic like

Academy like

Accelerate

Accelerate your

Accelerated

Accented with

Accept credit cards in minutes

Accept my/our offer

Accept your offers

Accept your proposal

Accepted business practices

Accepted by

Access proof

Access time

Access to all past issues

Accessible

Accessories included

Accident prone

Accidental

Acclaimed

Accompanied by

Accomplish your

Accomplished

Accomplishing a goal

According to

Accountability

Accountable

Accountant like

Accounted for

Accuracy and precision

Accuracy tested

Accurate information

Accurate methods

Accurate records

Accurately

Accused of

Ace in the hole

Achieve goals

Achieve instant credibility

Achieve the success you deserve

Achieve top rankings

Achieve your

Achieving success

Acknowledged by

Acknowledged expert

Acknowledged forerunner

Acknowledgment

Acquire your

Acquired taste

Acrobatic

Act now

Act now!

Act today!

Act upon

Act upon your suggestions

Act within "hour, days, etc."

Action

Activate your

Activated by

Activation fee

Active company

Active market

Active participation

Actor like

Actress like

Actual case studies

Actual people

Ad claims

Ad like

Adapt to

Adaptable

Adaptive

Add another income

Add emotional value

Add on

Add on business

Add on products

Add up

Add your

Add your own links

Added bonus

Added value

Addict like

Addicted

Addiction free

Addictive

Additional

Additional benefits

Additional income

Additional stream of income

Additive free

Addle

Address your

Addressed by

Adequate insurance

Adhered to

Adhesive like

Adjoin at

Adjust your

Adjustable

Adjusted

Administer

Administrated by

Administrator

Admirable

Admired

Admirer the

Admissible in

Admit that

Adoptive

Adorable

Adore the

Adrenaline

Adrenaline rush

Adsorbing

Adult

Advance

Advanced

Advanced equipment

Advanced formula

Advantage

Advantageous features

Adventure

Adverse reaction

Advertise

Advertise to millions

Advertise to thousands

Advertised

Advertisement free

Advertising allowance

Advertising impressions

Advertising related

Advertising space

Advertising strategy

Advice from

Advice jammed

Advisable

Advise your

Advised by

Advocated to

Aerial

Affected by

Affection prone

Affectionate

Affiliate

Affiliate bonus

Affiliate contests

Affiliate discounts

Affiliate newsletter	Agent run
Affiliate program	Agony
Affiliate selling	Agony free
Affiliation	Agree that
Affirm your	Agreement
Affirmations	Agreed to
Affirmative	Agreement
Affix your	Ahead of
Affluent in	Ahead of the game
Affluent times	Ahead of the pack
Afford luxury items	Aided by
Afford the	Aim at
Affordable	Aiming for
Affordable	Air conditioned
Affordable accommodations	Air cooled
Affordable price	Air heating
Afraid of	Air like
After hours	Air proof
After tax	Air sealed
After years of	Air tight
Against the wall	Airborne
Age old	Alarmed that
Agenda	Alarming

Alarming increase

Alarming speed

Alert!

Alien like

Alien proof

Alienate

Alienated by

Aligned

Alignment free

Alive and kicking

All about

All absorbing

All consuming

All day

All embracing

All female

All I can say is

All important

All in one place

All inclusive

All male

All natural

All new

All night

All of the resources

All or nothing

All powerful

All purpose

All round

All star

All systems go

All terrain

All the __ you'll need

All the business you want

All the difference in the world

All the ins and outs

All the tools you will need

All the way

All-time record

All walks of life

All washed up

All you do is advertise

All you need

All you need to know

Allergy free

Alliance with

Allocated by

Allow yourself

Allowance

Allowed to

All-purpose

Allure

Alluring terrain

Almighty

Almighty dollar

Almost controversial

Almost everyone has heard of

Almost perfect

Almost too good to be true

Altar your

Altered by

Alternated

Alternating

Alternative strategies

Always adding new products

Amazed amazement

Amazing

Amazing ability

Amazing advertising tips

Amazing amount

Amazing collection

Amazing discovery

Amazing features

Amazing improvement

Amazing results

Amazing scene

Amazingly effective

Amazingly simple

Ambition seeking

Ambitious

Ambitious growth

Amended

Ammunition filled

Amount to something

Amphibious

Ample

Amplified

Amplify

Amplify your orders

Amusement

Amusing

An absolute winner

An action plan for

An angel

An arm and leg

An astronomical living

An email from a customer

An extra surprise

An idea whose time has

An in depth look

An instant business

An internet fortune

An offer you can't refuse

An old age problem

Analysis

Analysis of

Analyzed

Ancestor

Ancestral

Ancestry

Anchor down

Ancient

Ancient myth

Ancient secrets

Ancient truth

Angel like

Anger free

Angered by

Angled

Anguish free

Animal like

Animated like

Ankle deep

Anniversary

Annoyance free

Annoyed by

Annoying

Annual earnings

Annual sale

Anonymous

Answerable

Answered by

Answering your questions

Answers hundreds of your questions

Anti-drug

Anti-virus

Anticipated by

Antique

Any budget

Any CEO will agree

Anybody

Anyhow

Anyone

Anyone can do it

Anyone can do this

Anyone who buys will

Anyone who is serious about

Anyplace

Anything

Anytime

Anyway

Anywhere

Apart from

Apocalypse

Apocalyptic

Apologetic

Apology

Apparent advantage

Appeal to prospects

Appeal

Appealing

Appealing alternative

Appealing choice

Appealing fragrance

Appearance friendly

Appliance like

Applicable

Application required

Appointed by

Appraisal proof

Appraised by

Appreciate by

Apprentice friendly

Approachable

Appropriate

Appropriate alternative

Approval rating

Approved

Approved by

Approved by major companies

Approximate value of

Archive your goals

Are you a ___who has been trying to?

Are you looking?

Are you looking for?

Are you ready to?

Are you serious about?

Are...?

Arm raising

Arm twisting

Armageddon

Armed with

Around the clock

Around the clock service

Arousing

Arranged by

Array of colors

Arrogant

Art like

Article mentioned

Artifact

Artificial

Artist signed

As good as it gets

As heard on

As mentioned on

As seen in

As seen on

As seen on TV

As soon as possible

Ask yourself

Ask yourself this question

Asking price

Ass kicking

Assassin proof

Assault

Assembled by

Assembles fast

Assembly less

Assert yourself

Assess your

Assessable to

Assessed by

Asset

Assigned to

Assists you

Associate

Associate program

Association

Assumable

Assume your

Assumed by many

Assure yourself of

Assured by

Astonishment

Astonishing

Astonishing ability

Astonishing size

Astounding

Astounding ability

Astounding collection

Astounding efficiency

Astounding miracle

Astounding power

Astronomical proportions

Astronomical sales

At a premium

At the age of x

At your fingertips

At your own pace

At your request

Athlete like

Athletic

Athletic looking

Atomic

Attachments

Attain celebrity status

Attainable

Attempt to

Attend today

Attention

Attention driven

Attention grabbing

Attentive service

Attest to

Attitude adjuster

Attract customers

Attract new clients

Attract prospects

Attracting business

Attractive

Attractive deal

Attractive incentive

Attractive investment

Attractive price

Auction like

Audible

Audio

Audit proof

Augmented

Authentic

Authentic antique

Authentic flavor

Authentic miracle

Authentication

Author of

Authored by

Authoring

Authoritative

Authoritative reports

Authority on

Authorization require

Authorized by

Authorized Version

Auto delivery

Auto pilot

Auto pilot income stream

Auto saved

Autographed

Autographed

Automate

Automate everything

Automate your follow up

Automate your product fulfillment

Automate your prospecting

Automate your site

Automated

Automated income

Automated profit generators

Automated tools

Automatic

Automatic marketing system

Automatic merchandising

Automatic sponsoring

Automatically deposited in your bank

Automatically submit

Automating	Awe
Automation	Awe inspiring
Autosuggestibility	Awe struck
Availability limited	Awed
Available	Awesome
Available funding	Awesome pay plans
Available in hard copy format	Awesome size
Avalanche of sales	Awful looking
Average	Awhile back I
Average sized	Babe magnet
Avid fan of	Baby like
Avoid costly mistakes	Back alley
Avoid mistakes	Back breaking
Avoid pain	Back end
Avoid problems	Back end profits
Avoid the big mistakes	Back handing
Avoid the costly mistakes	Back in the saddle
Avoid the costly pitfalls	Back order
Avoid the run around	Back when I was just
Award winning	Backdoor
Award winning presentation	Backdoor selling
Awarded	Backed
Award-winning	Backed by

Backed up	Bank like
Background	Bankable
Backlash	Bankrolled
Backlogged	Bankrupt proof
Backstabbing	Bankruptcy
Bad	Bankruptcy sale
Bad debt	Banned
Bad economy	Banner like
Bag like	Banner year
Bag of tricks	Bar like
Bags of cash	Barbecued
Bail out	Bare
Balance your	Bare basics
Balanced	Bare boned
Bald like	Bare truth
Ball and chain	Barely
Ball park figure	Barely scratched the surface
Ballistic	Bargain
Balloon your business	Bargain conscious
Bamboozle	Bargain hunter
Band like	Bargain price
Bandwagon	Bargained
Bang	Barn burner

Barrage

Barrier proof

Barring out

Barter deal

Base line

Base on a true story

Based in

Based on

Based on my experiences

Basement price

Basic

Basic advice

Basic guide

Basic survival

Basically you

Basics of

Basket full

Bastard

Bastard like

Battered

Battery powered

Battle hardened

Battle tested

Be a major player

Be a super affiliate

Be an affiliate

Be an expert

Be completely satisfied or

Be first to qualify

Be one of the first

Be rich and successful

Be selling in minutes

Be your own boss

Beach like

Beached

Bearable

Beast like

Beat competition

Beat down

Beat recession

Beat the system

Beatable

Beaten

Beating

Beating the competition

Beautiful

Beautiful scenery

Beautifully

Beautifully packaged

Beauty

Because

Because you

Become a bona fide expert

Become an expert

Become a millionaire

Become a paid subscriber

Become a pro

Become a super associate

Become an expert in your field

Become profitable

Become rich

Beef up

Been publishing since

Been well kept

Before and after

Before I share with you

Before they're gone

Before they're gone

Beg you

Begging

Begin by

Begin profiting now

Begin without any

Beginner

Beginner to advance

Behind closed doors

Behind the scenes

Behind the scenes look

Being a leader

Being an expert

Being educated

Being famous

Being in first place

Being informative

Being intelligent

Being organized

Being successful

Belief driven

Believability

Believable

Believably

Believe

Believe us or not

Belly buster

Belong to

Belonging

Belonging to a certain group

Below average

Below dealer price

Below is proof that

Below market

Below retail prices

Below wholesale prices

Bend the rules

Beneath you

Beneficial

Beneficial advice

Beneficial agreement

Beneficial influence

Beneficial ties

Beneficiary

Benefit

Benefits

Benefits you'll get

Bent over

Berry flavored

Beside yourself

Best

Best $ I every spent

Best home businesses

Best investment I've ever made

Best is yet to come

Best kept secret

Best managed companies

Best money can buy

Best money I have ever spent

Best price points

Best promotional tools

Best quality

Best selection

Best seller

Best selling

Best shot

Best value

Best-performing

Best-selling

Beta test

Beta test offer

Beta version

Better

Better late than never

Better paying

Better than

Between success and failure

Beware

Beware of

Beware!

Bewildering

Bewilderment

Bewitched

Beyond expectations

Beyond reason

Beyond your wildest dreams

Bible like

Big

Big and bold

Big bonus

Big breakthrough

Big business

Big check

Big company

Big corporation

Big deal

Big demand

Big enough

Big hearted

Big hitter

Big issue

Big name

Big reduction

Big residual checks

Big spender

Big stacks of money

Big ticket item

Big time

Big time operator

Big trends

Big wig

Biggest

Bill you later

Billed to

Billing cycle

Billing deferred	Blacklisted
Billion	Blast
Billion Dollar Company	Blast off
Billion Dollar Empire	Blatant
Billion dollar industry	Blazing
Billionaire	Bleak chances
Billions	Blended
Binary plan	Bless
Bind together	Blessed
Binding	Blessing
Binding commitment	Blew up
Binding promise	Blind like
Birth date	Blinded
Birthday	Blistering speed
Birthplace	Blizzard like
Bite sized	Blockbuster
Bitter sweet	Blocked
Bizarre	Blonde
Bizarre tactics	Blood
Bizarre twist	Blood and guts
Black and white	Blood red
Black colored	Blood stained
Black market	Blood thirsty

Bloodbath

Bloodcurdling

Bloody

Blossoming

Blow

Blow by blow

Blow it wide open

Blow the lid off of

Blow the whistle

Blow up

Blow up your profits

Blown apart

Blown away

Blown out

Blue collar

Blue colored

Blue ribbon

Blueprint

Blueprint for

Board of directors

Bodacious

Bodily harm

Body sculpting

Boggle your

Boggle your mind

Boil over

Boiled

Bold

Bold look

Bold offer

Boldly

Bolt out

Bomb

Bomb like

Bombard

Bona fide

Bonanza

Bonded by

Bonding

Bone chilling

Bone dry

Bone jarring

Bonkers over

Bonus

Bonus gift

Bonuses

Book like

Book value

Booked

Booked months ahead

Boom

Booming

Booming industry

Booming trade

Boost

Boost sales

Boost your

Boost your response

Boost your response rates

Bootleg

Borderline

Born again

Born and raised

Born on

Both are free

Bottled

Bottom

Bottom line

Bottoming

Bottomless

Bounce back

Bounce less

Bouncy

Bound and determined

Bound up

Boundary line

Boxed

Brace yourself

Braced by

Braided

Brain burned

Brain friendly

Brainy

Brand

Brand image

Brand loyalty

Brand name

Brand new

Brand positioning

Branded

Branding

Branding solution

Brass	Breakthrough
Brat like	Breakthrough discovery
Bratty	Breathtaking
Brave	Breathtaking display
Brazen	Breathtaking picture
Breach of	Breathtaking scene
Bread and butter	Breathtaking view
Break	Breezy
Break a leg	Bribe proof
Break away	Bricks and mortar
Break down	Brief
Break even	Bright
Break free from	Bright colors
Break in	Bright eye
Break new ground	Bright future
Break out	Brightly colored
Break out of your	Brightness
Break the bank	Brilliant
Break the ice	Brilliant color
Break up	Bring home the bacon
Breakable	Bring in
Breaking news	Brink of
Breakneck speed	Brinks

Brisk	Budgeted
Brittle	Buffed
Broad	Buffoon
Broad base support	Bug like
Broad experience	Bugged by
Broad minded	Build a client base
Broad spectrum	Build a global network
Broadened	Build an empire
Broke	Build business relationships
Broken	Build consumer trust
Broker friendly	Build profitable alliances
Bronze like	Build self confidence
Brought in over $	Build strategic alliances
Brown colored	Build your
Browse around	Build your business
Brutally honest	Building block
Bubble less	Built
Bubble wrapped	Built in
Buckle down	Built in affiliate program
Buckled	Built in business
Buddy	Built like a
Buddy like	Built to order
Budget	Built up

Bulk discount

Bulk of

Bull headed

Bullet proof

Bullet proof system

Bullet stopping

Bull's eye

Bullshit

Bully

Bully proof

Bum rap

Bumbling

Bumpy

Bunched together

Bundles of cash

Bureau of

Burglar proof

Burn rubber

Burned by

Burning desire

Burning issue

Burning question

Burst of cash

Bury the hatched

Business

Business alliance

Business as usual

Business building

Business consulting

Business equipment

Business from referrals

Business geniuses

Business information

Business law

Business leads

Business letter

Business like

Business machinery

Business model

Business name

Business needs

Business owner

Business partner

Business plan

Business planning help

Business relationships

Business secrets

Business seminar

Business vehicles

Business venture

Business veteran

Business wants

Bust onto the scene

Busted by

Busy

Busy time

Butt kicking

Buy

Buy a better car

Buy a bigger house

Buy a new car

Buy a new house

Buy again and again

Buy anything from you

Buy before midnight tonight

Buy direct and save

Buy it already

Buy now

Buy now!

Buy on impulse

Buy one get one free!

Buy one, get one free

Buy over and over

Buyer behavior

Buying power

Buying whatever they want

By leaps and bounds

By the book

By the numbers

By the truck full

Bypass

Cachet

Cadaver

Cahoots

Cajole

Cakewalk

Calculate your order

Calculated

Calculating

Caliber

Call

Call anytime

Call it like you see it

Call now

Call right now

Call right now!

Call the shots

Call today!

Call toll free

Call toll free -- anytime

Call your own shots

Camera ready

Camouflaged

Can be digitally download

Can I show you?

Can you

Can you handle?

Cancel anytime

Canceled on

Candy like

Canned

Can't imagine a better investment

Can't live without it

Can't match the sheer potential

Can't put it into words

Can't you

Capable of

Capitalize on

Captain of your own ship

Captivating results

Capture customers

Capture interested prospects

Carbonated

Career improving

Carefree living

Careful inspected

Careful supervision

Carefully selected

Caring

Caring service

Carnival like

Carries a lot of weight

Carry out

Carry the torch

Cartoon like

Carve out a niche

Carved in stone

Case by case	Cash on delivery
Case history	Cash on demand
Case in point	Cash or credit
Case sensitive	Cash paying customers
Case study	Cash rebate
Cases studies	Cash secrets
Cash	Cash starved
Cash at closing	Cash value
Cash back	Casino like
Cash bearing	Casual
Cash cow	Cat and mouse
Cash discount	Cat like
Cash flow	Cataloged
Cash generating	Catapult your sales
Cash grants	Catastrophe
Cash in	Catastrophic results
Cash in on	Catch 22
Cash in on your share	Catchy
Cash in your chips	Categorized by
Cash in your pocket	Causal
Cash incentive	Caution
Cash instantly deposited	Cautionary
Cash magnet	Celebrated by many

Celebrity status	Change your destiny
Cemented	Change your life
Censored	Changes
Center	Changes forever
Centered	Changes your life
Centralized	Changeable
Centuries old	Changed forever
Centuries owned	Changed my life
Ceramic	Channels of distribution
Certifiable	Chapter x will show you
Certified	Chapter x you'll uncover
Certified by	Charge it
Chairman	Charge the right price
Chairman of the board	Charity
Chalk up your	Charity giving
Challenge	Charmer
Challenged by	Charming
Challenging	Charming beauty
Chamber of	Charming hospitality
Champion of	Chat with us
Chance of a lifetime	Cheap
Change their beliefs	Cheap imitation
Change their mind	Cheapskate

Cheat proof

Check in

Check out these comments

Checked

Checked out what others

Checklist of

Checkout

Checks in your mailbox

Cheerful help

Chemical free

Cherish by many

Chide

Child like

Child proof

Chill out

Chilled

Chilling

Chilly

Chipped

Chock full of

Chocolate covered

Choose your own schedule

Choosing the right

Chopped

Chosen by many

Christmas sales

Chrome

Chronologically

Chunky

Cinnamon flavored

Circle

Circle the wagons

Circular

Circulated by

Circulation of

Circus like

Citrus

City like

City smart

Claimed by many

Clarified it with

Classed alone

Classic

Classic style

Classifiable

Classification

Classified	Clear sighted
Classified information	Clear solution
Classy	Clear thinking
Clean	Clear understanding
Clean bill	Clearance
Clean cut	Cleared
Clean the floor	Clearinghouse
Clean up	Clearly defined
Cleanest	Clearly explained
Cleansing	Clearly written
Clear	Clever
Clear communicator	Clever advice
Clear cut	Clever devise
Clear cut answers	Clever ideas
Clear cut proposal	Clever scheme
Clear cut report	Clever tactics
Clear examples	Cleverly designed
Clear eyed	Click here
Clear headed	Client attracting
Clear ideas	Client driven
Clear language	Climate safe
Clear policy	Climb on the bandwagon
Clear proof	Climbable

Clinical evidence

Clock like

Clocked at

Clockwork

Clone your sales

Close at hand

Close deals effectively

Close every sale

Close fitting

Close in

Close knit

Close out

Close sales faster

Close supervision

Close the deal

Close the sale

Close ties

Close up

Closed door

Closely guarded strategies

Closely monitors

Closes at "time"

Closing down soon

Closing forever

Club like

Clutter-free

Coached by

Coaching included

Coast to coast

Coastal

Coated with

Co-author

Co-authored

Cockamamie

Cocoon

Coded

Codger

Coefficient

Coffin like

Coiled

Coin operated

Cold

Cold blooded

Cold cash

Cold hard facts

Cold hearted

Cold shoulder

Cold sweat

Cold turkey

Colder

Coldest

Collaborated with

Collapse

Collateral free

Collect them all

Collectable

Collected by

Collectible

Collector's edition

Collector's item

College like

Collision proof

Colonial

Color

Color organized

Colorable

Colorful

Colorful demonstration

Colossal

Colossal amount

Colossal wealth

Combination locked

Combined with

Combustible

Combustible issue

Come and go

Come full circle

Come on strong

Come out ahead

Come out on top

Come out swinging

Come to a head

Come to grips with

Come to terms with

Come up with

Comeback to

Comes with free reseller program

Comes with the territory

Comfort

Comfort of home

Comfort zone

Comfortable

Comfortable accommodations

Comfortable fit

Comforting

Comical

Commendable

Comments from satisfied customers

Commerce friendly

Commercial

Commercially sold

Commission

Commission check

Commission on back end sales

Commission on repeat sales

Commissioned by

Commitment to

Committed

Committed to

Common

Common cause

Common in most

Common purpose

Common-sense approach

Commonsense to buy

Commonwealth

Communication oriented

Community oriented

Compact

Companionable

Company loyal

Company stock

Comparable to

Comparative

Compare it with other opportunities

Compare our product to

Compared by

Compassionate service

Compatibility

Compatible

Compelled them to buy later

Compelling

Compelling evidence

Compelling force

Compelling reason

Compelling testimonials

Compensate you

Compensated with

Compensating for

Compensation

Compensation package

Compensation plan

Compete with

Competitive advantage

Competitive advertising

Competitive drive

Competitive edge

Competitive industry

Competitive prices

Competitor proof

Compiled by

Complete

Complete authority

Complete confidentiality

Complete details

Complete facts

Complete honesty

Complete information

Complete instructions

Complete menu

Complete package

Complete perfection

Complete range of

Complete reliability

Complete setup

Complete support

Complete training

Complete truth

Completed

Completely

Completely confidential

Completely free

Completely free to join

Completing a project

Completing a task

Complex

Compliant with

Complimentary

Compliments your business

Compliments your product

Composed by	Computerize
Compounded	Computerized
Comprehensive	Concealed
Comprehensive index	Concealed by
Comprehensive instructions	Concept
Comprehensive inventory	Concerned
Comprehensive knowledge	Concise report
Comprehensive package	Conclusive evidence
Comprehensive range of	Conclusive proof
Comprehensive solution	Concrete information
Comprehensive support	Concrete solution
Comprehensive training	Condensed version
Compressed	Confession of a
Compromise	Confessions
Computable	Confide in your desires
Computed by	Confidence
Computer	Confident
Computer assisted	Confident that you'll
Computer equipment	Confidential
Computer like	Confidential location
Computer literate	Confirm your order
Computer repair	Confirmation provided
Computer training	Confirmed by

Confusion proof

Congratulations

Congratulations!

Conjoined

Connect the dots

Connected

Conscious of your

Consecutive awards in

Consider all alternatives

Consider these benefits

Consider your

Considerate

Consistent

Consistent accuracy

Consistent income

Consolidate

Consolidated

Constant communication

Constant interaction with

Constant promotional tool

Constant revenue stream

Constantly improving

Construct

Constructed by

Construction

Constructive

Constructive advice

Constructive approach

Consulted by

Consulting provided

Consumed by

Consumer help

Consumer protection

Consumer service

Contact information

Contact me/us/you

Contact us

Contact us by e-mail

Contagious

Contemporary

Content filled

Content rich

Contest

Continued support

Continuing relief

Continuous

Continuous flow of visitors

Contract protected

Contrary to popular belief

Contribute to

Contributing

Contribution of

Control

Control your income

Control your life style

Control your schedule

Controversial

Convenience

Convenient

Convention like

Conventional

Conventional size

Conversational

Conversion cost

Conversion ratio

Convert every lead

Convert into customers

Convert more prospects

Convert visitors to sales

Convert your

Convertibility

Convertible

Convince any skeptic

Convince yourself that

Convinced that

Convincing statistics

Cooked by

Cookie Cutter

Cool

Cooler

Coolest

Co-op

Cooperative

Coordinated by

Coordinated plan

Coot

Copy of my bank statement

Copyright

Coral

Core

Core market

Corporate

Corporate identity

Corporate image

Corporate secrets

Corporation

Corpse

Correct

Corruptive proof

Cosmetic

Cosmic

Cost

Cost accounting

Cost analysis

Cost conscious

Cost control

Cost effective

Cost effective advertising

Cost efficient

Cost of goods sold

Cost of living

Cost-effective

Costly

Couldn't live without it

Couldn't you

Counseled by

Countdown to

Counted by

Counter offensive

Counter productive

Counteract

Counteractive

Counterblow

Counterclockwise

Countered by

Counterpart

Counting on

Countless

Country wide

County smart

Coupon

Courage

Courageous

Course free

Courteous service

Courtesy driven

Cover virtually every

Cover your

Cover your butt

Coverage provided by

Covered by

Covering everything

Covers a lot of ground

Covers all the bases

Covers every detail

Covers everything

Covert

Cover-up

Coward

Cowboy like

Cozy

Crackdown on

Craft like

Crafty

Crammed

Crammed full of

Crank

Crank out

Crank up your promotion

Cranks out money

Crash and burn

Crave

Crave your product

Craw

Crazy

Cream of the crop

Creamy

Create a buying urge

Create a lasting impression

Create a media frenzy

Create a network

Create a traffic funnel

Create believable ads

Create credibility

Create impulse spending

Create interest

Create lifetime customers

Create monthly income

Create obscene wealth

Create profitable deals

Create profitable products

Create raving fans

Create residual income

Create your

Create your own

Create your own products

Created by

Creating a buzz

Creative

Creative alternatives

Creative invention

Credential supported

Credentials

Credibility

Credibility booster

Credible

Credible guarantee

Credible organization

Credible story

Credit

Credit card

Credit card processing

Credit cards accepted

Crime proof

Crime ridden

Criminal proof

Cringe at the thought

Crinkled

Cripple

Crisis

Crisis ready

Crisper

Crispy

Critic proof

Critical

Critical acclaim

Critical acclaimed

Critical decision

Critical factor

Critical issue

Critical mass

Critical material

Critical moment

Critical state

Critically acclaimed

Critically needed

Criticism proof

Crook proof

Crooked

Cross county

Cross merchandising	Crying free
Cross promotion	Crystal clear
Cross selling	Crystal clear sound
Cross the line	Crystal like
Crossed by	Crystallized
Crossover to a new	Cubed
Crowd pleaser	Cubic
Crowd proof	Cult like
Crowded by	Cultivated into
Crowned by	Culture
Crucial	Curable problem
Crucial function	Cure your
Crucial issue	Curiosity driven
Crucial stage	Curled
Crucial to own	Curly
Crumbly	Curmudgeon
Crunch the numbers	Currency converter
Crunch time	Currency exchange
Crunchy	Current
Crush	Current cost
Crush your competition	Current price is
Crushed	Currently we are offering
Crusty	Cursed by

Curved

Cushioned

Custom

Custom built

Custom design

Custom designed

Custom made

Custom packaging

Customer base

Customer care

Customer comes first

Customer complaints

Customer driven

Customer friendly

Customer loyalty

Customer oriented

Customer oriented company

Customer profile

Customer questions

Customer satisfaction

Customer service

Customizable

Customizable links

Customization

Customize

Customized

Customized affiliate web site

Customized for you

Customized information

Customized product

Customized version

Cut and dried

Cut and dry

Cut and dry answers

Cut and paste

Cut corners

Cut costs

Cut down

Cut out

Cut rate

Cut rate price

Cut throat

Cut to the chase

Cut you in on

Cut your loses

Cute

Cut-price	Dare you
Cutting costs	Dare you to
Cutting edge	Daring color
Cyber	Daring innovation
Cyber ready	Dark
Cyber space	Darken by
Cybermall	Darling
Cyberspace	Darn
Cycle like	Data supported
Cycled	Database chosen
Cyclone	Date of
Dagnabbit	Dawn of a new age
Daily	Day long
Daily Grind	Day of
Dainty	Day of Judgment
Dairy like	Day old
Damp	Day to day
Dandified	Daydream about
Dandy	Dazzling
Danger	Dazzling color
Dangerous	Dazzling compilation
Dangling hope	Dazzling event
Dare to be different	Dead broke

Dead deal

Dead end

Dead on

Deadbeat

Deadline

Deadlocked

Deadly

Deal of the

Dealer price

Dear ""Subscriber

Dear "industry" Consultant

Dear "industry" Customer

Dear "item" Dealers

Dear "item" Enthusiast

Dear "item" Seeker

Dear "their name"

Dear Associate

Dear Auction Seller

Dear Bargain Hunter

Dear Bidder

Dear Business Coach

Dear Business Investor

Dear Business Owner

Dear Business Tax Payer

Dear Buyer

Dear CEO

Dear Collector

Dear Copywriter

Dear Customer

Dear Editor

Dear Entrepreneur

Dear Executive

Dear Fellow Business Owner

Dear Friend

Dear Future ""

Dear Future Millionaire

Dear Home Worker

Dear Home-Based Business Owner

Dear Marketer

Dear Opportunity Seeker

Dear Publisher

Dear Reseller

Dear Sales Representative

Dear Supplier

Dear Surfer

Dear Visitor

Dear Webmaster

Dear Wholesaler

Dearly thankful

Death

Debated by

Debilitating

Debit or credit

Debt eliminating

Debt free company

Debt less

Debt ridden budget

Debt-free

Debugged

Debut

Decade long

Decadent

Decaffeinated

Decay proof

Deceased

Deceived by

Decent living

Decently priced

Deceptive competition

Decide now

Decided by

Deciding factor

Decipher

Decision

Decision makers

Decision making

Decisional

Decisive advantage

Decisive choice

Decisive influence

Decisive moment

Decode your

Deconstructed from

Decorated

Decreased price

Dedicate your

Dedicated

Dedicated team of

Deducted from

Deductible

Deduction friendly

Deed

Deep

Deep discount

Deep pocket

Deep rooted

Deepened

Deeper

Deepest

Defeat

Defeat your competition

Defective until

Defend your

Defendable

Defensible

Deferrable

Deferred billing

Deferred payments

Deferred till

Defined by

Definite answers

Definite benefits

Definite information

Definitely affordable

Deflective

Defrauding

Defrosted

Deft free

Defused the situation

Degree in

Delay paying till

Delegated by

Delete your

Deliberate discount

Delicacy

Delicate

Delicious

Deliciously

Delightful

Delightful scent

Delightful surprise

Delightful taste

Delightfully

Delighting

Deliver

Deliverable

Delivered fast

Delivered to your door

Delivers on their promise

Delivery guarantee

Delivery mechanism

Deluxe

Demo

Demographically

Demonstrate your

Demonstrated by

Demonstrated skills in

Demonstration

Demoted to

Denied by

Denounced by

Deodorized

Department of

Departmental to

Dependable

Dependable promise

Dependably

Dependency

Dependent upon

Deposit

Deposited in your bank

Depraved

Depreciated

Depreciation

Depressed market

Depressed over

Depth of

Descend upon

Descent

Described with

Description

Descriptive

Deserve

Design your

Designated by

Designed by

Designed to order

Designed to sell

Desirable

Desire

Desired results

Desperate deadline

Desperate measures

Destiny

Destroy

Destroy the competition

Destructible

Destruction of

Destructive

Detachable

Detail

Detail driven

Detail oriented

Detailed

Detailed analysis

Detailed description of

Detailed information

Detailed instruction

Detailed instructions

Detailed plan

Detailed report

Detailed research

Detailed sales statistics

Detailed table of contents

Detailed traffic statistics

Detailing

Detected by

Detective

Determination

Determine the

Determine your

Determined to help

Detrimental to

Devastating

Develop a recognizable brand

Develop your

Developed by

Developed new products

Developer tested

Developing new

Devilish

Devoted to

Diabolic

Diabolical

Diagnosed by

Diagonal

Diagrammed

Dial tone

Dial up access

Diamond in the rough

Diamond like

Did you

Did you feel?

Did you know?

Did you like?

Did you note that?

Did you realize?

Didn't you

Die hard customer base

Diet proof

Dietary

Difference

Different

Difficult economic times

Difficult situation

Difficulty

Digest version

Digital

Digital cash

Digital delivery

Dignified

Diligent

Dim

Dimensional

Diminish the

Dingy

Dinosaur like

Dip into

Diploma like

Diplomatic

Dire need

Direct

Direct access

Direct action

Direct marketing

Direct response

Direct selling

Direct to you

Directly

Directed by

Directional

Dirt cheap

Dirt poor

Dirty

Dirty secrets

Disability friendly

Disadvantages of

Disaffiliate with

Disagree with

Disappointed with

Disapproval of

Disassembles easily

Disaster proof

Disastrous

Disbelieve the competition

Discard your old

Disciplined

Disclaim any

Disclose any

Disclosed by

Discolored

Discontinue using

Discount

Discount coupon

Discount equal to sales tax

Discount rate

Discounted

Discover

Discover a step by step

Discover free

Discover how

Discover how to

Discover new tricks

Discover the mistakes that

Discover the most important

Discover the number one

Discover the secrets of

Discover what the

Discover which

Discovery"

Discovered by

Discrete packaging

Discretion advised

Disease proof

Disguised by

Disgusting

Dish out

Dishonest competition

Disinfected

Dislike your old

Dismiss as a

Dispatched to

Dispensable

Dispirited about

Display modal

Displayed by

Displeased with

Disposable

Disrupt

Disrupt your competition

Dissolvable

Distinct advantage

Distinct trend

Distinction between

Distinctive competence

Distinctly remembered

Distinguished

Distinguished ability

Distorted by

Distress about

Distributed by

Distribution

Distribution center

Distribution channels

Distribution rights

Distributor friendly

District run

Disturbed by

Ditch your

Diverse

Diverse background

Diverse experience in

Diversified

Dividable between

Divide and conquer

Divide your payments

Dividends

Divine

Do I have it right?

Do it yourself

Do something you love

Do you ask yourself?

Do you ever notice that?

Do you have a problem with?

Do you know anyone who

Do you know what?

Do you want?

Do yourself a favor

Do…?

Doctor approved

Doctor recommended

Doctrine

Documented

Documented facts

Doddering

Dodge the

Does…?

Doesn't have to be

Doesn't leave anything out

Doesn't…?

Dogma

Dollar

Dollar amount

Dollar for dollar

Domain friendly

Domestic

Dominant

Dominate the

Donate

Donation of $x

Don't be fooled by

Don't be left behind

Don't be left out

Don't cop out

Don't delay

Don't delay!

Don't even think of ""until

Don't fall for the hype

Don't go away empty handed

Don't know how I lived without

Don't let "subject" stop you

Don't let the chance slip by

Don't make another

Don't miss out

Don't miss out!

Don't miss the boat!

Don't need any employees

Don't press you luck

Don't take my word for it

Dooms day

Doorway to

Dormant

Do and don'ts

Dotcom

Double

Double barrel

Double digit advantage

Double digit response rates

Double edge

Double headed

Double header

Double hung

Double income

Double sales

Double take

Double trouble

Double whammy

Double your money back

Double your money!

Double your revenues

Doubled by

Double-your-money-back guarantee

Doubtful of

Down and dirty

Down economy

Down scale

Down the sales path

Down to

Down to a science

Down to earth

Down to earth advice

Down to the wire

Downgraded to

Downhill

Downline

Download a free version of

Download it in minutes

Download it now

Downloadable

Downside of not ordering

Downsizing

Downtrend

Dozens of

Drafted by

Drafty

Drag and drop

Drama like

Dramatic

Dramatic breakthrough

Dramatic discovery

Dramatically increase your sales

Draped

Drastic mistake

Draw the line

Drawback

Drawing wide interest

Drawn out

Dream like

Dream your

Dreams come true

Drench in

Dressed up

Dried

Driven

Driving force

Droopy

Drop

Drop dead gorgeous

Drop down menu

Drop shipping

Drop the ball

Drought stricken

Drowning

Drudgery

Drug free

Drum up business

Dry

Due by

Due to popular demand

Dumb

Duplicable

Duplicate my success

Duplicate our

Duplicate your business

Duplication proof

Durability

Durable

Duty free

Dwarfs other

Dyed with

Dire need of

Dynamic

Dynamics

Dynamite

Each and every

Eagerly

Eagerly anticipated

Ear piercing

Ear splitting

Ear steaming

Earful of

Early bird

Early on

Early retirement

Early stages

Earn

Earn an additional $

Earn great recognition

Earn money

Earn money selling

Earn money while you sleep

Earn more in less time

Earn more money!

Earn substantial income

Earn top dollar

Earn x times your current income

Earned income

Earned over

Earning about

Earning potential is enormous

Earth shattering

Earthbound

Earthy materials

Ease

Ease of distribution

Ease of use

Eased up

Easier

Easiest

Easiest way to make money

Easily

Easily add

Easily sell them

Easily understood

Easy

Easy "easily"

Easy access

Easy as pie

Easy come, easy go

Easy going

Easy installation

Easy money

Easy operation

Easy ordering

Easy payment

Easy payments

Easy plan

Easy prosperity

Easy reference

Easy renewal

Easy solution

Easy to follow

Easy to implement

Easy to install

Easy to read

Easy to read and follow

Easy to understand

Easy to use

Easy to use software

Easygoing

Easy-to-read instructions

Eat up your competition

Eat your heart out

E-book marketing

E-business

Ecommerce

Economic

Economic benefits

Economic change

Economic climate

Economic factors

Economic gain

Economic growth

Economic indicators

Economic survival

Economical

Economy

Ecstasy

Ecstatic buyers

Edge up

Edited

Educate your audience

Educated	Eight
Educational	Eighth
Effect of	Either or
Effective	Ejected from
Effected by	Elaborate
Effective	Elaborate comfort
Effective and efficient	Elaborate scheme
Effective approach	Elaborate style
Effective ideas	Elapse time
Effective immediately	Elastic
Effective scheme	Elastic material
Effectively	Elating
Efficient	Elderly
Efficient company	Elected
Efficient service	Election held
Efficiently	Electric
Effort	Electricity
Effort free	Electrifying performance
Effortless	Electronic
Effortless skill	Electronic currency
Effortlessly	Electronic marketing
Effortlessly	Electronic publishing
Ego less	Elegance

Elegant

Elegant shaped

Elementary

Elevate traffic

Elevate your

Elevated

Elevated level

Elevating

Eleven

Eligibility is limited

Eligible

Eligible for

Eliminate

Eliminate all the confusion

Eliminate debt

Eliminate stress

Eliminate work

Eliminate your

Eliminated

Eliminating debt

Elite

Elude your

Elusive

Elusiveness

Email alert

Email marketing

Embark on

Embarrass

Embarrass by

Embedded

Embrace our

Emerald

Emerge as

Emergence of

Emergency

Emerging

Emerging growth

Emerging market

Emotion driven

Emotional

Emotional appeal

Emotional response

Emotionally charged

Empathy

Emphasize

Emphatic

Empire like

Employ our

Employable

Employed

Employee friendly

Employer proof

Empty

Emulate the

Enable our

Enabled

Enchanted

Enchanting

Enchanting fragrance

Enchanting scene

Enchantment

Enclosed

Encoded with

Encounter our

Encourage yourself to

Encouraged

Encrypted

Encryption

Encyclopedia like

End cold prospecting

End of a

End procrastination

End skepticism

End the daily grind

End user

End your money worries

Endangered

Endeavor

Endeavor less

Endless

Endless demand

Endless possibilities

Endless selection

Endless stream of traffic

Endless supply

Endless supply of
information

Endorse

Endorsed

Endorsed by

Endorsements

Ends today

Endure

Endurance

Enduring

Enduring stability

Enduring success energetic

Energize

Energize your income

Energy friendly

Energy saving

Energy

Energetic

Enforced

Enforced by

Engaged

Engaged in

Engineered

Engraved

Engraved with

Engross yourself

Engulfed in

Enhance your

Enhanced

Enhances relationships

Enhancing

Enhancing performance

Enjoy

Enjoy a dream vacation

Enjoyment

Enjoyable

Enjoyable surprise

Enjoyed by

Enjoyment

Enlarge your

Enlarged

Enlighten by

Enlightened

Enlightening

Enlist our

Enlisted

Enormous

Enormous ability

Enormous help

Enormous industry

Enormous potential

Enormous savings

Enormous wealth

Enraged	Enticing
Enriched	Enticing choice
Enriched	Enticing incentive
Enriching	Enticing offer
Enroll in	Entire
Enroll now	Entire price of
Ensure yourself	Entirely up to you
Entangle	Entrancing
Entangled by	Entrepreneur
Enter here	Entrust
Entering a new	Entry level
Enterprise	Envious of
Enterprising	Environment
Enterprising entrepreneurs	Environmental
Entertain yourself with	Environmental concerns
Entertained	Environmentally friendly
Entertainer like	Environmentally safe
Entertaining	Environmentally sound
Entertainment	Envision
Enthusiasm	Envision having
Enthusiastic	Envy
Enthusiastic comments	Envied
Entice yourself with	Epic adventure

Epic proportions

Epidemic like

Equal

Equal terms

Equals

Equipment

Equipped

Equipped with

Equity

Era of

Erasable

Erased from

Erotic

Erotica

Errand free

Error proof

Error-free

Errorless

Error-proof

Erupt your

Erupt your cash

Escape proof

Escape your

Escaping the daily grind

Escorted by

Essence of

Essential

Essential component

Essential goods

Essential ingredients

Essential knowledge

Essential nutrients

Establish

Establish rapport

Establish yourself as

Established

Established classic

Established tradition

Estimated

Eternal problem

Eternity

Ethical

Ethical procedures

Ethically increase your profits

Ethics

Evaluated by

Evaporated

Even

Even for busy people

Even terms

Event of

Eventually you

Ever lasting

Ever present

Ever wonder how

Everlasting comfort

Everlasting profits

Every entrepreneur

Every little bit helps

Every minute counts

Every wonder

Every the customer will

Everyone experiences

Everyone is joining

Everyone is talking about

Everything exposed

Everything from __ to __

Everything provided/supplied

Everything still in tact

Everything you always wanted to know about

Everything you may have heard about

Everything you need

Everything you need to know

Evidence from

Evil

Exact

Exact instructions

Exact timetable

Exactly

Exactly how

Exactly how to

Exactly what

Exactly what I've been looking

Exactly what you get

Examination less

Examined by

Example

Examples of how

Exceed

Exceed your goals

Exceeding expectations

Excellence

Excellent

Excellent authority

Excellent craftsmanship

Excellent credentials

Excellent credit

Excellent offer

Excellent payment structure

Excellent quality

Excellent service

Excellent skills

Except

Except our

Exceptional

Exceptional ability

Exceptional antique

Exceptional condition

Exceptional facility

Exceptional honesty

Exceptional qualifications

Exceptional quality

Exceptional service

Exceptionally high incomes

Exceptionally reliable

Excess of

Excessively

Exchange it for

Excited

Exciting

Exciting adventure

Exciting challenge

Exciting destination

Exciting details

Exciting developments

Exciting discovery

Exciting invention

Exciting news

Exciting results

Exciting revelation

Exclude the $x

Exclusive

Exclusive

Exclusive access

Exclusive information

Exclusive news	Exhilarating adventure
Exclusive offer	Exhilarating news
Exclusive privilege	Existing customers
Exclusive product	Exotic location
Exclusive rights	Exotic taste
Exclusivity	Expand
Excruciating	Expand your marketers
Excuse me but	Expandability
Execute our	Expandable
Executed	Expanded
Executive	Expanding income
Executive like	Expands your knowledge
Executive strength	Expansion driven
Executive summary	Expansive
Exempt by	Expect a lot
Exempted	Expectations
Exemption	Expedited by many
Exercise free	Expendable income
Exercised by	Expenditures
Exhausted from	Expense
Exhibited at	Expensive
Exhilarated	Expensive experimentation
Exhilarated by	Expensive looking

Experience happiness	Experts won't share this
Experience included	Explained
Experience the	Explained by
Experienced	Explanation
Experienced as	Explicit
Experienced in all aspects of	Explode
Experienced in all facets of	Explode your orders
Experienced in all phases of	Exploding
Experiential	Exploded
Experiment like	Exploit
Experimented	Explore new opportunities
Expert	Explore your
Expert advice	Explosion in profits
Expert choice	Explosive
Expert in your field	Explosive growth
Expert only information	Explosive influence tactics
Expert opinion	Exported
Expert solutions	Exposed
Expert testimonials	Exposure
Expertise	Express
Expertise	Express ordering
Experts agree	Express service
Experts say	Expressed

Expressible

Exquisite color

Exquisite elegance

Exquisite pleasure

Exquisitely detailed

Extend your

Extended

Extensible

Extension

Extensive

Extensive experience

Extensive involvement

Extensive marketing

Extensive training

Exterminate

External

Extinct

Extinction proof

Extinguished by many as

Extra

Extra energy

Extra exposure

Extra incentives

Extra income

Extra insurance

Extra money

Extra source of income

Extracted from

Extraction proof

Extraordinary

Extraordinary collection

Extraordinary resemblance

Extraordinary success

Extrasensory

Extravagant

Extravagant gift

Extreme

Extreme accuracy

Extreme caution

Extreme persuasion strategies

Extremely hard to find

Extremely informative

Extremely versatile

Exude/ooze

Eye candy

Eye catching

Eye catching style

Eye opening

Eye opening advice

Eye pleaser

Eye popping

Eye startling

Eyebrow raising

Eye-catching

Eye-popping

Eyewitness accounts

Eyewitnesses

E-zine advertising

E-zine friendly

Fabricated proof

Fabulous

Fabulous adventure

Fabulous collection

Fabulous taste

Face up

Face up to reality

Face value

Faceless

Fact

Fact finding

Fact sheet

Facts

Factor in

Factoring

Factory direct

Factory like

Facts and figures

Factual

Factual material

Fad like

Fad proof

Fail

Fail proof

Fail safe

Fail safe system

Fail safe tests

Failure

Faint hit of

Fair

Fair and square

Fair market value

Fair methods

Fair price

Fair shake

Fair value

Faith

Faithful

Faithfully

Fake out

Fall back on

Fall in love with

Fallen to $x

Fame

Fame and fortune

Familiar

Familiarized by

Family

Family run

Famine proof

Famous

Fan driven

Fancy

Fancy shmancy

Fantasies

Fantasize learning

Fantasy

Far and wide

Far fetched

Far flung

Far more than I expected

Far out

Far reaching consequences

Far seeing

Far surpasses anything

Fascinate

Fascinating

Fascinating figures

Fascinating ideas

Fascinating information

Fascinating results

Fashion

Fashion conscious

Fashion friendly

Fashionable mix

Fashioned

Fast

Fast acting

Fast and easy access

Fast and furious

Fast break

Fast breaking news

Fast delivery

Fast distribution

Fast food

Fast growing

Fast growing collection

Fast growing market

Fast moving

Fast pace

Fast results

Fast rising

Fast service

Fast turn-around

Faster

Faster service

Fastest

Fast-moving

Fast-setup

Fat free

Fatal

Fate

Father from the truth

Favorable

Favorable image

Favorite

Fear of

Feared by

Fearless

Feasible ideas

Feast

Feast on

Feast or famine

Featured

Features

Features include

Federal

Fee less

Feeble

Feed yourself

Feedback friendly

Feel like a million

Felt by many

Fervor

Fester

Festival like

Festive

Few and far between

Few clicks of the mouse

Few disagree

Few employees

Fewer the better

Fiber like

Fictional

Field of

Fielded by

Figure driven

Figure pointing

Figured by

Fill in

Fill in the blank

Filled with

Filler

Fills the bill

Filmed at

Filter proof

Filthy rich

Final offer

Finalized today

Finance

Financed

Financial

Financial abundance

Financial advice

Financial advisor

Financial collapse

Financial crisis

Financial dreams

Financial freedom

Financial gain

Financial goal

Financial independence

Financial position

Financial security

Financial statement

Financially beneficial

Financially independent life

Financing available

Find extra cash

Find hidden profits

Find out an easier way

Find out how to

Find smarter ways

Find success

Find the answer to

Finder's fee

Fine

Fine accent

Fine and dandy

Fine antique

Fine craftsmanship

Fine grained

Fine quality

Fine reputation

Fine texture

Fine tune your

Fine tune your biz

Fine workmanship

Finely crafted

Finest

Finest quality

Finish by

Fire breathing

Fire like

Fire off

Fire proof

Fire sale

Fire the boss!

Fire your boss

Fired

Fired up

Fireproof materials

Firm

Firm action

Firm believer in

Firm commitment

Firm hold

Firm policy

Firm support

Firmly placed

First

First and foremost

First class

First class company

First come first served

First degree

First generation

First hand

First-hand experience

First hand facts

First hand report

First impression

First line of defense

First month free

First of its kind

First place

First priority

First prize

First rate

First round

First strike

First time offered

First-class

Firsthand experience

Fist punching

Fist squeezing

Fit

Fit for a king

Fits all

Fits in your pocket

Fits your budget

Five

Five star

Five star rating

Fix up

Fixable

Fixed price

Fixed rate

Flabbergasted

Flame proof

Flannel

Flaring

Flash

Flash by

Flashed

Flat

Flat fee

Flat rate

Flatter

Flattery

Flaunt it

Flavor less

Flawless

Flawless integrity

Flawless system

Flee from

Flex your

Flexible

Flexibility

Flimsy

Flip over

Flirt with

Flood of

Flood of money

Flood of visitors

Floodgates of success

Floored by

Floral

Flourishing business

Flowing

Fluent in

Fluffy

Fluid like

Fluke

Flurry of

Flush out

Fly by night

Focus

Focus on

Focused

Foldable

Follow though

Follow up

Follow up message

Follow your dreams

Follow your heart

Follow your instincts

Follow your passions

Followed through

Follows directions

Follows through

Fool

Foolhardy

Foolish

Foolproof

Foolproof ideas

Foolproof methods

Foot loose

Foot stumping

For a beginner or pro

For a novice or expert

For a number of years

For a one-time fee of...

For a select few

For beginners or veterans

For better or for worse

For example

For less than $ you can

For less than the cost of

For most any budget

For serious collectors only

For the hell of it

For the low price of $

For the month of

For the next x buyers we

For those of you planning

Forbidden

Forbidden luxury

Forbidden secrets

Force field of

Forced by forced matrix

Force-fed foul

Forecast

Forecasted by

Foreclose on

Forefront of

Foreign

Foremost expert on

Forensic like

Foreplay

Foresight in

Foretell the future

Forever

Forfeit your

Forge

Forgery proof

Forget about

Forgetful

Forgivable

Forgive us for

Forgotten

Form and substance

Formalized offer

Formatted with

Formed by

Former customer

Formidable challenges

Formula

Formula for success

Formulated with

Forthcoming

Fortunate

Fortunately

Fortune

Forum of

Fossil like

Foul

Foul smelling

Found out

Foundation

Founded by

Founders of

Four

Four star

Four wheeled

Fourth

Foxy

Fraction of

Fraction of the cost

Fraction of the price

Fragile

Fragile economy

Fragrance

Fragrance free

Framed

Framework

Franchised

Franchising

Frank

Frantic

Fraud proof

Freak of

Freak out

Freakish

Freaky

Free

Free advertising

Free advice

Free and clear

Free approval

Free articles

Free bonus

Free booklet

Free brochure

Free cassette

Free classified ad

Free consultation

Free consulting

Free coupon

Free delivery

Free demonstration

Free details

Free distribution rights

Free download

Free e-book

Free e-course

Free email consolidation

Free email support

Free enterprise

Free estimate

Free estimate

Free excerpt

Free exposure

Free e-zine

Free e-zine submission

Free flowing

Free from pain

Free gift

Free gift subscription

Free gift with purchase

Free ideas

Free internet access

Free issue

Free lesson

Free market

Free membership

Free newsletter

Free of charge

Free parts

Free personal help

Free publicity

Free quote

Free replacement

Free report

Free reprint rights

Free resell rights

Free ride

Free sample

Free samples or trials

Free seminar

Free service

Free shipping

Free software

Free standing

Free subscription

Free support

Free telephone consulting

Free to join

Free training

Free trial

Free trial download

Free trial offer

Free up your time

Free vacation certificate

Free web site

Free with purchase

Free written evaluation

Free your schedule

Freely

Free/no obligation

Freebie

Freedom

Free freebie

Freelanced

Freelancing as

Freely

Freeze dry

Freeze proof

Freeze up

Frenzy

Frequency

Frequent

Fresh

Freshly

Fresh and targeted

Fresh detail

Fresh information

Fresh insights

Fresh look

Fresh originality

Fresh perspective

Fresh scent

Fresh start

Fresh thinking

Fresher

Freshly made

Friction proof

Fried

Friend like

Friendly

Friendly advice

Friendly terms

Frighten by

Frightening

Frigid

Fringe benefits

Frisky

From rags to riches

From start to finish

From the bottom up

Front line

Fronted by

Frost like

Frosted

Frown upon

Frozen

Frugal

Frugal times

Fruity

Fuel efficient

Fuel to the fire

Fugitive like

Fulfill

Fulfilled

Fulfilling a dream

Fulfilling a fantasy

Fulfillment driven

Full

Full blooded

Full blossom

Full blown

Full bodied

Full bodied taste

Full circle

Full color

Full course

Full coverage

Full effect

Full faced

Full fledged

Full grown

Full hearted

Full independence

Full length

Full level intelligence

Full or part time

Full page ad

Full range of

Full scale

Full service

Full size

Full size book

Full solution

Full spectrum

Full term

Full throttle

Full time

Full-featured

Fully

Fully assembled

Fully automated

Fully documented

Fully explained

Fully insured

Fully prepared

Fully restored

Fully searchable

Fully trackable

Fun

Function less

Functional

Fund raiser

Fundamental

Fundamental business principles

Fundamental component

Fundamental goals

Fundamentals

Funded by

Fungus proof

Funky

Funnel

Funnel in business

Funny

Furious with

Furnished

Future

Future earnings

Future of

Futures market

Gadget

Gag gift

Gain

Gain an edge

Gain an enormous following

Gain authority

Gain control of your life

Gain instant

Gain instant recognition

Gain new leads and customers

Gain pleasure

Gain prestigious

Gain status

Gain the upper hand

Gain valuable experience

Gaining a promotion

Gaining a skill

Gaining a talent

Gaining an advantage

Gaining free publicity

Gaining freedom

Gaining knowledge

Gaining on

Gaining popularity

Gaining time

Galactic

Galaxy like

Gallery of

Gamble less

Gambling

Game like

Game plan

Gamesmanship

Gang up

Gangster like

Garage sale

Garbage proof

Garnish with

Gas generated

Gas less

Gas powered

Gated

Gateway to

Gathered by

Gauge your

Gear down

Gear less

Gear shifting

Gear up

Geared for

Geeky

Gel

Gelled together

Gem like

Gems

Gender friendly

Gender specific

General

Generate a huge response

Generate cash on demand

Generate consistent revenue

Generate instant cash

Generate leads

Generate more leads

Generate qualified targeted leads

Generate sales

Generated

Generic

Generosity

Generous hospitality

Generous offer

Generous portion

Generous terms

Genetic

Genius

Gentle

Gently

Genuine

Genuine commitment

Genuine improvement

Genuine offer

Genuine opportunity

Genuine satisfaction

Genuinely

Geographical

Germ free

Germ less

Get

Get $ worth of bonus gifts

Get a bang out of

Get a free subscription to

Get a high ranking

Get a load off

Get a maximum return

Get a piece of the pie

Get a sneak peek at some

Get an x% discount

Get across

Get ahead

Get all dolled up

Get an edge

Get around

Get away

Get back on your feet

Get direct access to

Get dozens of

Get every technique I use

Get every tool I use

Get everything you need to

Get expert advice on

Get free advertising

Get in

Get into the swing of things

Get it without delay

Get more traffic

Get on auto pilot

Get on the stick

Get one under your belt

Get out of debt

Get paid

Get paid forever

Get readers interested

Get reciprocal links

Get repeat visitors

Get results

Get results -- order now!

Get results fast!

Get results overnight

Get rich quick

Get rid of financial
frustration

Get rid of money problems

Get something extra

Get spectacular results

Get started immediately

Get started in minutes

Get started overnight

Get started today

Get the ball rolling?

Get the best!

Get the buzz

Get the facts

Get the final word

Get the freedom you want

Get the goods on

Get the inside track

Get the last laugh

Get the most for your money

Get the picture

Get the upper hand

Get them to buy

Get these incentives

Get to the top

Get together

Get top placement

Get top rankings

Get up the nerve

Get with it

Get x free gifts

Get x page views

Get x surprise bonuses

Get x% off of selling price

Get your feet wet

Get your foot in the door

Get your hands on

Get your prospect's attention

Getting a bargain

Getting a discount

Getting a raise

Getting intense interest

Getting over obstacles

Ghost like

Ghostly

Giant

Giant like

Gift

Gift certificate

Gift with purchase

Gifted

Gifted marketer

Gigantic

Gigantic industry

Gigantic profit

Gimmick proof

Give

Give and take

Give away

Give back

Give in

Give me a chance

Give up

Give you an insiders

Giveaway rights

Giveaways

Gives you more flexibility

Gives you new insight

Glad

Gladly

Glamorized

Glamour driven

Glare less

Glaring

Glass

Glass clear

Glassy

Glazed

Glimmer of

Glimmer of hope

Glimmering

Glitch proof

Glittering

Global

Global achiever

Global commerce

Global market

Global marketing

Globalize

Globe like

Gloomy

Glorified by

Glorious

Glory gloss

Glossy

Glowing

Glowing acknowledgments

Glowing forecast

Glowing reviews

Glowing testimonials

Glued together

Go

Go along for the ride

Go down in history

Go for broke

Go for it

Go for the gold

Go the distance

Go to town

Goal

Goal oriented

Goal setting

Gobbledygook

Goes both ways

Going away from

Going bananas over

Going like clockwork

Going on

Going public

Going through the roof

Going value

Gold

Gold digger

Gold medal

Gold mine at your fingertips

Gold mine of secrets

Gold plated

Gold rush

Golden

Golden opportunity

Gone instantly

Good

Good advice

Good afternoon

Good and ready

Good as gold

Good by

Good customer service

Good day

Good deal

Good evening

Good faith	Governed
Good health	Government
Good humored	Government established
Good investment	Governmental
Good judgment	Grab their attention
Good listener	Grab your
Good looking	Grab your share
Good luck	Grace period
Good night	Graceful
Good quality	Graceful acknowledgments
Good reasons	Grade a
Good reviews	Gradual adjustment
Good sense	Gradual increase
Good taste	Graduate
Good year	Graduated from
Goods	Grainy
Good-tasting	Grand
Goodwill	Grand adventure
Goof proof	Grand opening
Goofy	Grand prize
Goosebumps	Grand scale
Gorgeous	Grand slam
Gossip	Grand times

Grand tour

Grant yourself

Granted by

Grape flavored

Graphic

Grass roots

Grassy

Grateful

Gratification

Gratifying

Grave consequences

Gray colored

Greasy

Great

Great bargain

Great deal

Great deal of money

Great for beginners

Great for novices

Great significance

Great wealth

Greater

Greatest

Greed

Greedy

Green colored

Grenade like

Grief stricken

Grim results

Gritty

Grog

Gross

Gross earnings

Gross income

Gross revenue

Gross sales

Ground breaking

Ground breaking findings

Ground breaking solutions

Ground floor

Ground floor opportunity

Ground out

Ground shaking

Ground speed

Grounded

Ground-floor offer

Ground-floor opportunity

Group like

Group ware

Grouped

Grow

Grow up

Grow your business

Grow your practice

Growing

Growing commitment

Growing competition

Growing craze

Growing day by day

Growing demand

Growth

Growth fund

Growth industry

Growth patterns

Growth potential

Growth segment

Grueling hours

Guarantee

Guarantee your success

Guaranteed

Guaranteed delivery

Guaranteed income

Guaranteed lowest price

Guaranteed overnight delivery

Guaranteed return

Guaranteed success

Guaranteed to work

Guaranteed visitors

Guarantees

Guard against

Guarded

Guarded secrets

Guardian angel

Guess

Guesswork

Guest

Guffaw

Guide

Guided

Guided tour

Guiding force

Guilt	Hand blistering
Guilty	Hand blown
Gullible	Hand carved
Gunning	Hand crafted
Guru	Hand held
Gut like	Hand made
Gutsy	Hand painted
Gutter less	Hand picked
Haberdashery	Hand powered
Habit	Hand set
Habit buying	Hand stamped
Habit forming	Hand stenciled
Habitual	Hand woven
Hack	Hand written
Hacker proof	Handier
Haggle the price	Handle the volume
Hair raising	Handling
Hairy	Hands free
Half baked	Hands free income
Half hearted	Hands free system
Half off	Hands on
Half price	Hands on demonstration
Halftone	Hands on experience

Hands on information

Hands on training

Handsome

Handsome benefit

Handsome offer

Handsome profit

Handy

Handy guide

Handy order form

Handy reference

Hang onto your hat

Happy

Happy alternative

Happy feeling

Happily

Hard

Hard bitten

Hard core

Hard drive

Hard earned

Hard facts

Hard hearted

Hard hitting

Hard hitting appeal

Hard liner

Hard nose

Hard-nosed approach

Hard offer

Hard one

Hard pressed

Hard shelled

Hard to beat

Hard to find

Hard to get

Hard to pin down

Hard to resist

Hard up

Hard wired

Hard working people

Hardball

Hard-hitting

Hardship

Hardware

Hardworking

Harmful

Harmless

Harness

Harness the power

Harsh economic times

Harshly

Harvest

Has been

Hassle free

Hassle-free

Hate

Haunted by

Haunting beauty

Have a ball

Have a heart

Have access within minutes

Have fun

Have it made

Have money to burn

Have the time of your life

Have them in your pocket

Have you

Have you been trying to?

Have you ever asked
yourself?

Have you ever purchased an

Have you ever wanted?

Have you ever wished?

Haven't seen it anywhere else

Haven't you

Having a fulfilling career

Having authority

Having excellent credit

Having high investment
returns

Having things easier

Having things faster

Hayseed

Hazardous

Hazardous free

Haze

Head fast

Head over heels

Head spinning

Head start

Head to head

Head turner

Head turning

Headache proof	Heat proof
Head-and-shoulders above	Heat up
Headline	Heat up your sales
Heads up	Heated
Headway	Heaven
Healing	Heaven sent
Healing	Heaven sent opportunity
Healthy	Heavenly
Healthy	Heavier
Healthy flow of customers	Heavily armed
Healthy income	Heavy
Healthy portion	Heavy duty
Heard working	Heavy handed
Heart felt	Heavy hitter
Heart pounding	Heavy weight
Heart rendering	Hefty
Heart stirring discovery	Hefty gain
Heart to heart advice	Hefty profits
Hearty	Heighten
Heartfelt	Hell bent
Heartfelt appeal	Hell like
Hearty	Hell or high water
Hearty nutrients	Hello

Help

Help desk

Help you personally

Helpful

Helped many

Helpful invention

Helpful reference

Helpful service

Helping people like you

Helpless

Helps you

Helps you____every step of the way

Here are my credentials

Here is a summary

Here is how you can

Here to stay

Here's a fact for you

Here's a list of common

Here's a quick recap

Here's a small sample

Here's a summary of

Here's my actual check "your affiliate check"

Here's my web site stats

Here's proof

Here's something that will

Here's the bottom line

Here's what other say "testimonials"

Here's what you'll learn

Here's what you'll receive

Here's x reasons why you

Here's your opportunity to

Hero like

Heroic

Heroic status

Hesitant with

Heyday

Hi

Hidden

Hidden gold mine

Hidden secrets

Hidden strengths

Hidden wealth

High

High achievement

High and mighty

High budget

High caliber

High click through rate

High conversion ratio

High cut

High definition

High degree of

High demand

High end features

High energy level

High ethical standards

High expectations

High flying

High frequency

High grade

High hopes

High impact strategies

High income products

High intensity

High key agenda

High level

High level of expertise

High level strategies

High margin products

High octane

High paying

High payoff

High percentage

High performance

High pitched

High potential

High powered

High pressure

High priced

High priority

High probability

High productive output

High profile

High profile industries

High profit margin

High profit potential

High quality

High Quality Company

High quality goods

High quality products

High ranking

High results

High return

High return investment

High rise

High rise enterprise

High risk

High roller

High security

High speed

High speed traffic

High spirited

High standards

High status lifestyle

High strung

High tech

High tech innovation

High tech service

High tension

High ticket items

High turnover

High velocity

High voltage

High volume

High wage

High-class

Higher

Higher click rates

Higher conversions

Higher income

Higher paying

Higher profit margins

Higher sales conversion

Highest

Highest commission offered

Highest paid people

Highest paying clients

Highest quality

Highest recommendation ever

Highest recommendations

Highest response anywhere

Highest standards

Highest-rated

High-growth

High-impact

Highlight

Highlighted

Highly acclaimed seminar

Highly ambitious

Highly articulate

Highly competitive

Highly complex

Highly customizable

Highly endorsed

Highly guarded

Highly motivated

Highly organized

Highly persuasive

Highly prosperous people

Highly rated ____

Highly recommended

Highly regarded

Highly respected

Highly selective

Highly sensitive information

Highly skilled

Highly skilled marketers

Highly sophisticated

Highly specialized

Highly trained

Highly-rated

High-rolling

High-speed

High-tech

Hilarious

Hire us

Hired by

Historic

Historic treasure

Historical

Historical material

History making

History of prior successes

History rich

Hit and miss

Hit counter spinning

Hit or miss

Hit the bull's eye

Hit the jackpot

Hit their sweet spots

Hit's the spot

Hoax

Hobnob

Hold prospects attention

Holiday

Holiday favorite

Holiday price

Holiday sale

Hollow

Hollowed out

Holocaust

Home based business

Home business

Home grown

Home made

Home office

Home stead

Homemade

Honest

Honest methods

Honest truth

Honesty

Honor

Honorable

Honorary

Hook, line and sinker

Hope

Hopeful situation

Hordes of customers

Hordes of visitors

Horizon expanding

Horizontal

Horrendous figures

Horrible conditions

Horribly

Horrific

Horrified by

Horsey

Hospitable

Hospitality driven

Hosted by

Hostile competition

Hostile takeover

Hot

Hot and cold

Hot business model

Hot commodity

Hot issue

Hot product

Hot property

Hot selling

Hot tempered

Hot ticket

Hotheaded

Hotshot

Hotter

Hottest

Hour long

Hourly

How a simple

How and where to

How and why to

How anyone can

How come

How do you

How does

How I ___ in one week

How I get at least

How I made $

How I once

How I took a

How important is

How I've earned

How many times have you

How often to

How one man

How one person

How one woman

How to

How to absolutely

How to actually see

How to add

How to always

How to automatically

How to avoid

How to become an

How to build

How to buy

How to choose

How to come up with

How to create

How to decide

How to design

How to determine your

How to develop

How to double

How to earn

How to eliminate

How to ensure

How to establish

How to find

How to gain

How to generate

How to get

How to get rid of

How to get your hands on

How to give your

How to have

How to identify

How to increase

How to install

How to instantly

How to know exactly

How to know if

How to launch a

How to legally

How to literally

How to locate

How to maintain

How to make

How to manage

How to never again

How to obtain

How to operate

How to overcome

How to pick

How to present

How to produce

How to promote

How to pull in $

How to quickly

How to reduce

How to roll out

How to select

How to sell

How to send

How to set up

How to spend

How to spot

How to start

How to stop

How to take

How to tap into

How to tell if

How to triple

How to turn

How to use

How understanding the

How would you feel knowing?

How would you like to

How you can

How…?

Howdy

Huge

Huge amount

Huge collection

Huge compilation

Huge demand

Huge difference

Huge discount

Huge fortune

Huge industry

Huge money maker

Huge proportions

Huge quantities

Huge selection

Huge success

Human like

Humane

Humble

Humbling display

Humorless

Humorous

Hundreds

Hundreds sold

Hungry

Hungry crowd of customers

Hunky dory

Hurricane

Hurry

Hurry! Offer ends soon

Hustle and bustle

Hustle proof

Hygiene

Hyped up

Hyper feeling

Hyperactive

Hypnotic

Hypnotic effects

Hypnotize

Hypnotized prospects

Hypoallergenic

I "benefit" in X days

I "benefit" in X weeks

I "benefit" over X %

I "benefit" up to X %

I "benefit" X thousand in X weeks

I "benefit pounds in X months

I "benefits" less than X hours

I almost bought it again

I am about to tell you a

I am excited to

I appreciate your interest

I couldn't wait to

I don't care if you're

I don't care what

I don't have to convince you of

I don't want to waste

I first got involved in

I graduated from college

I grew up in "location" in the "year"

I have a confession to make

I have a degree in

I have first-hand experience

I heard from

I heard on "source" that

I highly recommend

I just have to say

I know from experience

I know this sounds

I know you

I know you don't have

I know you're busy

I know you're skeptical

I know you've been

I love it

I normally charge

I normally charge up to $

I picture you

I promise to

I rarely endorse products but

I rate it X out of X

I read in a "source" that

I remember back about
""years

I saw on "source" that

I sense you

I stand behind the product

I think you'll agree

I trust you'll

I was blown away

I was reluctant at first

I was skeptical but

I would have paid

Icon like

I'd like to make you a
promise

Idea

Idea driven

Idea generation

Ideal

Ideal choice

Ideal condition

Ideal customer

Ideas

Identical

Identifiable

Identification checked

Identified

Idiot proof

Idiotic

Idol

Idolized by

If I can do it you can

If I were you

If you

If you already

If you are looking for a
simple

If you are seriously

If you aren't familiar with

If you buy now

If you could have

If you decide

If you give me x minutes to

If you learn nothing else

If you like the idea of

If you really want to

If you thought

If you want a

If you want the answers to

If you want to know how

If you would like to

If you would like to learn

If you're currently

If you're like me

If you're like most

If you're looking for

If you're planning to

If you're ready to

If you're serious about

If you're tired of

If you've been looking

If you've been wanting to

If you've ever thought about

If you've ever wondered

If you've read every

If you've tried to

If you've watched

Ignitable

Ignite your

Ignite your profits

Ignite your sales

Ignorant proof

Ignore the

Ill advised

I'll also throw in

I'll assume you've

I'll be completely honest with you about

I'll bet you anything that

Ill feeling

I'll get straight to the point

I'll help you

Ill judged

I'll keep my word

I'll make you a promise

Ill mannered

Ill nature

I'll personally guarantee

I'll refund your money

I'll refund your purchase

I'll show you how to

I'll show you the following

I'll show you where

I'll teach you

I'll tell you exactly how to

I'll throw in X bonuses

Illegal

Illuminated

Illustrated

I'm about to reveal to you

I'm absolutely amazed

I'm confident that

I'm definitely impressed

I'm going to show you

I'm no rookie

I'm not going to waste your time

I'm not kidding

I'm sensing that you

I'm so "emotion" today

I'm speechless

I'm sure you agree with

I'm sure you heard of

I'm sure you know from experience

I'm sure you'll agree that

I'm sure you're

I'm very satisfied

Image driven

Imaginable

Imaginary

Imagination

Imagination friendly

Imaginative

Imagine making $

Imagine that

Imagined by

Immeasurable

Immeasurable importance

Immediate

Immediate access

Immediate action

Immediate cash flow

Immediate cash surge

Immediate change

Immediate response

Immediately

Immediately after you order

Immediately downloadable

Immense appeal

Immense fortune

Immense improvement

Immense relief

Immense satisfaction

Immense size

Immerse yourself with

Immobilize your

Immoral

Immortal

Immovable

Immune to

Impacted by

Impeccable

Impeccable guide

Impeccable policy

Impeccable reputation

Imperial

Implemented

Important

Important addition

Important factor

Imported

Impose your

Impossible

Impossible to fail

Impractical

Impress your

Impression driven

Impressive

Impressive ability

Impressive demonstration

Impressive findings

Impressive packaging

Impressive statistics

Impressive technology

Imprinted

Improper to

Improve

Improve customer retention

Improve customer service

Improve every area of your life

Improve link popularity

Improve your business

Improve your life

Improve your lifestyle

Improve your sales

Improved

Improved version

Improvement

Improvise

Impulse buying

Impulse like

Impulsive

In

In "month/year"

In "year"

In "year" I

In a big way

In a few minutes

In a flash

In business for "number" decades

In case

In charge of

In close

In constant demand

In demand

In demand product

In depth

In depth analysis

In depth report

In depth study

In excellent condition

In flesh and blood

In full swing

In hot pursuit

In house

In less than no time

In line

In minutes

In my humble opinion

In my opinion

In need

In order to ""you need

In prelaunch

In record numbers

In season

In seconds

In short supply

In stock

In store

In style

In the bag

In the black

In the lap of luxury

In the long run

In the next X minutes

In the nick of time

In the red

In this article you're going to

In this day and age

In this letter you're going to

In this report you're going to

In today's

In X or less

In your best interests

In your spare time

Inactive

Inappropriate

In-between jobs

Inbound

Incalculable profits

Incalculable worth

Incapable of

Incendiary

Incentive for buying

Incentive

Incentives

Inch by inch

Inched

Incidental

Included with

Includes a high tech formula for

Includes useful resources

Includes X issues

Income

Income enhancing

Income literally overnight

Income on the line

Income statement

Income stream

Income tax

Incoming

Incomparable

Incompatible of

Incomplete

Inconceivable

Inconclusive

Inconsiderate businesses

Inconspicuous

Incontestable

Incontestable proof

Inconvenient

Incorporate

Incorporated

Incorporation

Incorrect numbers

Increase

Increase affiliate
commissions

Increase leads

Increase leverage

Increase perceived value

Increase profits

Increase readership

Increase renewals

Increase sales

Increase sales anytime

Increase subscribers

Increase the dollar value

Increase their average order
amount

Increase your

Increase your bank account

Increase your cash flow

Increase your closing ratio

Increase your popularity

Increase your sales volume

Increase your success

Increased

Increasing

Increasing affiliate partners

Increasing profits

Increasing sales

Increasing traffic

Increasingly

Incredible

Incredible announcement

Incredible benefits

Incredible results

Incredible sight

Incredible sums of money

Incredibly easy

Incredibly easy to use

Incredibly low budget

Indebted to helping you

Indeed you can

Indefinite supply

In-demand

Independence

Independent

Independent company

Independent contractor

Independent professionals

Independence

In-depth

Indestructible

Indestructible material

Indexed by

Indispensable

Indispensable component

Indisputable evidence

Indisputable proof

Individual effort

Indoor

Indulge in

Industrial

Industrial strength

Industrialized

Industry

Industry experts

Industry leader

Industry leading

Industry secrets

Industry's leading experts

Ineffective

Inefficient

Ineligible for

Inestimable benefits

Inexpensive

Inexplicable

Infamous

Inferior to

Infiltrate your

Infinite benefits

Infinite possibilities

Infinity

Inflatable

Inflated prices

Inflation prone economy

Inflation proof

Inflation-beating

Influence

Influence buying behavior

Influence others

Influence your prospects

Influenced by

Infomercial

Inform yourself on

Informative

Informal

Information

Information highway

Information superhighway

Informational

Informed

Informed advice

Ingenious

Ingenious design

Ingenious mechanics

Ingenious methods

Ingenious tactics

Ingenious technique

Ingredient

Inhabited by

Inherit our

Inhuman

Inhumane

Initial

Initial public offering

Initially employed

Injury free

Inner

Inner circle

Innermost

Innocent

Innovated

Innovation

Innovative

Innovative approach

Innovative concept

Innovative creation

Innovative skills

Innovator in

Inopportune time

Ins and outs

Insane

Insane amounts of traffic

Insane not to buy

Insane prices

Insanely profitable

Insatiable

Inscribed with

Insecure

Inside

Inside knowledge

Insider

Insider discoveries

Insider information

Insider knowledge

Insider secrets to

Insidious

Insightful

Insightful

Inspected by

Inspection checked

Inspiration

Inspired

Installation free

Installed

Installed by

Installment plan

Instant

Instant access

Instant access product

Instant acclaim

Instant e-mail notifications

Instant fortune

Instant impacted

Instant magic

Instant message

Instant money machine

Instant reference

Instant relief

Instant results

Instant success

Instantaneous

Instantly

Instantly learn

Instituted by

Institution like

In -store repairs

Instructed

Instructional instructions

Instructive

Instrumental in

Insubstantial amount of

Insufficient

Insufficient income

Insulated

Insurable

Insurance

Insure yourself

Insured by

Intact

Intangible

Integral part

Integrate your

Integrated by

Integrity

Intellect

Intellectual

Intellectual atmosphere

Intellectual property

Intellectually

Intellectually appealing

Intelligence

Intelligent

Intense

Intense commitment

Intensify your sales

Intensive study

Intent on

Interactive

Interactive experience

Interchangeable

Interest free

Interest free findings

Interest less

Interest rate

Interest-free

Interest

-free financing

Interesting

Interesting adventure

Interesting developments

Interesting invention

Interfaced with

Interior designed

Interlocking

Intermediate

Internal problem

Internally secret

International

International acclaim

International attention

International best seller

International reputation

Internationally known

Internet

Internet access

Internet marketing

Internet marketing guru
internet presence

Interpreted by

Interrupt your

Intervention

Interview free

Interviewed by

Intimate moment

Intoxicating

Intriguing

Intriguing collection

Intriguing details

Intriguing features

Intriguing ideas

Intriguing results

Intriguing scene

Introducing

Introduction

Introductory offer

Introductory price

Introductory price of only

Introductory rates

Intruder proof

Intuition driven

Intuitive

Invalid

Invaluable

Invaluable advice

Invaluable facts

Invaluable help

Invasion

Invent your future

Invented

Invention

Inventive

Inventive tactics

Inventory controlled

Inverted

Invest in our product today

Invest now

Invest today and receive

Investment

Invested in

Investigate

Investigated by

Investigation

Investigative

Investing

Investment

Investment bank

Investment banker

Investment quality

Investor like

Invincible

Invisible

Invite your friends

Invited by

Inviting

Inviting offer

Invoiced by

Involuntary

Involve yourself

Involved in

Iron like

Ironclad

Ironclad guarantee

Irrefutable

Irreplaceable

Irresistible

Irresistible appeal

Irresistible magnetism

Irresistible sales letter

Irresistible temptation

Irresponsibility

IRS

Is ___ a problem for you?

Is it possible that

Is provided with

Isolate yourself from

Issued by

It actually delivers

It blows my mind

It can't be matched

It can't hurt

It could mean the difference

It could take you years

It doesn't matter how

It far exceeded my wildest

It has been about X years since

It is by far

It is for people that

It makes sense buy now

It over delivers

It seems that everywhere

It sells its self

It simply works

It surprises me how most people

It took "time" of research

It walks you through

It was just another typical day

It will boggle your mind

It would take several

It's "time" on a "day"

It's a breeze

It's a fact that

It's a must

It's a steal

It's absolutely crucial you learn

It's all covered in

It's all here

It's allowed me to

It's almost ""years old

It's better than nothing

Its common knowledge that

It's confidential

It's critical to have this information

It's important to understand that

It's in our X year

It's just what you need

It's more like a library

It's not for everyone

It's not the same old ___ you use to

It's numbered

It's quite obvious

It's sold over X copies

It's that easy

It's that good

It's the only ___ that ___

Itty bitty

I've discovered a

I've found the secret to

I've just put together

I've personally found

I've recently

I've recently developed a

I've sold over $

I've taught

I've taught " " seminars about

I've written

I've written over " " on

Jacked up fees

Jackpot

Jail

Jam packed

Jargon free

Jargon less

Jaw dropping

Jazz up your sales

Jealous feeling

Jealously guarded

Jeopardizing your

Jeopardy

Jerked around

Jesting

Jet lagged

Jewel like

Jim-dandy

Job satisfaction

Jobless

Join now

Join our affiliate program

Join our reseller program

Join the club

Join the winners!

Join the X% who

Join today

Joined by

Joint enterprise

Joint facility

Joint venture

Joint venture opportunities

Joyful

Judged by

Judgment

Judgmental

Judicial like

Juicy

Juicy profit

Juicy story

Jump on the bandwagon

Jump start your

Jump start your orders

Junky looking

Just $ for a membership

Just a few minutes

Just a taste of the

Just between you and me

Just cash the checks

Just cause

Just last week

Just one "benefit" will pay for

Just plug in and sell

Just published

Just released

Just sit back and relax

Just small sample of

Just the other day

Just the ticket

Just what the doctor ordered

Justice

Justice driven

Justifiable alternative

Justified price

Just-in-time

Keen delight

Keen insights

Keep 100% of each sale

Keep customers

Keep customers happy

Keep every penny

Keep prospects interested

Keep quiet about

Keep the free bonuses

Keep the profits rolling?

Keep their eyeballs locked

Keep them glued to your

Keep then on the edge of their seat

Keep this to yourself

Keep up with the competition

Keep up with the times

Keep x% of the profits

Keep your costs down

Keep your customers

Keeps you abreast of

Keeps you ahead of the game

Keeps you informed with

Kerfuffle

Key account

Key fact

Key issue

Keynote

Kick butt

Kick off

Kick start your business

Kid friendly

Kill two birds with one stone

Killer

Killer application

Killer marketing schemes

Killer prices

Killer reviews

Killer strategy

Killer tactics

Killer ways

Kind act

Kindhearted

King like

Kiss your boss goodbye

Kissable	Laced
Knee deep	Lackluster
Knee jerking	Ladylike
Knee slapping	Laid back
Knock on wood	Laid off
Knock out	Lame
Know how	Land locked
Know how to	Landmark
Know it all	Landmark announcement
Know the ropes	Large
Knowledge	Large amount
Knowledge about	Large collection
Knowledge base	Large company
Knowledge incentive	Large earning potential
Knowledge of	Large market
Knowledge sources	Large minded
Knowledgeable	Large package
Knowledgeable service	Large savings
Known by	Large scale
Lab tested	Large share
Labor less	Large size
Labor saving equipment	Larger
Laboring	Larger than life

Largest

Largest ever

Largest selection

Largest-selling

Lascivious

Laser like precision

Last

Last but not least

Last chance

Last gasp

Last minute

Last resort

Last stand

Last straw

Last week

Last year

Lasting

Lasting impact

Lasting impression

Lasting legend

Lasting reputation

Lasting solution

Lasting stability

Lasting success

Latch on to

Late notice

Late-breaking

Latest

Latest craze

Latest fad

Latest sensation

Latest technology

Launching

Launched today

Lavish

Lavish amount

Lavish gift

Lavish praise

Lavishly

Law abiding

Law like

Lawful

Lawsuit

Lay it on the line

Lay your cards on the table

Layaway

Layering

Lazy

Lazy mans

Lead generation

Lead in

Lead yourself to

Leadership

Leadership qualities

Leading

Leading case

Leading cause

Leading edge

Leading indicator

Leading motive

Leading name

Leading question

Leak proof

Lean

Leaner

Leaps and bounds

Learn

Learn about

Learn about all the

Learn closely guarded

Learn everyday

Learn everything from a to z

Learn everything from start to finish

Learn everything I've learned

Learn exactly what

Learn fresh tips

Learn from my experience

Learn from my mistakes

Learn from other pros

Learn how to

Learn little known resources

Learn new

Learn to

Learn to harness

Learn to write

Lease or buy

Lease to buy

Leasing is available

Least expensive

Least known

Leather like

Leave the rat race

Leaves no stone unturned

Lectured by

Led by

Left handed

Leg kicking

Leg pulling

Leg up

Legacy

Legal

Legal advice

Legal jointure

Legalized

Legally

Legally and ethically

Legally increase your sales

Legally steal business

Legend

Legendary

Legendary discovery

Legendary masterpiece

Legendary success

Legendary supreme

Legendary tycoon

Legislation proof

Legit

Legitimacy

Legitimate

Legitimate concerned

Legitimate opportunity

Legitimate source of cash

Leisure like

Leisurely

Lengthy study

Less hassle

Lessons learned

Let down

Let me introduce myself

Let me share with you

Let me tell you the story

Let your hair down

Lethal

Lethal mistakes

Let's examine the

Let's get down to business

Let's have it

Let's talk about

Level of service

Level off

Leveled

Levels of performance

Leveraging the media

Liability

Liberal

Liberated

Liberty

License to resell

Licensed rights

Licensing

Licensing agreement

Lick

Lies

Life and death

Life changing

Life changing secrets

Life giving

Life less

Life like

Life of riches

Life or death

Life saving

Life threatening

Lifeblood

Lifesaver

Lifestyle you deserve

Lifetime

Lifetime commission

Lifetime commitment

Lifetime guarantee

Lifetime income

Lifetime membership

Lifetime of wealth

Lifetime revenue

Lifetime traffic

Lifetime warranty

Lifetime money back

Light

Light minded

Light up your traffic

Light weight

Light years ahead of competition

Lightened

Lightning fast results

Lightest

Lightly scented

Lightweight

Light-weight

Likable

Like a million

Like a ton of bricks

Like clockwork

Like gangbusters

Like minded

Like new

Like no other

Like you, I have

Limber

Limit buying resistance

Limit your

Limited

Limited access

Limited availability

Limited budget

Limited edition

Limited number of affiliates

Limited supply

Limited time

Limited-time offer -- may be withdrawn at any time!

Limitless

Line of action

Line of communication

Line of credit

Line of duty

Line of products

Links to

Lip puckering

Lip smacking

Liquidated

Little

Little by little you

Little effort

Little known

Little known techniques

Little money

Little time

Little used

Live	Lock and key
Live dangerously	Lock out
Live now	Lock, stock and barrel
Live smarter not harder	Locked
Live very comfortably	Log in
Live your dream	Log on
Lively	Logic driven
Livelihood	Logical
Lively	Logical addition
Livid color	Logical choice
Living legend	Lollygag
Living proof	Lonely
Loaded	Long
Loaded with	Long abandon
Loan you	Long awaited
Loathsome	Long distance
Loaves of	Long established
Lobbied by	Long established industry
Local	Long haul
Localized	Long lasting
Locally sold	Long lasting influence
Locatable	Long lasting partnerships
Located in	Long lasting relief

Long legged

Long lived

Long lost edition

Long over due

Long range

Long range strategy

Long range threat

Long standing

Long standing commitment

Long standing policy

Long standing relationship

Long standing tradition

Long suffering

Long term

Long term business success

Long term commitment

Long term compensation

Long term gain

Long term hospitality

Long term remedy

Long term residual traffic

Long term vision

Long winded

Longevity

Look at our client list

Look at these case studies

Look at these comments

Look at what's inside

Look like a million dollars

Look out

Look up our

Look what's included

Looks so real

Looming

Loose

Loose cannon

Loose fit

Lose your

Loser

Lost

Lost cause

Lost opportunity

Lots of cash

Lottery like

Loud

Loud and clear

Lovable

Love

Love at first sight

Love it or leave it

Loved

Loved by many

Lovely accommodation

Lovely sight

Low

Low alcohol

Low budget

Low calorie

Low cut

Low factory prices

Low fat

Low interest

Low interest rates

Low key

Low keyed

Low level

Low maintenance

Low minimum

Low numbered edition

Low overhead

Low paying

Low payment

Low pressure

Low price

Low profile

Low rate

Low rates

Low risk

Low startup cost

Low strung

Lowdown

Lower

Lower class

Lower costs

Lower income

Lower prices

Lower your

Lowest

Lowest price

Lowest prices ever

Lowlife

Low-risk solution

Loyal	Lust
Loyal enthusiasts	Luxurious
Loyal followers	Luxurious accommodations
Loyal support	Luxurious comfort
Loyalty	Luxurious style
Lubricated	Luxury
Luck	Luxury of earning
Lucky	Lying
Lucky for you	Machine like
Lucrative	Machine made
Lucrative global business	Machine washable
Lucrative industries	Mad about
Lucrative industry	Made by
Lucrative internet business	Made in
Lucrative investment	Made to order
Lucrative line of products	Made untold millions
Lucrative partnerships	Magazine like
Lucrative situation	Magazine mentioned
Lump sum	Magenta colored
Lunatic	Magic
Lurking	Magic formula
Luscious	Magic like
Luscious colors	Magical

Magical remedy

Magical scene

Magically increase

Magnet like

Magnetic

Magnetizing

Magnificent

Magnificent collection

Magnificent color

Magnificent future

Magnificent ideas

Magnificent treasure

Mail today!

Mailing list tested

Main goal is

Mainstream

Maintain momentum

Maintain rapport

Maintained by

Maintenance free

Major

Major announcement

Major breakthrough

Major cause

Major commitment

Major company

Major corporations

Major influence

Major issue

Major objectives

Major priority

Major wealth opportunity

Majority of people

Make $

Make $ per hour

Make $ per month

Make $ per year

Make 100% commission

Make a bundle

Make a career change

Make a fantastic living

Make a fortune

Make a fortune overnight

Make a go of it

Make a killing

Make a living

Make a long story short

Make a lot of money

Make a minimum of $

Make a score

Make additional income

Make affiliate revenue

Make as much money as you want

Make at least $

Make back X times your purchase

Make believing

Make extra income

Make it big

Make it happen

Make it snappy

Make maximum use of

Make millions

Make money

Make money at home

Make money at will

Make money at your computer

Make money online

Make money your first day

Make more money

Make or break

Make over

Make people visit

Make reoccurring income

Make sales day and night

Make short work of

Make sure your

Make the move

Make them do your bidding

Make thousands

Make tons of money

Make up to $ each week

Make up your mind

Make waves

Make wheelbarrows of cash

Make X your investment

Make X$ commission

Make you rich

Make yourself

Make yourself a fortune

Make yourself a home

Makes a great gift

Making money

Making money automatically

Mall like

Mammoth

Mammoth collection

Man like

Man made

Man sized

Man slaughter

Manage a team

Manage your

Manageable

Managed by

Management advice

Management run

Mandatory

Maneuver

Maneuverability

Manhandled

Mania

Manifest your

Manipulated by

Manipulation proof

Mankind

Manual like

Manufactured by

Many ""have concluded that

Many people

Map like

Maple flavored

Marginal improvement

Marginal return

Markdown

Marked down

Market

Market capacity

Market demand

Market downturn

Market driven

Market driven company

Market identity

Market leader

Market moves

Market niche

Market oriented company

Market penetration	Markup
Market planning	Maroon colored
Market potential	Marquee
Market research	Marriage like
Market risk	Marvelous design
Market saturation	Marvelous opportunity
Market share	Masculine
Market value	Mashed
Marketability	Masked
Marketed	Mass
Marketing	Mass marketing
Marketing campaigns	Mass produced
Marketing ethics	Massive
Marketing etiquette	Massive amounts of money
Marketing help	Massive back end profits
Marketing masters	Massive collection
Marketing mix	Massive income
Marketing phenomena	Massive index
Marketing pioneers	Massive operation
Marketing rights	Massive reduction
Marketing savvy	Massive supply
Marketing success	Massive traffics floods
Marketing tools	Master

Master of your destiny

Master reprint rights

Master the art of

Master your own destiny

Mastermind

Masterpiece

Matched together

Matchless perfection

Matchless power

Material like

Maternal

Mathematical

Matter of fact

Mature

Maul

Mauve colored

Maverick

Maximize performance

Maximize your money

Maximized

Maximum

Maximum achievement

Maximum effectiveness

Maximum efficiency

Maximum income potential

Maximum results

Maximum security

Maximum strength

Maybe you can finally

Meal like

Meaningful

Meaningful benefits

Meaningful investment

Measurable

Measurable results

Measure the competition

Measure up

Measured

Measures approximately

Mechanical

Medal of

Media

Media attention

Media blitz

Media goals

Mediated by

Medical	Mentored by
Medicine like	Mentoring program
Medieval	Menu like
Medium	Merchandise
Meet deadlines	Merchandised
Meet me halfway	Merchant
Meeting friendly	Merchant account
Mega	Merger
Mega earnings	Mergers and acquisitions
Mega traffic techniques	Merry
Megabucks	Meshed together
Mellow	Mesmerize
Melt away	Mesmerize your customers
Melt the resistance	Messed up
Meltdown	Metal
Member	Metallic
Member of	Metric
Member sign in	Micro
Members only	Microchip
Membership site	Microwavable
Memorabilia	Microwave safe
Memorable	Mid life
Memorable surprise	Middle

Middle class

Middleman

Midway

Midweek

Mighty

Military

Military backed

Milk it for all it's worth

Millennium

Million dollar

Million dollar secret

Millions

Millions of people want

Millions of potential customers

Millions sold

Mind blowing

Mind boggling

Mind busting

Mind expanding

Mind opening

Mind rocking

Mind-boggling

Mindful

Mingled

Mini

Miniature

Minimal

Minimal instruction

Minimal investment

Minimal learning curve

Minimal promotion

Minimal resistant

Minimize

Minimize hassles

Minimize returns

Minimized

Minimum

Minimum effort

Minimum supervision

Minimum work

Minor adjustment

Minority owned

Mint

Mint condition

Miracle

Miraculous	Modified
Mired	Moist
Mission statement	Mom and pop business
Mistake	Moment of truth
Mistake proof	Money
Mistaken	Money back guarantee
Mistakes to avoid	Money from home
Mixable	Money in record time
Mixed	Money is no object
Mixture like	Money isn't everything
Mobile	Money just pours in
Modeled	Money less
Modeled organization	Money making concepts
Moderate	Money making ideas
Moderate cost	Money making opportunities
Moderated	Money making opportunity
Modern	Money making robot
Modern day	Money making web site
Modern device	Money management
Modern equipment	Money on demand
Modernized	Money saving
Modest income	Money saving coupon
Modifiable	Money talks

Money vacuum

Money well spent

Money while you sleep

Money-grubbing

Moneymaker

Money-making

Money-making facts

Money-saving

Monitored

Monologue

Monopoly like

Monster looking

Monthly

Monthly check

Monthly royalties

Monumental

Monumental collection

Morale

More bang for your buck

More clients than you can handle

More in less time

More than I ever expected

More than x hours of

More than x years

Mortal like

Mortgage

Mortgage broker

Most

Most accessible

Most advanced

Most businesses know

Most fail

Most important investment

Most overlooked

Most prized

Most trusted

Most underrated

Mother of all

Motherly

Motivate

Motivate prospects

Motivate your affiliates

Motivate your employees

Motivated

Motivation

Motivational

Motive driven

Mountain of cash

Mouth filling

Mouth opening

Mouth watering

Mouthwatering menu

Movable

Movers and shakers

Moxie

Much read

Much used

Multi colored

Multi-faceted

Multi grade

Multi-million dollar

Multi-million dollar business

Multi-national corporations

Multi user

Multi-brand strategy

Multifunctional

Multi-functional

Multilevel selling

Multimedia

Multiple

Multiple branding

Multiple income streams

Multiple products to sell

Multiple revenue streams

Multiple streams of income

Multiplied

Multiply my efforts

Multiply the results

Multiply your

Multiply your influence

Multiply your links

Multiply your repeat sales

Multiply your sales

Municipal

Murder

Mushroomed

Musical

Must attend event

Must have

Must read

Must see

Muted

Mutual

Mutual exceptions

Mutual fund

Mutual understanding

Mutually

My actual pay check

My bank deposit

My best investment

My biggest complaint is

My first reaction was

My gut reaction is

My highest rating

My most cherish possessions

My name is

My only regret is

My overall rating is

My reputation is on the line

My sales by months

My secret sources for

My sure fire method

My very first day I made

My x minute

My x part formula for

Mysterious

Mystery like

Mystic

Mystical

Myth like

Mythical

Nail biting

Nailed down

Naked

Naked truth

Named the

Nameless

Narrow

Narrow minded

Nasty

Nation wide

National

National brand

National craze

National treasure

Nationally

Nationwide

Natural	Necessary requirement
Natural born	Necessary tools
Natural color	Necessity
Natural finish	Neck breaking
Natural growth	Need be
Natural ingredients	Need I say more?
Natural quality	Needs
Naturally you will	Needy
Nature friendly	Negative
Naughty	Negative cash flow
Naughty secrets	Negotiable price
Navigated by	Negotiate
Navigation	Negotiated
Nazi	Neighborly
Near miss	Neon
Near perfect	Nerdy
Near perfect achievement	Nerve racking
Near record	Nest egg
Near you	Net
Neat	Net earnings
Neato	Net income
Necessary	Net profits
Necessary parts	Net revenue

Net sales

Net worth

Netiquette

Netted over

Network marketing

Network of customers

Network security

Networked

Networking like

Never

Never be laid off

Never been released

Never been removed from box

Never ceases to amaze me

Never cut corners again

Never ending

Never ending source

Never ending stream of green

Never ending supply

Never ending traffic

Never failing

Never get ripped off

Never have to deal with

Never heard of information

Never live pay check to pay check

Never opened

Never out dated

Never pay a penny

Never pay for advertising

Never say never

Never seen anything like it

Never seen before

Never seen before information

Never shell out money

Never struggle again

Never throw away money again

Never to be forgotten

Never used in circulation

Never wait for checks

Never worry about

Never worry about money again

New

New age

New and improved

New and used

New approach to business

New blood

New bread

New concept

New dimension

New economy

New found

New found wealth

New ground

New leads every week

New lease on life

New look

New niche

New order

New release

New standard

New style

New twist

New vision

New wave

New world

New Year

Newbie friendly

Newbies

Newer

Newest

Newest fad

Newest information

Newfound

Newly

News

News break

News case

News clip

News group

News mentioned

News release

News room

News service

News sheet

Newscast

Newsworthiness

Newsworthy

Newsworthy event

Next best

Next frontier

Next-day air available

Nice

Nice distinction

Niche

Niche market

Niche marketing

Niche markets

Nifty

Night long

Nightly

Nightmare

Nimble

Nine

Nippy

Nitty gritty

No

No 1

No ad budget

No additional charge

No additives

No advertising costs

No application fee

No application fees

No B.S.

No better time to invest in

No better way

No bottom feeding

No brainer promotion

No clutter

No commute

No complicated

No complicated system

No computer needed

No contracts

No cost opportunity

No cost technique

No costly overhead

No costly repairs

No costly supplies

No credit check

No damage

No degree required

No distribution costs

No doubt

No education required

No employee costs

No employees

No employees to manage

No expensive equipment

No experience

No experience necessary

No experience needed

No extra cost

No face to face selling

No fault

No fighting morning traffic

No fillers included

No financial risk

No financial stress

No financial worry

No fluff

No fly by night scam

No fulfillment costs

No gimmicks

No good

No guess work

No hands on work

No hard work

No hassles

No hesitation saying

No hidden fees

No hidden reserve

No holds barred

No html knowledge

No hype

No interest

No interest for one year

No internet connection

No inventory

No inventory to ship

No investment

No large investment

No learning curve

No loans

No long term commitment

No maintenance

No matter how much you

No matter what business

No matter what you're selling

No matter where you live

No matter who you are

No meetings

No merchant account

No merchant account needed

No minimum

No minimum order

No misinformation

No money down

No money needed

No money required

No money to risk

No monthly charges

No more 9 to 5

No more being flat broke

No more endless searching

No more everyday grind

No more guess work

No more headaches

No more rejections

No more sleepless nights

No more stress

No more supervisors

No more time clock

No nonsense advice

No obligation

No obligation required

No ongoing fees

No one will call

No operating costs

No or low overhead

No out dated information

No out of pocket expense

No out of pocket money

No out-of-pocket cash

No packaging expenses

No pain no gain

No payment for "x" months

No payment for one year

No phone calls

No postage necessary

No presentations

No previous experience

No problem

No product reproduction costs

No programming knowledge

No prospect can resist

No questions asked

No recycled information

No rehashed information

No rejection

No repairs

No reserves

No restrictions

No risk

No royalty fees

No salesperson will visit

No same old information

No scam

No secretary

No selling

No set up fee

No shipping fees

No side effects

No sign up fees

No skills required

No software needed

No software to download

No special education

No sponsoring

No staff

No strings attached

No sweat

No technical ability

No technical knowledge

No time like the present

No time required

No win

No work on your part

Noble

Noble service

Noble thought

No-hassles refund

Noise proof

Nonabrasive

Nonacid

Non-addicting

Non-addictive

Non-additive

Noncompetitive

Nonconforming

Nondisclosure

Non-effective

Nonessential

Nonexplosive

Nonfiction

Nonfictional

Nonflammable

Nongovernment

Nonhuman

Nonindustrial

Nonlethal

Non-mandatory

No-nonsense

Nonpayment

Nonprofessional

Nonprofit

Non-profitable

Nonrecurring

Nonrenewable

Nonresident

Nonrestrictive

Nonspecific

Non-spillable

Nonstick

Nonstop

Nonsurgical

Nonverbal

Nook and cranny

Normal

Nostalgic

Nosey

Not a fly by night scam

Not a franchise

Not a pyramid

Not a scam

Not available in stores

Not by a long shot

Not for everyone

Not in a thousand years

Not in stores

Not on your life

Not refurbished

Not sold in stores

Not to worry

Not totally convinced yet

Notability

Notable

Notable examples

Noted

Noted by

Noted expert

Noteworthy

Nothing better!

Nothing comes close

Nothing down

Nothing else to buy

Nothing to lose

Nothing ventured, nothing gained

Noticeable

Noticeable adjustment

Noticeable trend

Noticed by

Notorious

Nourishing

Novel

Novel idea

Novice friendly

Now

Now available

Now for the first time you

Now involved in

Now is the time to get

Now is the time!

Now or never

Now you can own

Nuclear free

Nude

Nudity

Null and void

Number x

Numeral like

Numeric

Numero Uno

Numerous

Numerous examples

Nurturing

Nutrient rich

Nutrients

Nutrition like

Nutritional

Nutritional discovery

Nuts and bolts

Nutty

Oak

Obese

Objectionable

Objective

Obligated

Obligation

Obligation to

Obliterate your competition

Oblivious to

Obnoxious

Obscene

Obscene amounts of cash

Obscene profits

Obsession

Obsession like

Obsessive over

Obsolete

Obtainable

Obtainable money

Obvious that

Obvious urgency

Obviously you can

Occasional

Occasionally customers

Occupational

Occurring commission

Odd

Odd looking

Odds and ends

Odorless

Of the year

Off and running

Off beat

Off center

Off color

Off duty

Off key

Off line

Off road

Off shore

Off the books

Off the shelf

Off the wall

Off to a running start

Off year

Offer ends "date "

Offer ends soon

Offer expires

Offer limited to first ___ orders

Offered by

Official

Official credentials

Official guide

Official version

Officially

Off-limits

Off-line

Offset

Offshore

Oily

Ok

Old age

Old fashion

Old school

Old schooled

Old style

Old time

Old tradition

Old world

Older

Oldest

Oldie but goodie

On a scale of 1 to 10

On a shoestring budget

On a silver platter

On a tight budget

On automatic pilot

On cue

On easy street

On sale

On screen

On site repair

On target

On the blink of

On the money

On the right track

On the spot

On time

Onboard

Once and for all

Once flourishing economy

Once in a blue moon

Once in a lifetime

Once in a lifetime opportunity

Once upon a time

Once you own our product

One

One and only

One and the same

One comment from "name"

One day workshop

One dimensional

One in a million

One level

One of a kind

One of a kind collection

One of the best

One of the most

One of those rare products

One on one coaching

One on one mentoring

One owner

One person business

One shot deal

One sided

One simple

One size fits all

One source

One stop

One stop resource

One stop shopping

One sunny day

One-time fee

One up

One way or another

One-hour service

One-time setup fee

Ongoing

Ongoing expansion

Ongoing profits

Ongoing training

Online

Online access

Online auction

Online campaign

Online mall

Online marketing

Online or off-line

Online ordering

Online recruiting

Online revenue

Online sales process

Online service

Only $x.99

Only "$" a month

Only "$" a year

Only "$" for a subscription

Only "$" for instant access

Only "$" for lifetime access

Only a pinch

Only for serious people

Only investing "$" benefit

Only investing "$" per chapter

Only one click

Only paying "$" per page

Only paying "$" per word

Only serious people apply

Only spending "$" pay day

Only spending "$" per tip

Only the current information

Only the tip of the iceberg

Only x left

Only x made

Oodles of

Open "x" days a week

Open "x" hours a day

Open and shut

Open book

Open ended

Open eye

Open field

Open invitation

Open market

Open minded

Open their wallets

Opening bid

Operate you own business

Operated

Operating advantages

Operating budget

Operating costs

Operating expenses

Operational

Operative

Opinion friendly

Opinionated

Opportunist

Opportunities

Opportunities open up

Opportunity

Opposition proof

Optic

Optical

Optimal

Optimal levels

Optimize your time

Optimized

Optimum

Optimum accuracy

Option to choose

Option to purchase

Optional

Or you pay me nothing

Orange

Orchestrate your

Orchestrated

Order

Order before "day, date, time"

Order direct

Order form free

Order grabbing

Order in the next

Order now

Order now and I'll include

Order now!

Order page

Order processing

Order pulling

Order pulling copy

Order ready web site

Order today!

Order while supplies last

Ordered by

Orders keep pouring in

Orders processed
automatically

Ordinary

Organic

Organization

Organization to specialize in

Organization wide

Organize your

Organized

Organized table of contents

Oriental

Oriented

Original

Original creation

Original mint

Original production

Originated

Others cost twice as much

Our clients say

Out of date

Out of pocket

Out of pocket expensive

Out of sight

Out of the ordinary

Out of this world

Out perform

Out produce

Out source

Outbreak of

Outburst

Outgoing

Outgrow

Outlandish

Outlast

Outlawed

Outline the benefits

Outlined

Outmaneuver

Outnumber

Out-of-sight

Outperform

Outperform your
competitors

Output

Outrage

Outrageous

Outrageous amount

Outrageous profits

Outrageously rich

Outright sale

Outscore

Outsell

Outsell the competition

Outshine

Outside

Outsmart

Outsmart your competition

Outsourcing

Outspend

Outspoken

Outstanding

Outstanding ability

Outstanding benefits

Outstanding credentials

Outstanding merits

Outstanding performance

Outstanding qualities

Outstanding quality

Over $ my very first month

Over and above

Over looked

Over powering

Over the counter

Over the past few years

Over the past year

Over x MB of information

Over x pages of testimonials

Over x searchable chapters

Over x tactics

Overactive

Overall

Overcome objections

Overcome your

Overcoming

Overcrowded

Overdrive

Overemphasis

Overexcited about

Overexposure

Overflowing

Overflowing profit

Overhaul your

Overhauled

Overhead costs

Overindulge

Overjoyed

Overlooked opportunities

Overnight

Overnight delivery

Overnight expert

Overnight shipping

Overnight success

Overpowering effects

Overrated

Overrides on sales

Overriding advantage

Overriding benefit

Oversized

Oversold

Overstate

Overstocked

Oversupply

Overtake the competition

Overtake your

Overwhelmed by

Overwhelming

Overwhelming display

Overwhelming force

Overwhelming impression

Overwhelming success

Overwhelming tasks

Overwhelming urge

Overwhelming variety

Overworked

Owe yourself

Own your own

Owned by

Owner of

Ownership

Pacesetter

Package deal

Package design

Packaged and delivered

Packaged goods

Packaging friendly

Packed

Packed with

Packs a punch

Padded

Padding included

Paid every week

Paid in full

Paid up

Pain free

Pain killer

Pain less

Painful

Painful process

Painstaking

Paint by numbers formula

Paint the town red

Painted

Paired with

Palace like

Pale

Pales in comparison

Palm sized

Pamper yourself

Pampered by

Panel of experts

Panic

Paper work free

Paperless

Paradise

Paralyzing

Paranoia-induced

Parent friendly

Parental guidance

Part time

Part time income

Participate in

Participation is limited

Particular

Partner with

Partner's world wide

Partnership

Party like

Passed by

Passion

Passionate

Passive

Passive income stream

Password

Password and user name

Password protected

Password protection

Password required

Past customers

Patched

Patent pending

Patented

Patience

Patriotic

Patrolled by

Patterned

Patterned after

Paved

Pay an arm and leg

Pay as you go

Pay bills on time

Pay later

Pay nothing

Pay nothing for "x" months

Pay now

Pay off

Pay off your bills

Pay off your credit cards

Pay only $x.95

Pay per click

Pay per lead

Pay per sale

Pay per use

Pay up now

Pay your bills on time

Pay zero

Payable

Payable to

Payback pound

Payday

Paying benefits

Paying bills before they're due

Paying clients

Payload

Payment free

Payment systems

Payroll

Pays dividends

Pays dividends for years

Pays for itself

Pays on multiple levels

Pays out fast

Peace like

Peace of minds

Peaceful

Peak at

Peak efficiency

Peak level

Peak performance

Peaked

Peculiar looking

Pending your order

Penetrate their minds

Penniless

Penny pincher

Pennyworth

People friendly

People from all over the world have bought it

People have paid up to $

People helping people

People just like you

People pay $

Peppermint flavored

Peppery

Perceived by

Perceived value

Percent of

Perfect

Perfect accent

Perfect asset

Perfect compliment

Perfect condition

Perfect detail

Perfect fit

Perfect ideas

Perfect match

Perfect size

Perfect solution

Perfect souvenir

Perfect timing

Perfected system

Perfectible

Perfection

Perfectly legal

Perfectly suited

Performance	Person to person
Performance tested	Personal
Performed by	Personal fortune
Perhaps you're wondering	Personal growth
Peril	Personal insights
Periodic discounts	Personal mentor
Periodical improvements	Personal promise
Permanent	Personal security
Permanent commitment	Personal selling
Permanent income	Personalized
Permanent influence	Personalized list of
Permanent monthly income	Personally refund
Permanent relief	Perspective
Permanent satisfaction	Persuade
Permanent solution	Persuade anyone, anytime
Permanently owned	Persuade buying decisions
Permanently retire	Persuade people to spend
Perpetual	Persuade skeptical customers
Perpetual income	Persuade your prospects
Perpetual promotional	Persuaded by
Perplexing phenomenon	Persuasion like
Persistence free	Persuasive
Person friendly	Pet friendly

Petite	Peace of mind
Petrified	Piece of the wealth
Phased out	Pierced by
Phenomenal	Pig like
Phenomenal breakthrough	Piggyback offer
Phenomenal level	Piggybacking
Phone today!	Pile up
Photograph of	Piles of cash
Photographed by	Pillar of success
Photos of	Pin down your
Physical	Pine scented
Physically changing	Pink colored
Physique	Pinpoint achievement
Pick and choose	Pinpointed by
Pick up the pieces	Pins and needles
Pick your	Pint sized
Picked by	Pioneer
Pictorial	Pioneered
Picture investing	Pipe lined
Picture of	Piped in
Picture perfect	Piranha
Pictured by many as	Pitched
Pie in the sky	Pitches in

Pitfall	Play
Pivotal	Play for keeps
Pivotal component	Play hardball
Pivotal decisions	Play it safe
Pivotal event	Playable
Placed __the	Played
Places to	Played by
Plague	Playful
Plagued by	Pleasant accent
Plain	Pleasant sent
Plain and simple	Pleasing personality
Plain truth	Pleasing results
Plan of action	Pleasing sound
Planet like	Pleasurable
Planetary	Pleasure
Planned	Pledge to
Planned out	Plow new ground
Planning phrase	Plucked from
Plant like	Plug in
Plant the seeds	Plug in cash machine
Planted by	Plummet
Plastic plated with	Plunge
Platinum	Plunge into

Plural

Plus

Plus get

Plus size

Plush

Pocket

Pocket sized

Pocket up to

Poem like

Poetic

Point and click

Point blank

Point of purchase

Pointless

Poised

Poised for

Poison free

Poison

Poisoned

Pummel

Poker faced

Polar

Policed by

Polished

Polished looked

Polished performer

Polished skills

Polished style

Polite

Political

Politically correct

Pollute less

Polluted by

Pollution proof

Pool of experts

Poor

Poorer

Poorest

Pop up

Popped

Popular

Popular acclaim

Popular myth

Popularity

Popularity

Popularized by

Population accepted

Portability

Portable

Portfolio

Portion of

Position yourself

Positioning

Positional

Positioned by

Positive

Positive future

Positive impact

Positive influence

Positive outlook

Positively

Possess every

Possess knowledge of

Possibilities are endless

Possibly you should

Post-holiday

Postage and handling

Postage free

Potent

Potent force

Potent influence

Potential

Potential bargain

Potential benefits

Potential demand

Pounding

Pouring money

Pouring money down the drain

Poverty proof

Poverty stricken

Powdered

Power

Power packed

Powerful

Powerful company

Powerful impact

Powerful incentive

Powerful technology

Powerhouse

Powerless

Practicable alternative

Practical

Practical benefits

Practical choice

Practical information

Practical methods

Practical solution

Practically with no effort

Practice free

Practice what you preach

Praised by

Praiseworthy

Prank proof

Pre-owned

Pre-publication opportunity

Pre-qualified

Pre-qualified customers

Pre-qualified traffic

Pre release

Pre-sale

Pre written

Preached by many

Prearrange

Precious

Precious asset

Precious free time

Precious opportunity

Precise

Precise adjustment

Precise detail

Precise function

Precise standards

Precise timing

Precision

Precision

Precision quality

Preconception that

Predator like

Predatory

Predetermine

Predict

Predict new trends

Predictable

Preemptive

Preface driven

Prefect tools

Preferred by many

Preferred member

Prehistoric

Premier

Premier collection

Premier offering

Premium

Pre-paid

Prepaid

Prepare to discover

Prepared by

Prepay now

Preposterous

Prescription free

Preselected

Presell

Presentable

Presentation

Presentational

Presented by

Preserve

Preserve your

Preserved

President

Presidential like

Press covered

Press release sample

Pressing issues of

Prestige

Prestigious organization

Presuppose you ordered

Pretend earning $

Pretend your

Pretty

Pretty penny

Prevent

Prevention

Preventive

Preview

Previously released

Price break

Price comparison

Price conscious

Price cutting

Price friendly

Price includes shipping

Price list

Price points

Price range

Price reduction

Price war

Priced right

Priceless

Priceless help

Priceless knowledge

Priceless masterpiece

Priceless opportunity

Priceless treasure

Prices below competitors

Prices cut in half

Prices slashed!

Pricing strategy

Prickly

Pride

Pride and joy primary

Prime earning

Prime location

Prime position

Prime time

Primed

Prime-quality

Primer on

Primitive

Principal

Principle

Principle and interest

Print on demand

Print out edition

Printed

Priority

Prison

Pristine

Privacy

Privacy policy

Private

Private broadcast

Private consultation

Private invitation

Private membership

Private sector

Private stock

Privately funded

Privately held

Privilege

Privileged

Privileged access

Prize appealing

Prize winning

Prized collection

Prized institution

Prize profit

Pro

Proactive

Proactive professional

Proactive thinker

Problem free

Problem free delivery

Problem laden

Problem less

Problem solved

Processed by

Proclaimed by many

Procrastination proof

Produced by

Product

Product class

Product creation

Product design

Product development

Product diversification

Product driven

Product Empire

Product life

Product life cycle

Product line

Product mix

Product package

Product placement

Product selling formulas

Production

Productive

Productivity

Productivity friendly

Profession less

Professional

Professional advice

Professional guidance

Professional installed

Professional looking

Professional organization

Professional product graphics

Professional results

Professional services

Professional standards

Professional teacher

Professional trends

Professional values

Professional web site

Professionally checked

Professionally designed

Proficiency

Proficient

Profile of

Profiled by

Profit

Profit and loss

Profit boosters

Profit center

Profit driven

Profit for life

Profit from

Profit generating

Profit levels

Profit making

Profit margin

Profit model

Profit motive

Profit oriented

Profit potential

Profit producing

Profit right away

Profit sharing

Profit system

Profitable

Profitability

Profitable

Profitable advice

Profitable as possible

Profitable asset

Profitable business ideas

Profitable firm

Profitable formula

Profitable information

Profitable investment

Profitable membership

Profitable price

Profitable product idea

Profitable projects

Profitable response

Profitable strategies

Profitable ventures

Profit-generating

Profits everyday

Profits month after month

Profits through the roof

Profits with minimum risk

Profound

Profound impact

Profound though

Profusely

Program

Program their mind

Programmable

Programmed

Programmer friendly

Programming proof

Progressive

Prohibited

Project friendly

Projectable figures

Projected by many

Prolific

Prolong use

Prominent

Promise the moon

Promise you

Promises I'll make you

Promising

Promising company

Promising future

Promising ideas

Promising outlook

Promising solution

Promising times

Promo

Promote

Promote it in x minutes

Promote your business

Promote your site

Promote yourself

Promoted

Promoted to

Promoting any product

Promotion

Promotional

Promotional phenomenon

Promotional planning

Promotional software

Promotional tool

Prompt action

Prompt service

Promptness

Prompted by

Promptly shipped

Prone to

Proof

Proofread by

Propaganda proof

Propel

Propel visitors

Propel your traffic

Proper

Prophet like

Proportional

Proposal accepting

Pros

Pros and cons

Prospect like

Prospecting

Prospective

Prospective clients

Prospects galore

Prospects on demand

Prospects to paying customers

Prospects won't resist

Prosper during a recession

Prosper in bad times

Prosperity

Prosperity

Prosperous business

Prosperous future

Prosperous lifestyle

Protect your business

Protected

Protected by our

Protection

Protective

Prototype

Proudly presents

Provable figures

Prove it to yourself

Prove your

Proved

Proven

Proven and tested

Proven effective

Proven fact

Proven in the field

Proven leader

Proven marketing system

Proven name

Proven performer

Proven revenue models

Proven solutions

Proven step by step formula

Proven to work

Proven track record

Proven ways

Provided by

Provided technical assistance to

Provisional

Provocative

Psychedelic

Psychological

Psychotic

Public access

Public policy

Public relations

Publicize your business

Publicized

Publicly held

Published "date"

Published by

Publisher of

Puffy

Pull all the stops

Pull in an additional $ this year

Pull like crazy

Pull more than $

Pull your weight

Pulled

Pulling power

Pulsating

Pulverize the competition

Punctual

Punish

Punish proof

Punk like

Purchasable

Purchase today

Purchased by

Purchasing power

Pure

Pure and simple

Pure blooded

Pure convenience

Pure delight

Pure fact

Pure gold

Pure luck

Pure profit

Purebred

Purple colored

Purposed by

Push

Push button

Push the envelope

Push the right buttons

Push their hot bottoms

Put down any about

Put money on it

Put two and two together

Put up or shut up

Put your money where your mouth is

Quadruple

Quadruple profits

Quadruple the results

Quadruple your earnings

Quadruple your sales

Quake proof

Qualified

Qualified choice

Qualified guide

Qualified leads

Qualified responses

Qualified source

Qualify prospects

Qualify yourself

Qualifying

Quality

Quality assurance

Quality awareness

Quality control

Quality crafted

Quality enhancing

Quality management

Quality materials

Quality visitors

Quality-minded

Quantity driven

Quantity pricing

Queen like

Quenching

Quest driven

Question friendly

Questionable

Quick

Quick break

Quick buck

Quick cash

Quick change

Quick decline

Quick fire

Quick fix

Quick operation

Quick recovery

Quick reference

Quick response

Quick return

Quick shifting

Quick solution

Quick tempered

Quick tips

Quickly

Quickest

Quiet

Quieter

Quilted

Quit feeling

Quit making peanuts

Quit your day job

Quit your job

Quite old

Quiz like

Quota driven

Quotable

Quoted by

Racked to sell

Radar like

Radiant

Radiant color

Radiant future

Radical approach

Radical concept

Radio like

Rags to riches

Rain or shine

Raise eyebrows

Raise the bar

Raise your

Raise your friend's eyebrows

Raise your sights

Raised to

Raising this price to $

Rake in

Rake in an extra $

Rake in over $

Rake in the dough

Rake in the profits

Random

Randomly selected

Ranked as the

Ranked at the top

Rant and rave

Rapid action

Rapid change

Rapid delivery

Rapid fire

Rapid growth potential

Rare

Rare craftsmanship

Rare delight

Rare design

Rare find

Rare formula

Rare information

Rare insights

Rare moment

Rare opportunity

Rare pleasure

Rare power

Rarely

Rarely seen

Rarely used tactics

Rarest ___ that exists today

Rascal

Rat race

Rate of growth

Rate of return

Rated by

Rated number x

Rates as low as

Rational choice

Rational purpose

Rave reviews

Ravenous

Raving fans

Ravish

Raw

Razor

Razor like

Razor sharp

Razzle dazzle

Reaccept

Reach a new milestone

Reach for the sky

Reach for your

Reach new levels

Reach your full potential

Reach your goals

Reachable dreams

Reaction friendly

Reactions from repeat customers

Reactive

Read all about it

Read below to learn

Read between the lines

Read our FAQ

Read these endorsements

Read these facts carefully

Read these testimonials

Read this jam packed

Readable

Readable dates

Readable serial number

Reader response

Readers agree that

Readers say

Ready and able

Ready and willing

Ready made

Ready to act prospects

Ready to buy customers

Ready to sell

Ready to ship

Ready to use

Ready, willing and able

Reaffirm your commitment to

Real

Real comfort

Real freedom

Real life examples

Real secrets

Real success

Real time

Real world

Real world examples

Real world experience

Real world tested

Realign your goals

Realistic expectations

Realistic ideas

Realistic income

Realistic objectives

Reality

Realize your dreams

Realize you're potential

Reap

Reap the benefits

Reap the financial rewards

Reap the rewards

Reason to order

Reasonable

Reasonable price

Reassert yourself as

Reassure your

Reassuring

Reassuring answers

Rebate

Rebel like

Rebuild your

Recalculate

Recall making

Recall when

Recapture your dreams

Receipt provided

Receive coupon with payment

Receive free

Receptive to your offer

Recession

Recession busting

Recession proof

Recession resistant

Recession wary

Recession-proof refund

Rechargeable

Reciprocal

Reciprocal links

Reckoning

Reclaim your dreams

Reclaim your freedom

Recognizable brand

Recognizable identity

Recognize by many as

Recognized expert

Recommended by

Recommended for professionals

Recommit to

Reconsider investing in

Reconsolidate your

Reconstructed with

Record amount

Record breaking

Record breaking response rates

Record breaking sales

Record high

Record year

Recordable

Recoup your investment

Recyclable

Red colored

Red hot

Red tap

Redecorate your

Redeem it at

Redesigned as

Redistributed by

Reduce business costs

Reduce charge backs and
returns

Reduce refunds

Reduce the costs

Reduce your

Reduce your dependence

Reduced

Reduced

Reduced material costs

Reduced price

Reduced rates

Reevaluate your options

Refer just x people

Refer others

Referable

Reference like

Referral

Referral generating

Referrals

Referred as

Refinance now

Refined as

Refinished

Reflect back on buying

Reflective

Reformed

Refreshed

Refreshing

Refreshing alternative

Refreshing facts

Refreshing news

Refreshing taste

Refugee

Refund every penny

Refund friendly

Refundable

Regained your

Regardless of being

Regardless of your education

Regardless of your experience

Regenerate your

Regional

Registered with

Registration free

Regular

Regular communication

Regulated by

Reinforced

Reinstated by

Reinvent the wheel

Reinventing the wheel

Rejuvenate your

Related to

Relaxing

Released today

Relentless

Reliable

Reliable equipment

Reliable expert

Reliable guarantee

Reliable promise

Reliable source

Reliable tracking

Relief

Remarkable

Remarkable craftsmanship

Remarkable information

Remarkable performance

Remarkable rates

Remarkable story

Remarkable timing

Remedy the situation

Remember having

Remember when

Remixed

Remodeled

Remote access

Remote control

Removable

Remove buying defenses

Remove life's obstacles

Remove their objections

Renegotiated

Renew at only "$"

Renew today

Renewable

Renewal free

Renovated

Rent free

Rent to own

Rental

Reoccurring income

Reorder at a discount

Reorganized package deal

Repair free

Repairable

Repairs included

Repeat customers

Repeat sales

Repeat traffic

Repeat visitor

Repeatable

Replaceable

Replaceable equipment

Replaceable parts

Replaced by

Replacement parts

Replay for free

Replenish your

Reply before "date"

Report included

Reported benefits

Reprehensible

Represented by

Reprint rights

Reproduced

Reproduction rights

Reprogram your

Reputable

Reputation is on the line

Request our

Requested

Requested by

Required by law

Requirements of

Requires absolutely no

Resale for

Resale rights

Research

Research and development

Researched

Resell for profit

Reseller package

Reseller program

Reserve before

Reserve your appointment now

Reserve your copy

Reserve your package

Reserve your spot

Reshape your

Residence friendly

Residential location

Residual

Residual benefits

Residual checks

Residual income

Residual revenue stream

Residual value

Resistance free

Resolvable problem

Resource box

Resourceful

Respectable

Respected authorities

Respected by many as

Respected genius

Respected guru

Respected name

Respected representative

Respond now

Responds quickly

Response is incredible

Response rate

Response required

Responsibility

Responsible

Responsive to your

Restock your

Restored

Restriction free

Restrictive to

Restructure your

Restructured by

Restyled

Result proven

Resulted in

Results

Results overnight

Resurging

Retail

Retain customers

Retain more clients

Retain more customers

Retire

Retire early

Retire rich

Retire young

Retired by

Retirement

Retiring early

Retroactive

Retrospective

Return friendly

Return it and owe nothing

Return on investment

Return on sales

Return policies

Returnable

Returns

Revamp your business

Revamped

Revealing

Revealed

Revealing

Revealing details

Reveals all

Revelation

Revenge

Revenue

Revenue bond

Revenue enhancing

Revenue generating

Revenue month after month

Revenue sharing

Reverse your fortune

Reversed

Reversible

Review our super

Reviewed by

Reviewing

Revised

Revised and updated

Revisit soon

Revitalized

Revived

Revolting

Revolutionary

Revolutionary information

Reward employees

Reward oriented

Reward yourself

Rewarded

Rewarded by

Rewarding

Rewarding challenge

Rewarding industry

Rich

Rich accent

Rich collection

Rich color

Rich detail

Rich diversity

Rich experience

Rich flavor

Rich menu

Rich nutrient

Richly

Richly detailed

Richly textured

Ridiculous

Right

Right and wrong

Right at your finger tips

Right away

Right hand man

Right handed

Right now

Right thinking

Rigorous

Rigorous examination

Rinky dink

Rip roaring

Ripe

Ripe experience

Ripped

Ripped off

Rip-roaring

Ripsnorter

Rise and fall

Rise in costs

Rise in sales

Rising demand

Risk free

Risk nothing!

Risk proof

Risk reversal

Risk taker

Risk-free trial

Risky

Risky business

Rival competition

River of cash

Riveting

Riveting package

Road map to success

Road to wealth

Roaring

Rob you of

Robotic

Robust

Robust industry

Rock bottom

Rock bottom price

Rock hard

Rock solid

Rock-bottom prices

Rocket launch your profits

Rocket like

Rocketed

Rocky

Rocky times

Rogue

Roll out

Romance

Romantic

Rookie friendly

Rooting tooting

Rotational

Rough

Rough edged

Round

Round table

Rounded

Rousing success

Royal

Royalties	Ruthless
Royalty free	Sabotage
Royalty free products	Safe
Royalty free reprint rights	Safe and secure
Rub shoulders with	Safe investment
Rugged	Safe to the environment
Rugged tests	Safeguarded
Ruining your traffic	Safety
Rule less	Safety requirements
Rules and guidelines to	Said and done
Run a home business	Salary driven
Run around	Sale
Run it from anywhere	Sale of the century
Run of the mill	Saleable product
Run the show	Sales appeal
Running within hours	Sales call
Runs like new	Sales copy
Rural	Sales driven
Rush delivery	Sales force
Rush hour	Sales forecast
Rush ordering	Sales galore
Rust resistant	Sales generating
Rusty	Sales goal

Sales intensifiers

Sales letter

Sales material

Sales modifiers

Sales over and over

Sales pitch

Sales process

Sales promotion

Sales pulling

Sales quota

Sales ratio

Sales reps

Sales stimulus

Sales through the roof

Salesman

Salivate at

Salty

Same as

Same as cash

Same day

Same old story

Same-day delivery

Same-day service

Sample

Samples of

Sanctimonious

Sandy

Sanitary

Sassy

Satisfaction

Satisfaction guaranteed

Satisfactory

Satisfied customers

Satisfy your craving for

Satisfying

Satisfying pleasure

Satisfying solutions

Savable

Save

Save a small fortune

Save a ton of money

Save for college

Save hundreds

Save money

Save thousands

Save time

Save your business

Save yourself years of research

Saves you from mistakes

Saving time

Savings

Savor

Savvy

Sawed off

Scaled

Scaled down

Scandal proof

Scandalous

Scarce

Scare proof

Scarf out

Scary

Scented

Schedule proven

Scheduled

Scheme proof

Schism

Scholarly

School of

Schooled by

Scientific

Scientific discovery

Scientific fact

Scientific material

Scientific studies

Scientifically proven

Scientifically tested

Scientifically verified

Scorching

Scream

Screened by

Scripted by

Scrumptious

Seal of approval

Sealed air tight

Seamless

Search for

Searing

Searing heat

Seasonal

Seasoned

Seasoned pro

Second

Second income

Second place

Second rate

Second to none

Secondary

Secondary market

Secret

Secret formula

Secret recipe

Secret selling blueprints

Secret technique

Secret tip

Secret weapon

Secrets

Secretive

Secrets

Secrets of

Secrets of the pros

Secrets revealed

Secrets to a successful

Sectional

Secure

Secure a top spot

Secure accommodations

Secure investment

Secure mail

Secure ordering

Secure ordering system

Secure server

Secured by

Secured opportunity

Security

Security measures

Security policies

Seduction

Seductive appeal

Seductive offer

See before you buy

See eye to eye

See for yourself

See it to believe it

See the light

See the savings

See yourself selling

Seed capital

Seeded with

Segmented

Seize the day

Seize the moment

Seldom heard

Seldom known

Seldom used

Select goods

Select mixture

Select winning products

Selected

Selected from

Self-absorbing

Self-adjusting

Self-appointed

Self-assured

Self-centered

Self-cleaning

Self confidence

Self-correcting

Self-development

Self-duplicating

Self-educated

Self employed

Self-funding

Self-generating

Self-indulgence

Self-made millionaire

Self-mailer

Self-proclaimed

Self-reliant

Self-rising

Self sufficient

Self-support

Self-supporting

Self-updating

Self-worth

Sell

Sell a boatload

Sell again and again

Sell an unlimited number of copies

Sell as many copies as you want

Sell at warp speed

Sell bucket loads of products

Sell in hard times

Sell like crazy

Sell more by raising prices

Sell or give away

Sell out

Sell products fast

Sell x and make back your money

Sellable

Seller's market

Selling costs

Selling experience

Selling history

Selling like crazy

Selling like hot cakes

Selling machine

Selling multiple products

Selling principles

Selling skills

Sells itself

Semiautomatic

Seminar like

Semipro

Send for free details

Send no money now

Send today

Send your name

Senior

Seniority chosen

Sensational

Sensational news

Sensible agenda

Sensible alternative

Sensible choice

Sensible ideas

Sensible plan

Sensible solution

Sensitive intelligence

Sensual

Sentimental

Separate

Separate but equal

Separate from the competition

Separate winners from losers

Separate yourself

Separately

Separates winners from losers

Sequel

Serge in

Serial number

Series of

Serious

Serious bids only

Serious commitment

Serious faced

Serious minded

Serious people only

Serious profit potential

Serious task at hand

Seriously you can

Served over x

Service

Service provider

Serviceable

Serviced X

Set your own hours

Setting high standards

Seven

Seven figure company

Several "months, days, years" ago

Sex

Sexual

Sexy

Shake a leg

Shameless

Shameless pleasure

Shape up or ship out

Shape your own tomorrow

Shape your prosperity

Share of the market

Shared by

Shark like

Sharp

Sharp distinction

Sharp increase

Sharp insights

Sharp tongued

Sharply

Sharper

Sharpest

Shatter

Sheer pleasure

Shelf life

Shell out

Shellacking

Shenanigans

Shimmering

Shining future

Shinny

Shipping included

Shocked at

Shocked at how cheap

Shocking

Shocking difference

Shocking strategies

Shoestring

Shoestring budget

Shop now

Short

Short cut

Short lived

Short order form

Short range

Short run

Short sited

Short term

Shorted

Shorten

Shortly

Short-term lease

Show piece

Show stopper

Show the world

Showcased

Shredded

Shrink resistant

Sick and tired

Sick and tried

Sight unseen

Sign of things to come

Sign on

Sign up

Sign up instantly

Signature free

Signed and sealed

Signed by ___

Signed, sealed and delivered

Significant

Significant acquisition

Significant claims

Silky

Silly

Silver colored

Silver lining

Simmering

Simple

Simple adjustment

Simple approach

Simple instructions

Simple marketing system

Simple no cost ways

Simple plan

Simple pleasures

Simple solution

Simple steps

Simple to follow outline

Simple to use

Simplified

Simply explain

Simply powerful

Simultaneous

Simultaneously increase sales

Since the age of x

Sincere

Sincere desire

Sincerely

Sinful

Sinful luxury

Single

Single edged

Sink or swim

Sink your teeth into

Sit back and

Sit on your butt

Sit up and take notice

Six

Six figure company

Six figure operation

Six figure revenue

Six-figure

Sizable

Sizable income

Sizable portion

Size up

Sized right

Sized to fit

Sizzle

Sizzling

Skedaddle

Skill

Skilled

Skillful

Skillful maneuvers

Skillfully managed

Skinflint

Skullduggery

Sky high income

Skyrocket

Skyrocket your profits

Sky-rocketed

Sky's the limit

Slapdash

Slash costs

Slashed

Slashing prices

Slaughter

Slave

Sleazy

Sleek

Sleeping

Slender

Slice of the pie

Sliced

Slick

Slight accent

Slim

Slimy

Sloe-eyed

Slow

Slow economy

Slow growing

Slow moving

Slow poke

Slow times

Slowdown

Sluggish economy

Sly

Small

Small business

Small company

Small enough

Small fortune

Small fry

Small investment

Small minded

Small package

Small size

Small time

Smaller

Smallest

Smallest ever

Smart

Smart decision

Smart money

Smart strategy

Smarter

Smash

Smash hit

Smash your competition

Smashing success

Smell the

Smelly

Smile because

Smoke filled

Smoke out

Smoke proof

Smoked

Smoking

Smooth

Smooth adjustment

Smooth feeling

Smooth flavor

Smooth spoken

Smooth texture

Smoothed

Smoother

Smothered in

Smug

Smuggled

Snake like

Sneak preview

Sneaky

Sneer

Sniveling

Snob	Solar
Snooty	Sold
Snotty	Sold millions
So called	Sold out
So what	Sold thousands
Soaked in	Solely
Soapy	Solid
Soar	Solid angle
Soar your sales	Solid background
Soaring	Solid business
Soaring demand	Solid cash
Soaring level	Solid choice
Social	Solid claims
Sodium free	Solid commitment
Soft	Solid credentials
Soft colors	Solid firm
Soft market	Solid footing
Soft sell	Solid foundation
Soft shoe	Solid gain
Soft spoken	Solid ground
Softened	Solid information
Softer	Solid investment
Softest	Solid record

Solid reputation

Solid research

Solid reward

Solid study

Solution

Solve

Solve your cash flow problems

Solve your problems

Solved

Solving a problem

Some actual results of

Some customers have told us

Something for nothing

Sooner or later

Sooner the better

Soothing

Soothing scene

Soothing sound

Sophisticated

Sophisticated equipment

Sophisticated facility

Sophisticated investor

Sophisticated procedure

Sophisticated tests

Sore to new heights

Sorted

Sought after

Sought after collection

Sought after expert

Sought after strategies

Sound advice

Sound alternative

Sound investment

Sound management

Sound off

Sound proof

Sound strategies

Sound workmanship

Soupy

Sour

Souvenir

Space age

Spam free

Spank

Spare no expense

Spare parts

Spare time

Spark

Spark your sales

Sparkling

Spearheaded

Special

Special alert

Special bonus

Special discounts

Special edition

Special gift

Special offer

Special pick

Special rebate

Special report

Special touch

Special training

Specialized"

Specialist

Specialize

Specialized

Specialized skills

Specializing in

Specialty

Specific

Specific examples

Specific mission

Specifically

Specifically designed

Specified

Spectacular

Spectacular color

Spectacular income

Spectacular story

Speechless

Speed

Speed delivery

Speed up your success

Speedy

Speedy relief

Speedy service

Spellbound

Spend time doing what you love

Spend wisely

Spending money

Spending money without worry

Spending spree

Spent countless hours researching

Spent time and money researching

Spice up your

Spicy

Spiffy

Spiked

Spill my guts

Spill over

Spill their guts

Spineless

Spiral

Spirit enhancing

Spirited

Spiritual

Spiritual value

Splendid

Splendid color

Splendid gift

Splendid ideas

Spliced

Split run

Split second

Split up

Spokesman said

Sponsoring the

Sponsorship

Spontaneous

Spook

Spoon fed

Spoonful of

Sport

Sport utility

Sporty

Spotless perfection

Spotlight

Spotted

Spread like wildfires

Spread out

Spreading

Spreads like a/the

Spring like

Spring loaded

Springboard your upsells

Sprint

Spruce up

Square

Squeaky

Squeaky clean

Squeezing your profits

Squishing your sales

Stability

STABLE

Stack the deck

Staffed by

Stage worthy

Staged

Staggering

Staggering achievement

Staggering figure

Staggering findings

Stained with

Stainless steel

Stampedes of traffic

Stand-alone products

Stand by

Stand out from the crowd

Stand the test of time

Stand up and be counted

Standard

Standard procedure

Standardized

Star crossed

Star like

Star studded

Star studded event

Stardom"

Starlight

Starry eyed

Start a dotcom business

Start a thriving business

Start earning today

Start expanding

Start from scratch

Start making money in

Start up

Start-up capital

Start with little or no money

Start with no money

Start with nothing

Start you own business

Start your empire

Starter kit

Startling

Startling announcement

Startling discovery

Startling headline

Startling truth

Startlingly simple

Start-up

Startup costs

State approved

State of the art

State of the art facility

State of the art tests

State-of-the-art

Statistical

Statistical methods

Stay ahead of competition

Stay competitive

Stay connected

Stay in power

Stay successful

Stay up late

Staying power

Steadfast help

Steady expansion

Steady flow of subscribers

Steady income

Steal the show

Steal the spotlight

Stealth like

Steam powered

Steamy

Steel

Stenciled

Step by step

Step by step affiliate training

Step by step directions

Step by step instructions

Step by step system

Step up to the plate

Step-by-step

Sterile

Sterilized

Stern masterpiece

Stewing

Sticky

Sticky sweet

Stiff armed

Stiff necked

Still in package

Still in the wrapper

Stimulate your sales

Stimulated

Stimulating

Stimulating ideas

Stomach filling

Stomach turning

Stop

Stop hesitation

Stop losing money!

Stop procrastinating

Stop spending time searching for

Stop spinning your wheels!

Stop the presses

Stop wasting time with

Stop wasting time!

Stop what you're doing

Stop worrying

Storable

Stories of success

Storms of leads

Story book success

Story like

Story struck

Straight

Straight to the point information

Straightforward

Straightforward answers

Straightforward technique

Strange

Strange and unusual

Strange phenomenon

Strangle

Strapped for cash

Strategic

Strategic partnerships

Strategically maneuver	Strike up a deal
Strategy	Strike while it's still hot
Strawberry flavored	Striking achievement
Stream of referrals	Striking beauty
Streamed together	Striking collections
Streaming	Striking design
Streamline	Striking difference
Streamline your business	Striking features
Streamlined	Stripped
Streams of income	Strive for perfection
Streams of traffic	Strong
Street like	Strong ability
Strength	Strong arm
Strengthen your profits	Strong bonds of trust
Strengthened	Strong close
Stress free	Strong commitments
Stress proof	Strong consumer demand
Stretch every dollar	Strong credibility
Stricken by	Strong demand
Strict deadline	Strong evidence
Strictly confidential	Strong foundation
Strike gold	Strong hold on
Strike out	Strong impact

Strong interest

Strong minded

Strong skills

Strong solution

Strong willed

Stronger

Strongest

Struck

Structural

Structured

Stuck up

Student friendly

Studied submitted

Studied tons of

Studies prove that

Study at home

Stunning

Stunning announcement

Stunning presentations

Stunning secrets

Stunning sight

Stupid

Sturdy

Sturdy materials

Style conscious

Styled with

Subcontracted

Subliminal

Submerse yourself in

Submitted by

Subscribe now

Subscribe to

Subscriber log in

Subscribing is easy

Substance filled

Substantial

Substantial addition

Substantial advantage

Substantial benefits

Substantial gain

Substantial income

Substantial increase

Substantial savings

Substantial wealth

Substantially increase business

Substantiated by

Substituted with

Succeed

Succeed in a big way

Succeed in business

Succeed quickly

Succeeded in

Success

Success and wealth

Success oriented

Success secrets

Success stories

Successful"

Successful

Successful analysis

Successful antidote

Successful at

Successful company

Successful Corporation

Successful firm

Successful habits

Successful talent

Successfully follow up

Successfully promote any product

Suck

Sudden change in

Sudden death

Sudden economic change

Sufficient

Sufficient funding

Suggested by

Suggestions welcomed

Suit and tie

Suitable

Summarized

Summer like

Super

Super achiever

Super affiliate

Super bargain

Super charge you profit

Super-efficient

Super profitable

Super sale

Super strength

Super successful	Supervised by
Super swift	Supplemented
Superb	Supplied by
Superb accommodations	Supplies limited
Superb condition	Supply and demand
Superb design	Supply is limited
Superb flavor	Support
Superb investment	Support friendly
Superb miracle	Support services
Superb performance	Support systems
Superb selection	Supported by
Superb view	Suppose you could just
Supercharged	Supreme
Superficial	Supreme authority
Superhighway	Sure fire
Superior	Sure fire income
Superior choice	Sure remedy
Superior living	Sure to fit your budget
Superior location	Sure-fire
Superior methods	Surely you will
Supernatural	Surge
Supersensitive	Surging
Superstar	Surging business

Surpass your goals

Surpassed

Surpassing beauty

Surpassing elegance

Surprise

Surprise bonus

Surprise bonuses

Surprise gift

Surprising advantage

Surprising amount

Surprising answers

Surprising collection

Surprising information

Surprising offer

Surveyed by

Survival proof

Survive a slow economy

Survive and prosper

Sustainable

Sustainable career

Sweaty

Sweeping power

Sweepstakes

Sweet

Sweet profits

Sweet smelling

Sweet sounding

Sweet tasting

Sweeten with

Sweeter deal

Swift

Swift action

Swift moving

Swiftest

Swiftly flowing

Swing into action

Symbolic

Symbolic value

Sympathetic to your

Synchronize your business

Synchronized

Synthetic

System like

Systematic

Systematic observation

Systematic results

Tabulate your order

Tabulated by

Tactics

Tag team

Tailor made

Tailored

Tailspin

Take a load off

Take a look at all

Take a peek

Take a risk

Take a shot

Take action now!

Take advantage of

Take all the

Take apart

Take care of

Take care of business

Take control of your life

Take dream vacations

Take it or leave it

Take no prisoners

Take orders in minutes

Take orders instantly

Take the plunge

Take you by storm

Take you by the hand

Takes care of itself

Takes full advantage of

Takes the guess work out of

Takes x minutes of your time

Takes you step by step

Taking over

Talented

Talented team of

Talk of the internet

Talk of the town

Talk to an expert

Tall

Taller

Tallest

Tamed

Tamper proof

Tan colored

Tank

Tantalize your senses

Tantalizing

Tantalizing facts

Tantalizing mixture

Tantalizing taste

Tap into the

Tapered

Target audience

Target market

Target other potential
markets

Target price

Targeted

Targeted exposure

Targeted traffic

Tasteful

Tasteful color

Tastes like

Tawdry

Tax advantage

Tax benefits

Tax deductible

Tax exempt

Tax free

Tax free money

Tax incentive

Tax savings

Team building

Team like

Team of experts

Team up with

Team work

Tearjerker

Technical

Technical help

Technique's"

Technology

Technology sensitive industry

Technology training

Teetering

Teeth chattering

Teeth grinding

Teeth jarring

Tempting menu

Tempting offer

Tender

Terms of sale

Terrific

Territorial

Terror

Terrorist

Test drive

Test everything automatically

Test the waters

Tested

Tested marketing system

Tested techniques

Testimonials

Tests prove

Thank you

Thank you for checking out this

That's how good it is

That's just what you need

The #no ___

The "#no" best

The absolute best way

The actual ""I used to

The advantages of owning

The best of both worlds

The best thing since

The big problem with

The biggest names in

The biggest problem with

The bus stops here

The clock is ticking

The complete authority on

The complete guide to

The comprehensive guide to

The countdown begins

The country's top

The critical information

The difference between

The disadvantages of not

The easiest way

The exact steps

The fact is

The fail safe way to

The fastest method of

The fastest way

The final countdown

The first thing

The following is just

The following rewards

The going value

The grand master of

The hidden secrets

The hidden truth

The impossible dream

The inside story

The key is knowing how to

The latest information

The little known

The location of

The major highlights of

The mechanics of

The most important thing

The nation's foremost authority

The next level

The nuts and bolts of

The one mistake you

The one specific

The only ___ like it

The only ___ you'll need

The only game in town

The original sells for "$"

The parts of a

The perfect business

The pitfalls and mistakes of

The powerful advantages

The pros and cons

The proven

The question is

The real deal

The real keys to

The real reasons

The real thing

The risk is on me

The run down on

The safe route

The safe way to

The secret weapon

The secrets behind

The shocking truth

The simple question

The simple technique

The single most

The success you dream

The surprising facts

The thing that impressed me

The things you'll receive

The time is now

The time is right

The top x most

The topics included are

The truth about

The truth is

The very first thing

The whole shebang

The whole works

The word is out about

The x elements every

The x ingredients

The x laws of

The x priorities of

The x steps

The x things you

Theft proof

There are a lot of myths about

There are very few people

There is no better time

There is nothing quite like

There is nothing wrong with

There's is nothing to it

There's never been a better time to

There's no free lunch

There's no tomorrow

There's no turning back

There's nowhere else to go

There's nothing else like it!

Thermal

Thermal lined

They have outdone their self

Thick

Thickest

Thin

Think about

Think about spending

Think of it as you're personal

Thinner

Third

Third class

Third degree

Third dimension

Third place

Third rate

Thirst quenching

This ___ has just about all the

This ___ is for

This fact is supported by

This fact is verified by

This is no gimmick

This is the complete

This probably comes as no big surprise

Thorough

Thorough analysis

Thorough knowledge

Thorough process

Thoroughly inspected

Thoroughly researched

Thought out

Thought stopping

Thousands

Thousands of extra dollars

Thousands sold

Three

Three dimensional

Three easy payments of $

Three time looser

Through thick and thin

Thrifty

Thrilling

Thrilling news

Thrilling results

Thrilling secrets

Thrive in a bad economy

Thriving industry

Thriving market

Throaty

Throw away

Ticket to success

Ticky tacky

Tidy

Tight

Tight cut

Tight deadline

Tight hold

Tight lipped

Tight security

Tightwad

Tilt the odds in your favor

Time bomb

Time clock

Time consuming

Time efficient ways

Time honored

Time honored custom

Time honored solution

Time is money

Time is of the essence

Time is running out

Time released

Time saving

Time saving device

Time saving ideas

Time tested

Timeless

Timeless appeal

Timeless classic

Timeless gift

Timeless masterpiece

Time-limited information

Timely

Timely help

Timely ideas

Timely information

Time's running out

Time-saving

Time-tested

Timing is everything

Tinted

Tiny

Tip of the iceberg

Tip the scales

Tip top shape

Tippled

Tire burning

Tire spinning

Titanic energy

To die for

To summarize

To the fullest

To the max

Toll free

Tomfoolery

Tongue hanging

Tongue tied

Tongue wagging

Tons of marketing tools

Too hot to handle

Toodle-do

Toodles

Took me two seconds to decide

Took me years to research

Took x hours to create this

Tool like

Toolbox like

Toots

Top

Top achievers

Top corporate giants

Top dog

Top dollar

Top executives

Top experts

Top flight

Top level

Top marketing experts

Top name

Top notch

Top of the line

Top placement

Top priority

Top prize

Top producing

Top quality

Top rated

Top recruiters

Top sales producer

Top secret

Top selling

Topic driven

Total

Total comfort

Total freedom

Total satisfaction

Total secrecy

Total transformation

Total winner

Totally confidential

Totally untouched

Tough

Toxic

Trade secrets

Tradition bound

Traditional

Traditional approach

Traffic building techniques

Traffic growth

Trail blazing

Trained by

Training system

Transferable

Transformed into

Transient

Transportable

Trap

Travel discounts

Traveled

Treasure

Treasure chest

Treasure map

Treasured by

Treasured forever

Treat yourself

Treatable

Tremendous

Tremendous amount

Tremendous asset

Tremendous bargain

Tremendous breakthrough

Tremendous experience

Tremendous help

Tremendous impact

Tremendous profits

Tremendous satisfaction

Trendy design

Trial

Trial and error

Trial offer

Trial size

Tricks of the trade

Tried and true

Trillion

Triple

Triple Crown

Triple play

Triple sales

Triple your money back

Tripled

Triumphal announcement

Trouble free

Trouble free delivery

Trouble shooting help

Trouble-free

Troubleshooting

Truckloads of cash

Truckloads of leads

True collector's piece

True facts

True financial security

True life

True story

Trust me you have to

Trusting

Trusted

Trustworthy

Truth

Truthful

Try before you buy

Try it, you'll like it

Tug-of-war

Turbo boost

Turbo boost your sales

Turn around your business

Turn nothing into something

Turn over a new leaf

Turn your dream into a reality

Turned on

To mentioned

Twinge

Twisted

Two for the price of one

Two free bonuses

Two level

Two sided

Two tier

Two way

Two way street

Two wheeled	Unbridled enthusiasm
Tycoon	Uncanny intelligence
Ugliest	Uncensored
Ultimate	Uncensored media
Ultimate authority	Unclaimed fortune
Ultimate collection of	Unclaimed treasure
Ultimate gift	Uncommon
Ultimate independence	Uncommon information
Ultimate time saver	Uncommon techniques
Ultra	Unconditional
Umpteen	Uncontrollable urge
Unadulterated	Uncover
Unauthorized	Uncover a faster method
Unbeatable	Uncover insider techniques
Unbeatable offer	Uncover the
Unbeatable price	Uncover uncommon
Unbelievable	Uncovered by
Unbelievable bargains	Uncut
Unbelievable invention	Uncut version
Unblemished reputation	Undeniable evidence
Unbounded energy	Under adverse conditions
Unbridled	Under aged
Unbridled energy	Under close scrutiny

Under cut

Under priced

Under privileged

Under the gun

Under the table

Under utilized

Underground

Underground economy

Underhanded

Underpriced

Underrated

Understand the importance of

Understanding

Underutilized asset

Undetectable sales boosters

Undreamed of

Unearth gold

Unearth more profits

Unedited

Unfair advantage

Unfair competition

Unfathomed secrets

Unforgettable

Unforgettable experience

Unforgettable impression

Unheard of

Unheard of level

Unheralded prosperity

Unimaginable

Unimaginable luxury

Unique

Unique antique

Unique blend

Unique concept

Unique methods

Unique moment

Unique offer

Unique opportunity

Unique policy

Unique qualifications

Unique selling point

Unique status

Unique system

Unique visits

Uniquely qualified

United

Universal

Universal acclaim

Universal phenomenon

Universal recognition

Unleaded

Unleash

Unleash the power of

Unleashed

Unless you already know

Unlike any other

Unlike anything

Unlike anything you've seen before

Unlimited

Unlimited access

Unlimited budget

Unlimited demand

Unlimited fortune

Unlimited innovation

Unlimited potential

Unlimited profit producers

Unlimited resources

Unlimited uses

Unlimited warranty

Unlimited wealth

Unlock

Unmarked

Unmatched

Unnecessary paperwork

Unofficial guide

Unordinary

Unorthodox

Unorthodox methods

Unparalleled

Unparalleled success

Unpreceded

Unquestionable proof

Unquestioned

Unquestioned honesty

Unquestioned originality

Unquestioning trust

Unreal

Unrelenting formula

Unrestricted access

Unspoken

Unspoken advice

Unstoppable

Unsung hero

Unsurpassable

Unsurpassed

Unsurpassed perfection

Unsurpassed reputation

Untainted

Untapped

Untapped market

Untapped opportunities

Untapped resources

Untapped wealth

Untarnished

Untarnished reputation

Untaxed

Unthinkable

Untold

Untold fortunes

Untold riches

Untold wealth

Untouchable

Untraceable

Unused condition

Unusual

Unusual for me to endorse a product

Unusual information

Unusual insights

Unusual phenomenon

Up and coming

Up for grabs

Up sell

Up the ante

Up the corporate ladder

Up to date

Up to date data

Up to date information

Up to date methods

Up to date on the latest

Up to speed

Up to the minute

Up to the minute updates

Upbeat

Updated

Updated weekly

Upgrade

Upgrade your business

Upgraded

Upholstered

Uplifting

Up line

Upper class

Ups and downs

Upscale

Urban

Urgency

Urgent

Urgent action

Usable

Use your credit card

Useful

Useful gifts

Useful information

Useful purpose

Useful searching

Useful tools

User friendly

Utility

Utilize

Utilized by

Utmost urgency

Vacancy

Vacant

Vacation anytime

Vacation money

Vacuum packed

Vaguely mentioned

Valid

Valid methods

Valid proof

Valid threat

Validated by

Valuable

Valuable addition

Valuable asset

Valuable collection

Valuable coupon

Valuable information

Valuable insights

Valuable knowledge

Valuable resources

Valuable service

Value

Value added

Value added service

Value conscious

Value driven

Value for your dollar

Valued by

Vandal proof

Vanilla flavored

Vanishes instantly

Vanishing

Vanishing formula

Vaporize

Vaporizing

Variable climates

Variable cost

Variable expenses

Varied

Variety

Various choices

Varnished

Varying styles

Vast amount

Vast asset

Vast compilation

Vast examples

Vast industry

Vast sums of

Vaulted to number x

Velvet covered

Vender friendly

Venom

Ventilated

Venture capital

Verbal warning

Verbalized

Verdict driven

Verified by

Verify

Versatile

Versatility

Vertical

Very good condition

Very good shape

Very hot

Very light

Very proficient

Veteran like

Veto proof

Vetoed

Vibrant

Vibrant colors

Vibrant display

Vibrating

Victim

Victim less

Victorious

Videotaped

View yourself

Viewable

Viewpoint

Vigilant

Vigorous training

Villain like

Vindicated

Vintage

Vintage craftsmanship

Vintage year

Violet colored

Viral

Viral marketing

Virtual assistant

Virtual presence

Virtual reality

Virtual storefront

Virtually no cost

Virtually zero risk

Virus like

Visibility

Visible plan

Vision

Versioned by

Visit

Visited by

Visitor friendly

Visitor to sales ratio

Visitor tracking

Visual control

Visual less

Visualize buying

Visualize yourself

Vital	Voided
Vital agreement	Volatile
Vital component	Volcanic
Vital force	Voltage
Vital function	Volume proof
Vital help	Volume resistance
Vital issue	Voluntary
Vital mission	Volunteering
Vital parts	Voucher friendly
Vital process	Vow to
Vital purchase	Vulnerability
Vital support	Vulnerable
Vivid	Vulture like
Vivid accent	Vying for
Vivid color	Wacky
Vivid design	Wads of cash
Vivid detail	Wage less
Vivid reminder	Wage war
Vocal less	Wager your
Vocational	Waist high
Voice cracking	Wait and see
Voice less	Wake up anytime
Voiced their opinion	Wake up call

Wake up late

Wallet opening

Want more proof

Wanton

War like

Warehousing

Warm

Warm colors

Warm hearted

Warning

Warp speed

Warrant

Warrant a pay check

Warranty

Was I surprised?

Wasteful

Water boiling

Water proof

Water steaming

Watered down

Wave of the future

Way back in "year"

Way the ball bounces

Ways and means

Ways to use the

We aim to please

We do all the work

We do all the work for you

We guarantee you'll

We have all heard about

We need your help

We pay postage and handling

We pay shipping and handling

We process all orders

We really care

We reserve the right to

We spilled the beans

We take the orders

We will foot the bill

We will not sell your name

We will show you

Weak

Weak market

Weak willed

Weaker

Weakest

Wealth

Wealth building

Wealth multiplying strategies

Wealth of information

Wealthy

Wealthy mindset

Wear what you want

Weathered

Web

Web designed

Web hosted

Web master

Web page

Web site

Web site award

Web site marketing

Web traffic

Weekends off

Weekly freedom

Weeknights off

Weighed

Weighs approximately

Weighs in at

Weird

Welcomed to

Well

Well advanced

Well advised

Well balanced

Well being

Well beloved

Well bred

Well built

Well chosen

Well connected

Well-constructed

Well crafted

Well documented

Well dressed

Well educated

Well established

Well established company

Well established institution

Well favored

Well groomed

Well-guarded

Well informed

Well-kept secret

Well known

Well-known figure

Well liked

Well made

Well marked

Well off

Well oiled

Well organized

Well planned

Well preserved

Well qualified prospects

Well regulated

Well rounded

Well set

Well spoken

Well stocked

Well thought out

Well thought out strategy

Well to do

Well trained

Well worked

Well worn

Well worth the price

Well worth what I paid

Well written

Wet

We've been online for x

We've sold x copies

What "customer" said?

What a deal

What are you waiting for?

What could

What do you?

What does it mean to?

What every person

What have you got to lose?

What I am about to share

What I have to tell you

What if I told you?

What if someone said to you?

What if you could finally?

What I'm about to

What I'm about to show you is

What I'm about to tell you is

What impressed me the most?

What it takes to

What others are saying

What the doctored ordered

What the experts are saying

What to do when

What type of?

What would an extra

What would you do if?

What you need to know

What you should

What you've been looking for

What you'll discover

What you'll get

What you'll receive

What…?

Wheel and deal

Wheeler dealer

When I first started out in

When will you

When you order by

When you order today

When…?

Where to find

Where to get a

Whether you're looking to

Which of the

Which…?

While supplies last

While you are sleeping

While you're on vacation

Whinny

Whip

White collar

White colored

Whiten

Whittle

Whiz

Who…?

Whole new ball game

Wholesale price

Wholesome advice

Wallop

Whoop-de-do

Whopping

Whopping increase

Whopping success

Why being an

Why creating a

Why I'm an expert

Why is

Why most

Why people are

Why people buy

Why some people

Why x% of businesses fail

Why you can be

Why you must get

Why you must use

Why you need

Why you should never

Why you should trust me

Why you shouldn't

Why you've got to

Why…?

Wicked

Wide

Wide availability

Wide awake

Wide distribution

Wide implications

Wide open

Wide open market

Wide range of

Wide range of products

Wide ranging

Wide selection

Wide spectrum

Wide variety

Widened your

Widespread

Wild

Wild extravaganza

Wild success

Wildly profitable

Will go over big

Will make a great gift

Will make or break you

Will never be leased

Will never be rented

Will never be sold

Will pay for its self

Will pay for your purchase

Will stretch your mind

Will supply you with

Will work for you

Willpower

Win

Win out

Win some lose some

Win their mind

Win them over

Win/win deal

Win/win offer

Win/win situation

Winning ad

Winning edge

Winning ideas

Winning personality

Winning products

Winning solution

Winning strategies

Wired

Wireless

Wisdom

Wise advice

Wise choice

Wise investment

Wish it was available sooner

Wish like

Wish list

Wishful

Wishy washy

With an added bonus

With flying colors

With handwritten letter

With little effort

With no startup money

With our product you can

With serial number

Withdraw this offer at anytime

Withheld

Within minutes from now

Without a big investment

Without all the hype

Without any of the frustration

Without any of the hassle

Without any of the stress

Without any string attached

Without any work

Without breaking a sweat

Without effort

Without failing

Without investing money

Without investing time

Without lifting a finger

Without paying outrageous fees

Without raising a figure

Without spanning

Without spending a fortune

Without spending one red cent

Without working hard

Without working harder

Withstand a slow economy

Witty

Woman like

Won over

Wonderful

Wonderful organization

Wonderful selection

Wonderful sight

Wondrous

Won't be here tomorrow

Word of mouth

Word-of-mouth

Words can't describe

Words of wisdom

Work a few hours a week

Work at home

Work at home on your computer

Work for yourself

Work free

Work from home

Work from your basement

Work from your bedroom

Work from your kitchen

Work from your living room

Work in your bathrobe

Work in your pajamas

Work in your sweats

Work in your underwear

Work less

Work loaded

Work of art

Work smarter not harder

Work the hours you want

Work were you wish

Work while you travel

Work with

Workable

Workable ideas

Workable objectives

Workable plan

Workaholic

Worked by

Worked closely with

Working for

Working from home

Working less

Working relationship

Works every time

Works in minutes

Works like crazy

Works like new

World class

World class faculty

World class standard

World class status

World famous

World premier

World renowned

World shaking

World wide

Worldwide phenomenon

Worldwide reputation

World Wide Web

Worlds greatest

Worlds largest

World's leading experts

Worlds oldest

Worldwide

Worldwide recognition

Worn down

Worn out

Worry

Worry free

Worry free investment

Worry free retirement

Worship the

Worst case scenario

Worst ever

Worth a fortune

Worth a hundred times the cost

Worth every

Worth every dollar I spent

Worth gold

Worth its weight in gold

Worth its weight in gold

Worth over $

Worth substantial sums

Worth the price and then some

Worthwhile

Worthwhile cause

Worthwhile charity

Worthy acquisition

Worthy addition

Worthy of

Worthy purpose

Would be crazy not to buy

Would you

Would you like to

Wouldn't you like to

Wounded

Woven with

Wow your prospects

Wrapped

Wrapped with

Wrath

Wrinkle free

Write it off

Write you a blank check

Write your own check

Written for today's

Written guarantee

Written in everyday language

Written in plain English

Written so a baby could understand it

X affiliate sales will pay for it

X cents

X characteristics of

X customers in X days"

X day free trial

X day trial pass

X day's free access

X different

X different ways

X easy payments of

X elements you can

X examples

X feet

X figure income

X foot

X free bonuses worth $

X freebies valued at $

X friends of mine

X full years of

X gallon

X grams

X helpful links

X hits in less than X hour's"

X hot reasons

X inches

X information packed pages

X information rich chapters

X items you

X karat

X key principles you

X key questions

X kinds of

X knowledge packed lessons

X leads in X weeks"

X lesson course

X mistakes that

X months ago

X out of every X

X piece

X piece collection

X places to

X pounds

X proven strategies

X quart

X quarters

X resources

X rules you must

X sales in X months"

X sales will pay for it

X sections on

X simple formulas

X step system

X strong

X subscribers

X century

X things to consider

X tips and tricks

X types of

X ways to

X ways to use our product

X year subscription

X years ago

X years in the making

X years later in "year"

X% commission

Yackety-yack

Yammer

Yard long

Year end

Year in year out

Year round

Yearly

Yearning for

Year-round

Years of experience

Years of research

Year's practical experience

Yellow colored

Yellow-bellied sapsucker

Yellow-belly

Yes

You

You ain't seen nothing

You already recognize

You are about to discover how to

You are about to realize

You better believe it

You can do this

You can literally start

You can own my brain for

You can too

You can't possibly lose

You can't afford

You can't fail

You can't lose

You do not need experience to

You don't have

You don't have to be an expert

You don't know it yet

You don't need

You get

You have a

You have no risk

You have nothing to lose

You have to start here

You just have to see it

You know all those people who

You know that you

You may have already heard

You may realize you

You may want to

You might be thinking

You might want to

You never have to

You never know

You only need to do

You owe it to yourself

You probably feel

You qualify

You select

You the customer comes first

You will also receive

You will be

You will have learned

You won't find this in "location"

You won't have to

You won't see this everywhere

You'll be sorry

You'll discover

You'll find out

You'll get instant access

You'll get unlimited

You'll get x bonuses

You'll have a great reputation

You'll improve your

You'll know

You'll learn

You'll learn it all

You'll never find a better way to

You'll sell a ton of them

You'll treasure this

Young

Young un

Your

Your choice

Your choice of

You're crazy not to invest

Your ethical duty

Your moral duty

You're not alone

You're only paying $

Your very own product

You're a creative marketer

You're an intelligent person

You're a skilled webmaster

You're a smart person

You're a talented entrepreneur

You're a wise investor

You're about to uncover

You're asking yourself

You're going to get

You're likely thinking

You're on the clock

You're probably tired

You're right on the money

Yours for no charge

Yours for the taking

Youth like

Youthful

You've probably heard

Youza

Yuk

Zapped

Zeal

Zealot

Zero advertising budget

Zero based

Zero delivery cost

Zero growth

Zero in on

Zero install

Zero to implement

Zest

Zestful

Zesty

Zig zagged

Zilch

Zillion

Zipped

Zoned by

Zoo like

Zounds

Zowie

Made in the USA
Columbia, SC
26 April 2021